INNOVATION

INNOVATION

The Creative Impulse in Human Progress

INDUSTRY - ART - SCIENCE

WILLIAM KINGSTON

Thinking outside of the box

The Leonard R. Sugerman Press
Washington DC
www.lrsp.com

Published by The Leonard R. Sugerman Press Inc.
1050 Connecticut Avenue N.W.
Washington D.C. 20036
United States of America
www.lrsp.com

Printed on acid-free paper

ISBN 0-9726484-2-9 Hardcover

Library of Congress Control Number: 2003106887

This is a new edition, with added text*, of a book of the same title that was first published in Great Britain 1977 by John Calder (Publishers) Ltd., 18 Brewer Street, London W1R 4AS

*Chapter III Reprinted from *Research Policy,* (29) 2000 William Kingston, *Antibiotics, Invention and Innovation,* 679-710 with permission from Elsevier.

Typeset by Chris Coles
Dust Cover Design by Chris Coles
and David Tarbutt
Printed in the United States of America

CONTENTS

CHAPTER III   *Antibiotics, Invention and Innovation*   70

To Mary

PREFACE TO THE FIRST EDITION

Interest in innovation is growing in both Europe and America, but for somewhat different reasons. Many Europeans feel that increasing domination by the United States, in cultural as well as in economic terms, is due in some way to better understanding by Americans of the innovatory process - `getting new things done', as distinct from `finding new things'. In America, apart from interest among actual innovators, there is now as well a contrasted and growing uneasiness about the meaning and value of much contemporary innovation. This sometimes amounts to outright rejection of the social structures which are associated with its existence there in such plenty.

From the viewpoint of the present book, it is possible both to understand these different attitudes and to reconcile them. Innovation is simply one way in which human creative energy is expressed, but it has been characteristic of recent stages in the culture of the West that this particular type of energy has tended to run into technological and technical innovation, rather than into survival or liturgy or art or literature. These are all areas of life in which very much the same kind of energy has spent itself, just as unequally, in different places and at different times in the past.

Consequently, although it is in technological innovation that much of one particular kind of excitement is to be found today, innovation is a great deal more than this, and in fact, a better understanding of it even in relation to technology is obtained by studying it in a wider meaning. The present book is the result of such a shift in the perspective from which it is usually examined.

PREFACE TO THE NEW EDITION

I have made only minor changes in the Chapters which deal with the book's central topic, that is, innovation as an aspect of the way in which human creativity is expressed. The factors which affect this do not change, and the addition of the case study, `Antibiotics, Invention and Innovation', now illustrates and puts flesh on the discussion.

Not surprisingly, it is in relation to the Chapter on `Innovation and Money' that there have been developments since the earlier edition. Business has become progressively more international. Branding has also become an even more important way of protecting investment in innovation through the power to gain lead time over competitors. Intellectual property has grown enormously in its range in recent years. New material in this Chapter suggests that these developments call for reforms, and discusses the shape some of these might usefully take.

Another area where there have been remarkable changes in recent years is the provision of seed capital, the very first money which is put behind a new idea to turn it into concrete reality. These include the Small Business Innovation Research Act in the United States, now by far the best source of seed capital in the world. The brief description of this which I have now added shows that the prospects for obtaining backing for new ideas – if only in the U.S. - are not as bleak as they appeared to be at the time of the first edition.

Naturally, what has changed most in the time between the two publications is the extent of my intellectual indebtedness to others, in particular to Dr. Hermann Kronz, formerly of the European Commission, and to Professors Richard Nelson of Columbia, Jerome Reichman of Duke, Douglass North of Washington University, St. Louis, and Don Kash and James Buchanan, both of George Mason University, as well as to my academic colleagues here in Dublin.

And of course I am particularly grateful to Chris Coles for his initiative in founding the Leonard R. Sugerman Press, devoted to the publication of `thinking outside of the box', and for considering that my book justified inclusion in his list.

WILLIAM KINGSTON,
School of Business Studies,
Trinity College, Dublin.
wkngston@tcd.ie

CHAPTER I

Between the Dreamer and the Mandarin

Artist, inventor, innovator, entrepreneur, trader - all words which describe people doing things. One senses something in common between them, the meanings of any adjacent pair of words in the group shade off into each other, and yet there is an evident contrast between the extremes. Individuals doing what artists do are obviously not doing what traders do, yet it is perfectly possible to think of people to whom several of the descriptions in the list could have been applied during their lifetime. Serge Diagilhev, who made the Russian ballet known throughout the world, was undoubtedly artist., innovator and entrepreneur all at once. Leonardo da Vinci was outstanding in the first three roles; Edison was everything but an artist at different times. The meanings of these words are worth dwelling on, since it is one of them –`innovator' – that is to be examined at length.

Considering the extremes first, it is easy to see the activity of both artist and trader as having in common a combination of `seeing' and `doing'. We speak of an artist's `vision', yet an artist does not stop at seeing, but endeavours to express a vision in some communicable form. A trader may not have vision in the same degree, but neither does he act blindly. He starts off with some idea of what he can achieve through action. The difference between the two activities comes from the balance between idea and action. What matters most in the work of art is the vision., that is, what happens *inside* the artist; the greatest art involves technical mastery, but there is no worthwhile art which consists of technique alone. What matters most in trading is what happens *outside* the trader. There is nothing especially world-shaking about the idea that `sandal-wood, cedarwood or sweet white wine' may be more valuable in a place where they are scarce than where they are plentiful; what makes a trader is that he actually does something about it, and makes the vision, limited though it may be, a complete reality. Another way of marking the contrast is to call attention to the way in which a trader's activity is socially conditioned, whereas that of the artist resists being modified by the surrounding social culture, if indeed it does not actually seek to modify it.

Expressing Vision

Both artists and traders, then, have `vision' and express it in some concrete way. In one case, the ideas or feelings dominate, and the change in the concrete, tangible world is comparatively unimportant; in the other, the change in the concrete, tangible world is more important than the idea. This may be expressed visually as follows:

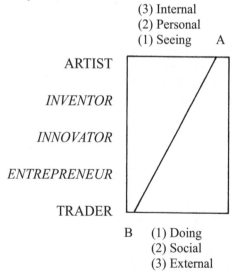

(3) Internal
(2) Personal
(1) Seeing   A

ARTIST

INVENTOR

INNOVATOR

ENTREPRENEUR

TRADER

B   (1) Doing
(2) Social
(3) External

In this rectangle, those who carry on the activities are listed at the side, and the contrasted pairs of attributes at the top and bottom. The slanted line AB can then be drawn to show the relative proportions of each attribute in each activity. Thus, artistic activity is more `seeing' than `doing', more `internal' than `external', more `personal' than `social'. Trading's proportions are the opposite in each case. It will be found that the other three activities of inventor, innovator and entrepreneur, can also be fitted into this diagram.

We speak, for example, in praise of an artist's or composer's `fertility in invention', referring to skill at discovering new and pleasing combinations of paint or sound. But in the even more common sense of the word, an inventor is one who discovers something new and useful or practical, something that *works*. There is rather more of the element of `doing' in this activity than there is in what an artist does. In a parallel way, we know that the material with which an entrepreneur works is generally much the same as that of a trader. In the case of the entrepreneur, however, something is added - standing out from the crowd of traders, taking higher risks for higher rewards, following a line which in some way puts his personal stamp upon some aspect of economic life. To this extent, what he does is less socially conditioned than what the trader does, it depends more upon what happens in his own mind and heart.

The Innovator

And what of the innovator? We commonly speak of innovation in the arts or in literature, as well as in technology. If we reflect upon the way in which the word is used, we find that it generally has the connotation, not so much of originating ideas, but of taking up an idea and developing it, realising its potential, or turning it into concrete reality. For these reasons, the position of innovator on the scale is above that of entrepreneur, but below that of inventor. An innovator may take the ideas with which he works from an inventor - as Matthew Boulton took up Watt's steam engine - but there is nevertheless a stronger element of `seeing' in his activity than there is in an entrepreneur's.

Thus, not alone can the five activities be ranked at the side of the rectangle, but many other pairs of contrasting words can be listed, and the same slanted line (AB) will still roughly designate the relative proportions of each pair in any of the activities.

In the following diagram, the first of each pair belongs to the top of the rectangle, the second to the bottom of it, as indicated by the arrows:

Seeing	- Doing
Personal	- Social
Individual	- Crowd
Imagination	- Verifiable facts
Ideas	- Concrete realities
New things	- Familiar things
World as it might be	- World as it is
Untried methods	- Established techniques
Long time-scale	- Short time scale
Element of chance	- Predictable
Spontaneity	- Learned behaviour
Inarticulate need	- Formulated want
Emotion	- Intellect
Revolution	- Evolution
Concern with future	- Concern with past or present

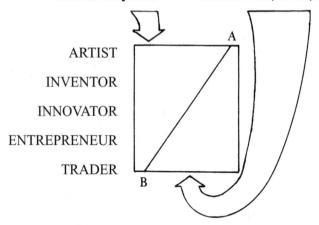

If we consider the types of person listed, the lower they are on the diagram, the more their activity deals with concrete realities on a basis of verifiable facts, by established techniques, on a short time-scale with everything largely predictable. The higher they are on it, the more their activity is concerned with ideas and imagination, with the world as it might be rather than as it is, and uncertainty plays a large part; it is more subject to chance, and longer time is needed before the full implications of the activity become clear.

To illustrate this, select the opposed concepts of `established techniques' - `untried methods'. Obviously, at the bottom of the rectangle, a trader operates as far as he possibly can along lines which he knows well, but an entrepreneur is such precisely because of breaking away from the familiar. In the case of the innovator, the break is a radical one. The idea may not be new, *per se;* what is new is the concrete realisation of it which he is seeking to bring about. When we come to the inventor, even the idea is new. However, to the extent that it has a bearing on practical life, it will be made up of elements that are previously known.

It is at the level of artistic activity that the `untried' aspect is most obvious, but even here the connection with `established techniques' is by no means broken. Only through the use of some form of language shared with the public - which is such a technique - can an artist attempt to communicate a personal vision. Much the same can be said of the pair of words `evolution/revolution'. At the level of art, change comes about simply through a single individual, quickly and sharply; at the level of trading, change is invariably slow, by careful steps, generally taken at much the same time by several people.

Low-grade Art

In this, as in all the pairs of words listed, reflection will confirm that the activity of the innovator is characterised by roughly equal proportions of the contrasted attributes. The importance of this is to establish how far innovation needs the vocabulary of Art for its proper description. We cannot hope to understand innovation - even economic innovation - without stepping outside the categories and definitions that apply to trading or even to entrepreneurship.

It may have been noted that the line AB is not a diagonal of the rectangle. This is because all the activities named contain some proportion of each pair of attributes listed at the top and bottom. Artistic activity is never without some element of `doing', however much `seeing' may predominate; trading, however much it may be socially conditioned, is never altogether without some personal contribution on the part of the trader, some notional idea in mind. However, the list can be extended at each end, so as to include peripheral activities, in each of which the proportion of one of each pair of characteristics has become so small that it can be ignored.

On the principle that something is only fully understood when its implications have been driven to their absolute limit, it is worth while adding to the list at either end, even though the respective activities may be of little practical concern.

Beyond art, for example, all the elements listed at the top of the rectangle can be found in a way which to all intents and purposes exclude the characteristics listed at the bottom. `Mystic' is by far the best description of a person acting in this way, but its use in a precise way would involve too much explanation in the present context. In its place, `dreamer' will serve well enough, and it is obvious that what distinguishes such a person's `vision' from that of an artist is that in this case the vision is altogether private and incommunicable, whereas in the other it can be communicated to others, at least in part. To the extent that it is communicable, there is a `social' aspect to the artist's activity. All art does include an element of dream, but it is always more than dream. Even at its most imaginative and personal, the work of an artist is never altogether unconcerned with doing, that is, with externalising an inner vision, in a way which allows it to be communicated to others. Nor can it be altogether `apart' from the world as it is, nor from established techniques.

It is the same with other elements. Imagination which has no anchor in reality turns into hallucination, insistence upon change through revolution implies equal rejection of the changes that can come about through evolution, and so on. In the psychiatrist's shorthand, the neurotic is a person who is partially out of touch with reality, the psychotic is one who is wholly so. It is only at the point of psychosis that the line AB on the diagram, which defines the relative shares of `vision' and `reality', will finally reach the maximum for one and zero for the other. Short of this point, reality keeps breaking in to one degree or another.

The limiting Cases

`Dreamer', may not be the ideal word for one limiting case, but `Mandarin' is for the other. The reality whose shape is being groped for in using it, cannot be unfamiliar. The Mandarin class was the bureaucracy of old China, noted for its reverence for traditional norms of behaviour and for a meticulous concern to maintain conformity with these norms in every aspect of life:

> This extreme conservative outlook was shared by the whole official hierarchy ... The type of mind that entered the Civil Service was a mind closed to all idea of progress, almost incapable of grasping the possibility, still less the need for change ... The system was self-perpetuating, seemingly immutable'.[1]

In any field, there will always be people whose activity hardly goes beyond repeating patterns which may once have been highly significant, but which are now no longer so. Preoccupation with ritual, with performing set routines imposed by convention or precedent, unquestioning acceptance of the world as it is, obsession with things made familiar by long association, reluctance to depart from the concrete and the predictable - all these add up to a well known type of human activity.

What the Mandarin does is as exclusively public as what the dreamer does is exclusively private. One is the extreme example of individuals who take the world as they find it; the others live in an imaginative world of their own making. Only in the case of mandarin-like behaviour, then, does the line AB in the diagram reach the point where `doing' is all, and `seeing' nothing. As long as it is successful, trading never gets to the stage where it can be said to be utterly lacking in imagination, ideas, subjection to chance, or concern with the future rather than the present. As trading approaches the point where it does increasingly lack these attributes, it becomes correspondingly unsuccessful. Most people have at one time or another encountered businesses or shops where such `hardening of the arteries' is perfectly evident, where the management has become completely mandarin like, loyally

[1] C. P. Fitzgerald *Society in China,* quoted in P. Woodruff *The Guardians* (1954) 356.

following through routines which were once successful but which have little relevance to contemporary situations, so that they are serving an ageing and declining group of customers. In this case, the trading has moved into an extension of the rectangle of the diagram, in which the line AB has become a diagonal, and the end of the business *has* come in sight.

Extended Rectangle

The rectangle may therefore be drawn again to include these additional activities. The area to which these refer is shown in hatched lines to stress that they are peripheral, and we may also plot the relationship of each activity to change in the 'external' world. The limiting cases in this spectrum have been called the dreamer and the Mandarin, for want of better words to describe the activities in question. Some may be reminded of Arthur Koestler's Yogi and Commissar, but the continuum that is being discussed in one case is quite different from that in the other. Koestler's extremes both describe contrasted ways of bringing about change, the Yogi representing *change from within,* the Commissar *change from without.* In the present spectrum, they represent, not fundamentally different approaches to the bringing about of change, but the very *absence of change* in the real world.

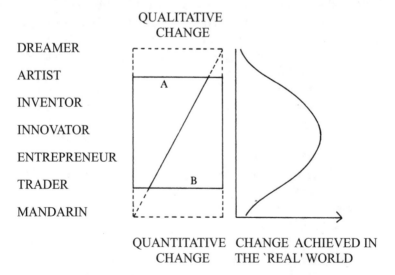

QUALITATIVE
CHANGE

DREAMER

ARTIST

INVENTOR

INNOVATOR

ENTREPRENEUR

TRADER

MANDARIN

A

B

QUANTITATIVE   CHANGE ACHIEVED IN
CHANGE   THE 'REAL' WORLD

Dreamers can bring about no change in this because their activity is not at grips with tangible reality; Mandarins bring about no change in it either, because for them, there is no tension between their thought and the immediately tangible.

Re-arranging the World

One pair of contrasted attributes on the rectangle which is worth special attention when considering innovation, is 'world as it is'/'world as it might be'. Vision - as long as it remains within the main rectangle - is always seeing a possible re-arrangement of the world as known. It is because artistic activity is always so rooted, and always contains some element of rendering what is seen, tangible or communicable, that

> As imagination bodies forth
> The forms of things unknown, the poet's pen
> Turns them to shapes, and gives to airy nothing
> A local habitation and a name.[2]

Artistic activity begins with the artists' own visions of the world, and it can go beyond mere perception of a possible re-arrangement of the world as it was previously known to them. In the outstanding cases of success in expressing this vision in some way which makes it accessible to others, the result is an imaginative world of such power that it can rival - or even surpass for a time - the world of day-to-day experience. The difference between the artist and the inventor, then, is that the inventors creativity never leads towards such *rival* worlds. Their ideas are firmly related to the existing world, and are limited to that world as it might be in the future. The artist sees and makes a different world, but the inventor is one who sees the possibility of some new relationship between aspects of the existing world, and the innovator makes this new relationship a reality.

Sometimes to the activity of artist or inventor there is added that of entrepreneur or trader. Shakespeare was a supreme artist, but he also traded and invested very shrewdly.

[2] Shakespeare *A Midsummer Night's Dream* Act V, Scene i.

Bernard Shaw showed remarkable 'trading' ability when it came to making money from his writing. In the other direction, the way in which the art dealer Durand-Ruel fought the cause of the Impressionist painters against a solid phalanx of critical scorn goes far beyond mere entrepeneurship. His lonely intensity of perception of their worth will be seen later on to be typical of innovators. However, in general, entrepreneurship - and trading even more so - is more a question of accepting the world as it is, and bringing about a change in only a few aspects, or perhaps even in no more than a single one, than it is of giving some form of tangible reality to a particular vision of a radical re-arrangement of things.

In trading, the element of seeing a possible re-arrangement of the known world may be every bit as small as the element of actively bringing about such a re-arrangement in concrete terms may be in art. For a trader, seeing a possible re-arrangement of the world as known may go no further than adding in the last component which makes a thing have value, measurable in money terms, for someone. Frequently this last component is the holding of stocks, or the physical movement of goods from a place where they cannot easily be used to one where they can, thus enhancing their value. For all this to take place, the goods must first exist. No one can hold stocks of other people's *perceptions* of possible re-arrangements for the world as known, nor can he make a business of moving these perceptions, in the abstract, about the world. To the same extent that the artist is concerned with the world of his own imagination and the inventor is concerned with the world of the future, the trader is concerned with the world of the present.

The Entrepreneur

On the 'inventive-artistic' side of trading in the rectangle is the activity of entrepreneurship, which therefore makes higher demands upon imagination, resourcefulness and constructive capacity. Like trading, it concerns itself with things which already exist in the concrete, and both these activities are directed towards a re-arrangement of the world as known. But this re-arrangement is more radical in the case of the entrepreneur. It depends much more upon some form of inner vision than the smaller changes brought about by the trader, whose activity of re-arranging the world is less a matter of realising his own mental constructs in some concrete way, than upon interpreting and reacting to external signals; for example, those from his customers in the act of defining their needs.

If it is characteristic of trading to fill in the last gap which makes an existing commodity capable of realising more value, it is characteristic of entrepreneurship to fill many gaps and even to arrange for the commodity itself to be brought into commerce in the first place. `Gap-filling' and `input-completing' capacities have, in fact, been designated as the unique characteristics of the entrepreneur.[3] The sociologist Sombart identified what he called `the conqueror strain' in the business leader, and contrasted it with the `instinct of bargaining' which he found, for example, in the Florentines, a contrast which again illustrates the difference between entrepreneur and trader.[4] The rewards for success in entrepreneurial activity and the losses in the event of failure, are correspondingly greater than in the case of trading. What an entrepreneur does cannot be performed merely by reacting to events as they happen; it only takes place against a background of a preconceived plan to control events, it is the realisation in concrete terms of ideas as to new ways of arranging the real world.

As suggested earlier, although the entrepreneur is imposing a re-arrangement on the world, his activity is limited to re-arranging things which already exist - he builds with concrete realities, which he does not have to make from his own ideas before he can even start. The individual performance of all the components with which he deals is generally fully known, so that the `newness' of his re-arrangement is limited. It undoubtedly takes entrepreneurial skill to bring about the successful establishment of a new manufacturing subsidiary of a firm in another country, but much, if not most of the information required will be available from experience in the parent firm's factories.

---

[3] H. Liebenstein, in *American Economic Review* (Papers & Proceedings) (1968) 75.

[4] F.W. Taussig *Inventors and Moneymakers* (1915) 86.

There is uncertainty, definitely more than in the case of trading, but nevertheless mitigated by the amount and reliability of the information which is available. The area of the activity which is not reasonably predictable in the light of what is known about the performance of the components, is constrained. Present realities bulk as importantly as the changes to be brought about in the future.

Difficulties of Innovation

When it comes to innovation, however, all of the practical difficulties encountered in entrepreneurship are still further intensified. An inventor may be content to remain at the level of mental activity, but it is the precise characteristic of the innovator that he does not do so. Innovation is the actual re-arrangement of the world which invention or discovery has made possible. Innovation thus straddles the worlds of mental and physical activity, `newness' and `uncertainty' are more in evidence even than with entrepreneurship, the area where imagination has to make up for the absence of reliable `hard' information is greater, and the work is much more concerned with the future than it is with the present.

For the entrepreneur, the components, the `building blocks', already exist and do not have to be developed. What is new is the way they are to be put together. For the innovator, some, if not all of the components, will themselves be no more than ideas. These will have to be turned into concrete reality, with all the difficulties and hazards which that involves, before their incorporation in the overall new arrangement can even begin. This is one reason for the observable time lag between invention and innovation - the realisation of the idea has to await the availability of every component, not just in theory but in dependable practice, and even the lack of a single one can close a whole area to innovation. Innovation is intrinsically more difficult than entrepreneurship, because the uncertainties of performance of its raw materials are always so much greater.

The position of the innovator, then, is mid-way down the rectangle, flanked by artists and inventors on one side, and by entrepreneurs and traders on the other. Innovation links two human worlds, two kinds of human activity; it might even be said, two kinds of people. There are those whose activity is characterized primarily by its mental character, and these are the ones who uncover new potential in the world as known. There are others who are unreflective, for whom living in the imagination has no attraction. It is these who are the doers, most often, the active ones. Both groups share the capacity to become emotionally involved in what they are doing, that is, they are linked by feeling, but they do not feel for the same things. The first group finds the world of thought and imagination real and satisfying, to the extent that some members of it feel little need at all for their thoughts and visions to be expressed in concrete form. The second group has hardly any use for a reality that remains on a mental level. Characteristically, its members demand of something new that it can be touched or measured before they will take it seriously. What characterizes innovators is membership of both groups. They have to have a strong feeling for ideas as such, often to the extent of being capable of being dominated or obsessed by them, and they must be able to make them a part of themselves - it will become clear later on to what a great extent this factor is an identifiable one in the performance of people who have proved themselves as innovators. Yet they cannot be content with a reality which is purely conceptual or imaginative, and their energy is therefore directed towards its embodiment in some concrete way.

More Than Technology

Looked at from this aspect, innovation is vastly more than *technological* innovation, which is the sense in which the word has been most generally used in recent years. Much of the literature on innovation limits itself to the consideration of technology, and suffers accordingly. But our understanding of the meaning of innovation is condemned to remain inadequate, unless we attain a wider context in which to integrate it. There is a second reason why the meaning of innovation has become narrowed in practice. This is that a particular pattern of law which has developed in Western countries during the past century and a half, has been conducive to innovation in technology to an extent that is without parallel in history. There has never been an era in which so many perceptions of possible changes in technology as known were realized, and consequently it was probably inevitable that the meaning generally given to the word `innovation' should acquire overtones which relate almost exclusively to technology. In spite of this, the broader meaning of the word remains unchanged, and even from the point of view of understanding technological innovation, there are advantages in bearing in mind that it has a much wider application.

Joseph Schumpeter

This is especially necessary for the task of raising a sound intellectual structure on the excellent foundation laid by the outstanding writer on economic innovation, Joseph Schumpeter. He and Marx are the two great exponents of a type of economics in which changes in the ways of doing and making things are fundamentally important - in contrast to Keynes, whose thought assumes throughout a technology which is essentially static,[5] and is correspondingly less relevant to the modern world. It is tempting to think that Schumpeter gave pride of place to innovation in his economics because of his own wide culture, which left him aware of how much more widespread creativity is in human life than is often thought. He had been the first Finance Minister of post-Habsburg Austria before settling at Harvard in the early 1930s, and he wrote two novels.[6]

What fascinated Schumpeter about business life was the way in which innovation provided the dynamic element through the `incessant rise and decay' of firms.[7]

For him, new ways of doing things `do not and generally cannot, evolve out of the old firms, but place themselves side by side with them and attack them ... The competition that counts is the competition from the new commodity, the new technology, the new source of supply ..., which strikes not at the margins of profit and the outputs of the existing firms, but at their foundations and at

---

[5] P. Sylos-Labini *Oligopoly and Technical Progress* (English trans. 1962) 152.

[6] cf. S. E. Harris (ed.) Schumpeter, *Social Scientist* (1951).

[7] J. A. Schumpeter *Business Cycles* (1939) 92-6.

their very lives'.[8] In the process whereby new things emerge, he was careful to distinguish invention from innovation, describing many cases of innovation where invention as such was not involved.[9] `It is not the knowledge that matters' he said, `but the successful solution of the task *sui generis* of putting an untried method into practice ... Successful innovation ... is a feat not of intellect, but of will. It is a special case of the social phenomenon of leadership.'[10] The most succinct expression of this aspect of his thinking is to be found in an article which appeared in 1947, in which he stressed that:

> It is particularly important to distinguish the entrepreneur from the `inventor'. Many inventors have become entrepreneurs and the relative frequency of this case is no doubt an interesting subject to investigate, but there is no necessary connection between the two functions. The inventor produces ideas, the entrepreneur `gets things done', which may but need not embody anything that is scientifically new. Moreover, an idea or scientific principle is not, by itself, of any importance for economic practice; the fact that Greek science had probably produced all that is necessary in order to construct a steam engine did not help the Greeks or Romans to build a steam engine; the fact that Leibnitz suggested the idea of the Suez Canal exerted no influence whatever on economic history for two hundred years. And as different as the functions are the two sociological and psychological types. Finally, `getting new things done' is not only a distinct process but it is a process which produces consequences that are an essential part of capitalist reality. The whole economic history of capitalism would be different from what it is if new ideas had been currently and smoothly adopted, as a matter of course, by all firms to whose business they were relevant. But they were not. It is in most cases only one man or a few men who see the new possibility and are able to cope with the resistances and difficulties which action always meets with outside of the ruts of established practice.[11]

---

[8] J.A. Schumpeter in *Economic Journal* (1928) 384; *Capitalism, Socialism & Democracy* (1943) 84

[9] J.A. Schumpeter *Business Cycles* (1939) 84.

[10] J.A. Schumpeter in *Economic Journal* (1928) 64-5.

[11] J.A. Schumpeter *Journal of Economic History* (1947) 152.

Distinctive Types

He was also aware that innovation lost meaning through having too strict limits placed upon its application:

> Seen in this light, the entrepreneur and his function are not difficult to conceptualize; the defining characteristic is simply the doing of new things or the doing of things that are already being done in a new way (innovation). It is but natural, and in fact it is an advantage, that such a definition does not draw any sharp line between what is and what is not 'enterprise'. For actual life itself knows no such sharp division, though it shows up the type well enough. It should be observed at once that the 'new thing' need not be spectacular or of historic importance. It need not be Bessemer steel or the explosion motor. It can be the Deerfoot sausage. To see the phenomenon even in the humblest levels of the business world is quite essential though it may be difficult to find the humble entrepreneurs historically.[12]

It will be noted that although Schumpeter is careful to distinguish innovation from invention, he makes little or no distinction between innovation and entrepreneurship. This is because his concern is with innovation as a subject for study by economists. But Schumpeter's own definition of the innovator as the man 'who gets new things done' can be applied to whole areas of life in which the economic element is comparatively unimportant, where 'no satisfaction from pecuniary success or worldly recognition equals the absorbed interest of trial, experiment, novel problems, happy solutions'.[13]

The Impressionists, for example, made a whole new way of dealing with light in painting a factor in the taste of all subsequent generations. This was undoubtedly innovation, but it had nothing whatever to do with business or entrepreneurship. The characteristic concern of innovators is with the embodiment of ideas. If the ideas become more important for them than their embodiments, they turn into inventors or even artists. If the ideas that are interesting to them can be measured according to whether they do or do not

---

[12] ibid.151.

[13] F. W. Taussig *Inventors and Moneymakers* (1915) 21, 23.

make money, to that extent they become entrepreneurs. Life readily enough yields examples of people moving in both directions. Matthew Boulton moved towards inventing as he grew older but he deteriorated correspondingly as a business man. In contrast, Samuel Morse was a landscape painter before he turned to making money, which he did by making the electric telegraph practical. Werner Siemens moved from electrical innovations through applied science (metallurgy) to pure science.

Irregular Advance

One feature which seems to be common to all types of innovation is that advances are not made along a smooth front, but take place in a decidedly jerky way. This reflects the pattern of the `artistic' end of the rectangle, where elements that are unpredictable and revolutionary, are dominant. It is of the essence of works of art that they would not have come into being without the existence of a particular artist (the author of qualitative change is always identifiable) whereas it is of the essence of a trading transaction that it would have happened in much the same way irrespective of the existence of any particular trader (quantitative change is characteristically anonymous). Once again, the insights of Schumpeter get to the heart of things. He saw innovation as always involving a `jump', a clear discontinuity with what had been there before. He was fascinated by this phenomenon of uneven progress, in sharp contrast to Marx, whose view of the way change occurs leant towards evolution rather than revolution.

The reason is doubtless because Schumpeter's thought gave such importance to human personality in the economic process, whereas Marx tended to think of what masses of people do and feel in common, not what separates individuals out from the crowd. In Schumpeter's thought, there invariably are more implications to the `jump' than are realized in practice immediately.

Kinds of Response

It is consequently necessary to distinguish between the A-phase and the B-phase in all innovation. The A-phase is the bringing into being of the initial major discontinuity with the past, the `jump' in some positive form, so that the `new thing' can be seen for the first time in some substantially complete way. The B-phase is the process, generally long drawn-out, of extracting all the implications of the A-phase. What economists call the `new production function' established by the A-phase, is initially much more of an ideal than a reality. The B-phase consists in making the `real' production function correspond to the `ideal' one. In contrast to the A-phase, which is usually exciting and dramatic, the B-phase involves a large number of comparatively humdrum changes and adjustments, individually unimportant but cumulatively of very great importance indeed. In fact, such evidence as is available is that the B-phase of innovation is economically at least as important as the A-phase, because it is only in it that the scarcest factor is economized the most.[14]

Schumpeter also has the following way of describing these two types of innovative activity:

> Whenever an economy or a sector of an economy adapts itself to a change in its data in the way that traditional theory describes, we may speak of the development as *adaptive* response. And whenever the economy or an industry or some firms in an industry do something else, something that is outside the range of existing practice, we may speak of *creative* response.[15]

In his mind, creative response has three essential characteristics: It can only be understood *after* it has taken place, hardly ever before. It shapes the whole course of subsequent events and their long run outcome - `it creates situations from which there is no bridge to those situations that might have emerged in its absence'. And thirdly, it obviously has something to do with the quality of available personnel, both absolute and relative, and thus with individual decisions, actions and patterns of behaviour. Such a view

---

[14] J.L. Enos in R.R. Nelson (Ed.) *The Rate and Direction of Inventive Activity* (1962) 317.
[15] J.A. Schumpeter in *Journal of Economic History* (1947) 150.

of creative response identifies it with innovative activity as it has been described above. Bearing in mind that an entrepreneur can be defined as `an innovator acting in an area of life where the appropriate measure is money', Schumpeter's conclusion that `a study of creative response in business becomes coterminous with a study of entrepreneurship'[16] is fully in line with the general view of innovation which is being developed here.

Since it is the personal element which has most effect upon how change takes place, it would not be surprising to find that a similar dual-phase pattern is also to be found in those activities which rank higher in the rectangle than innovation. Every great artist has imitators, the more creative of whom do not simply repeat what they have done, but develop it still further. Chopin, for example, wrote music for the piano which was highly original, but which can nevertheless be regarded from one point of view as drawing musical consequences from a `leap' which had been made by Beethoven. In literature, there has been an immense amount of work which may be regarded as the B-phase of a view of personality and particularly of relations between the sexes, of which the A-phase is to be found in the writings of D.H. Lawrence.

Invention Parallel

The same dual pattern in invention was recognized as long ago as 1908 by A.F. Ravenshear, who distinguished `originative' from `intensive' invention, the first being the big, dramatic insight, the second the series of subordinate ideas building upon this, and necessary if all its implications are to be drawn out.[17] Ravenshear's categories clearly correspond to Schumpeter's A and B phases, as indeed they do to `technological' and `technical' innovation. The first of these refers to a change of such a magnitude that it becomes increasingly pointless to carry on the line of development which was being followed before its occurrence. The second refers to the series of small improvements by which the potential of the new way of doing things is fully realized. Technological change sets the direction which development

[16] ibid.
[17] A.F. Ravenshear *The Industrial and Commercial Influence of the English Patent System* (1908) 22.

will take; technical change establishes the rate at which it will proceed. Much confusion is caused by the frequent use of 'technological' when what is meant is 'technical', not least by people seeking a more prestigious label for their work.

Incremental Changes

Both of these can be illustrated by the way in which the possibilities inherent in the design of a particular machine emerge over time as a result of countless modifications, each small in itself, but with great cumulative effect. In the 1930s, Rolls-Royce began work on P.V. (for Private Venture) 12, an aero-engine of radical design. This became the R-R Merlin, which powered nearly all British aircraft and some American ones during the War. Its power was less than 2000 h.p. in 1939, but this had grown to 4000 h.p. by the end of the War, and reliability, as evidenced by hours between overhauls, was 'stretched' correspondingly. P. V. 12 involved 'originative' invention (primarily qualitative change) the development of the Merlin was 'intensive' invention (primarily quantitative change) and, in economic terms, one was evidently as important as the other. Another example of the results of intensive invention is the price of a Kilowatt of electricity, which in America in 1882 was 40c., in 1897 20c., and in 1947 less than 2c., the reduction being very largely due to B-phase developments in turbine technology. B-phase innovation is also illustrated by L.T.C. Rolt's parallel between the place of Whitworth in machine-tool history and that of Henry Royce in automobile engineering:

> Neither man was an inventive genius but both possessed standards so exacting that even the best was never good enough. With unerring judgement they sought out the best features of contemporary design, improved upon them and combined them in one masterly synthesis. This is a conscious and deliberate process not to be confused with the kind of unconscious syntheses Henry Maudslay achieved when he built his first screw-cutting lathe. Works of the latter kind require inventive genius because the fact that they are combinations of preconceived ideas only becomes evident to the historian.[18]

[18] L.T.C. Rolt *Tools for the Job* (1965) 117.

F.W. Lanchester, the outstandingly inventive engineer to whom, amongst other things, many of the fundamentals of aerodynamics are owed, was to Royce what Rolt holds Maudslay was to Whitworth. Rolt's comments are particularly interesting in the light of what Schumpeter has to say about `creative response' only becoming intelligible in retrospect, whereas `adaptive response' is a logical and therefore largely predictable development out of existing practice.

`Clustering' of Innovations

Schumpeter also called attention to the way innovations tend to `cluster'. When there is an innovation in one area of life, it tends to be followed rather quickly by a number of others, some of which may be important in their own right and not merely B-phase developments of the first one. The tendency to `cluster' and the fact that a B-phase follows an A-phase in innovation, both have the same cause: a change in the risk of failure in breaking new ground.[19] When the work of any pioneer is seen to be fruitful, others will then start investigating neighbouring territories with the object of sharing in the perceived insights or rewards. Because of this success, their own risk in doing this is - at least subjectively - less than when the pioneer started the original exploration. If they in turn are seen to succeed, those investors who are only able to follow the lead of others start crowding in. Technology and even mundane business have their Klondyke rushes, too.

[19] O. Lange *Review of Economics &Statistics* (1941) 192.

These various concepts may be set out as follows:

DESCRIPTION	CHARACTERISTICS
(1) Schumpeter's A-phase or Ravenshear's `originative' invention or Qualitative change or Technological innovation	One and big; a `leap ' or discontinuity; and establishes a new production function; and understandable only with hindsight; and changes the course of development irrevocably; and needs high creativity.
(2) Schumpeter's B-phase or Ravenshear's `intensive' Invention or Quantitative change or Technical innovation	Many and small; each change arises from its predecessor, and determines its successor; and moves along a theoretical production function to make it a reality; and deterimines the rate of change, not its direction; and is ultimately as economically important as (1) because it optimizes the use of scarce resources; and does not require creativity to be high.

Social Conditioning

Returning to the rectangle, it will be recalled that as one moves downwards through the list of activities, they are increasingly conditioned by the surrounding social culture. In the case of the innovator, whilst the personal component is considerable, the breakthrough, if it is to be successful, must be done as the forerunner of the crowd, that is, it must be `socialized'. The same is even more true of entrepreneurs, who are thus the classical type of debtor to society, for two reasons: It is in social life that they uncover dormant possibilities which they can turn into actuality, secondly, it is society which provides them with the actual productive resources which they can re-arrange into a new pattern.[20]

---

[20] A. Taymans *L' homme agent du développement économique* (1951) 36.

Innovators, being further up the scale in the `private' direction, are less in debt to the surrounding culture, but nevertheless cannot carry on their characteristic activity except within it. There seems to be a quite definite tendency on the part of innovators to try to escape from this aspect of their work. The drift of the innovating temperament is in the direction of invention, rather than towards entrepreneurship, and this is one reason why so many innovating companies eventually fall out of the control of their founders, and become victims of bankers and accountants who have taken care not to let themselves be seduced in the same way. The cause of this `drift' can be nothing else than the charm (sometimes amounting to fatal intoxication) that creative experience has for humankind. The entrepreneur who has taken one idea to business reality, then seeks a bigger challenge and finds it in some form of innovation; it can happen that because the time-scale in the latter is so much longer than in the former, financial resources will not stand the strain, so that a firm gets taken over by another which has kept to a less imaginative path. Or the firm which has made a success of technically innovating some ideas of others, is tempted to originate its own through a major research programme (i.e. it tries its hand at qualitative change) and finds that it has moved from a world where the risks, though high, are acceptable, to one where the chances of success are just about the inverse of what business is used to.

Gilfillan and Rossman

The fact that the innovator's action is `socialized' raises the question as to how important is his individual contribution at all? S.C. Gilfillan, whose *Sociology of Invention* - although written in 1935, it is still one of the key works in this field - holds as far as invention is concerned that:

> There is no indication that any individual's genius has been necessary to any invention that has had any importance. To the historian and social scientist the progress of invention appears impersonal. Yet invention can only come at the hand of some sort of inventors and its directions, frequency and efficiency are determined wholly through deliberate actions by these men, in some proportion to their absolute numbers, intelligence, moral traits,

strength of motives for inventing, time free for it, and mental and mechanical equipment for it.[21]

Invention, for Gilfillan, is:

> ... a sociological phenomenon, a complex of folkways. It has probably no existence, i.e. definition at all, except what is imposed upon the engineering objects by the standardising tendencies of social man ... if an invention really fits into a civilisation, so that it is freely used, it is not apt to fit into a widely different civilisation ... The heaviest and the hardest block of steel is moulded into its form by human interests and emotions. The inner culture sets the goals, for which the inventor contrives the appropriate tools of civilisation, while also in turn doing his part to modify the culture, providing a material basis for changed ideals.[22]

Another pioneer in this area, Joseph Rossman, held that 'our inventions are the result of social accretions to prior inventions'.[23] He adds a useful distinction between the private and social aspects of invention:

> A man, for example, may construct a pump which to his knowledge is absolutely new. He has never read about such a pump and has never seen one in use. This man has actually created this machine by his own mental processes without receiving direct suggestions from any source whatever. Let us assume that he has spent years of his time and thousands of dollars to build and perfect his pump ... But if we should search the Patent Office records we would find an exact description of the same pump made a hundred years before. Our inventor has in this case reinvented the machine, and, as far as he is concerned, and from the psychological viewpoint, he is a true inventor. But what has he added to our fund of knowledge and to our cultural achievement? Nothing. From the cultural viewpoint, therefore, this man has made no invention. The relative meaning of invention is often overlooked. Invention must pass the cultural test of novelty in order to be recognized as a new invention.[24]

---

[21] S.C. Gilfillan *The Sociology of Invention* (1935) 10.

[22] ibid. 26, 34, 45.

[23] J. Rossman *The Psychology of the Inventor* (1931) 3.

[24] ibid. 13.

Cultural Test

Rossman's vocabulary contributes to making precise the difference between invention, innovation and entrepreneurship. The latter has to pass a test which is not merely a cultural one, but which also involves making money; innovation has to pass the cultural test, though not necessarily the money test - in any event in the short term; invention, psychologically considered, need not pass the cultural test at all. The fact that we generally speak of inventions that do face up to, and pass the cultural test, i.e. those that are actually innovated, is one cause of confusion between invention and innovation. Most inventing, in the psychological sense, is actually re-inventing, in the social sense, but there cannot be such a thing as re-innovation within the same culture.

Innovation's position in the rectangle implies that social values will count equally with personal ones. The activity of innovation requires intense personal activity, certainly, but in a socially meaningful context. Innovators can never cease to keep the cultural test in the forefront of their mind, since they have accepted the satisfaction of some social need as their objective.

A human need is never satisfied as such. What can be satisfied is a want, which is need articulated in a particular way by cultural factors. At one time the human need for mobility may express itself in terms of a want for a fast horse, at another it may be a want for a fast car. Innovators who see what they think is a better way of satisfying a particular need are therefore involved in modifying the want that articulates it, that is, they are involved in bringing about cultural change. The form this cultural change will take will reflect both the innovators' personality and the ways of articulating that particular need into wants that are available to them.

It is important to stress that the innovators' satisfaction is found precisely in satisfying the cultural test. It is not enough for them that the possibilities of an idea can be imagined and planned out, in no matter what detail, or how vividly in the imagination. Until they can experience the idea in its embodiment, in actual concrete, working terms, in performance, in something that has taken on a life of its own by being inserted in the appropriate niche in the surrounding culture, something which can now exist in some sense apart from them, (even though for a long time whether it would ever come to anything seemed to depend upon them and them alone) they will not be satisfied.

Multiple Inventions

One of the arguments on which those who argue that the social factors in this area outweigh the personal ones overwhelmingly, rest their case, is the evidence of multiple invention - and, of course, there is even stronger evidence of multiple innovation. Rossman quotes one list of 148 important inventions and discoveries which were made independently by two or more people, and a second one, containing `practically every important advance in medicine' of another 150 important multiple discoveries. An even stronger argument for the social nature of invention and innovation could be that different, but effectively equivalent ways of satisfying the same perceived need frequently arise at the same time.[25] Since want is defined by social patterns, it only requires one individual (possibly of outstanding ability) to perceive it and arrange for it to be satisfied. But even individuals of outstanding ability are distributed through the population by the normal probability curve, it is argued, so that there will always be more than one individual capable of seeing and satisfying wants, and no individual may therefore be regarded as essential to any innovation.[26]

The solution to this problem may not be quite so simple and clear-cut as the sociologists claim it to be, and reference back to the rectangle helps to illustrate why. It may be taken for granted that at the bottom end of it, the elements of understanding and predictability of needs are so strong that at any time, in any population, there will inevitably be many who can see how a need can be articulated into a want for a particular product, and have the ability to arrange for it to be satisfied. This is why all traders think their own business is always overcrowded and too competitive, and it is also why whatever happens in trading is virtually independent of whether

[25] S.C. Gilfillan *The Sociology of Invention* (1935) 151.
[26] cf. W.F. Ogburn *Culture and Social Change* (1964).

any particular individual acts or not. Towards the top end of the rectangle, the time it takes outstanding artists in any field to become accepted is evidence of how little the need which they satisfy has been previously articulated in *their* special way into a want. An artist satisfies need by sharing his own experience of the world. What we want from a painter is to share his eyes, and it is his eyes he gives us through his painting. In so far as this is so, statistical considerations do not apply, since no matter how large the population, one person and one only can satisfy this particular want. There can be no law of large numbers and no normal probability curve. In the intermediate area, between the artist and the trader, the individual's contribution is not unique, as the artist's is, but neither is it swamped by the social element, as is the trader's.

For invention, perception alone is not enough: `besides the necessity', as Rossman puts it, `we must have an individual who reacts with the proper emotional intensity to the need'.[27] Fessenden (who was Edison's Secretary) quotes a long list of scientists who had been working for years on sound waves, using recordings made by a mark traced by a pointer on lamp-black; none of them was the inventor of the phonograph, because only Edison thought of running the arrangement backwards - presumably because only he wanted to achieve it enough.[28]

This capacity to respond emotionally to wants is even more important in the case of innovation, because of the cultural test which has to be passed. This is why Schumpeter was right when he stressed that it was `a feat, not of intellect, but of will'. The importance of the contribution of identifiable individuals to the insertion of inventions into the surrounding social culture can therefore be seen. To begin with, perception of the way in which an invention or new idea articulates, or can be made to articulate, a need into a want for a particular product is rare. Of the few who may perceive it still fewer will be motivated to take action. Difficulties will eliminate all but the most determined, until in the end one will emerge as the innovator.

---

[27] Rossman op. cit. 87.
[28] R. Fessenden *The Deluged Civilization of the Caucasus Isthmus* (1923) 99.

Consider the seventeenth-century Canal du Midi linking the Atlantic with the Mediterranean across France - `nothing on so grand a scale had been built by man since the fall of the Roman Empire'.[29] This was talked about for generations, but it was not actually done until a quite remarkable man, Pierre Paul Riquet, devoted himself and his money to the project so completely as to earn the cynics' comment that `he had made a canal so as to drown himself and his family'. Riquet's career also raises the intriguing question of age and innovative work. Many empirical studies suggest that inventing may be best done in youth, as indeed may all absorption of ideas and information from outside. Mathematicians are known to `peak' in their twenties, Keynes thought that few could take in new ideas after the age of twenty-five or thirty; Schumpeter himself always spoke of `the sacred fertile third decade'.[30] But if Riquet is at all typical, the same may not be the case with innovation. He was fifty when he took up the task, sixty-one by the time building actually commenced, and seventy-three when he had to throw his whole personal fortune into the scales to ensure that it was finished.

Unique Contribution

Thus, without a particular individual, even if an innovation might still have come about, it would very probably not have done so at the same time or place. The uniqueness of the innovator's contribution is to be found in the fact that some change in the arrangement of the world as known was realized at a particular time in a particular place, rather than elsewhere and at another time. It is possible also to add `realized in a particular way', since the personal element in innovation will certainly bring some related flavour to the way in which the realisation takes shape, even if it is no more than to give a name to it, as the Hall-Herault process of extracting aluminium perpetuates the names of the American and the Frenchman who originated it virtually simultaneously. While every innovator is well aware that what he is involved in might have come about anyway, to have been the cause of the precise time and place (and possibly even mode) in

---

[29] L.T.C. Rolt, *From Sea to Sea* (1973) 2.
[30] J.M. Keynes *General Theory of Employment, Interest & Money* (1936) 387.

which it came about, is not an achievement to be despised. No doubt the jet engine would have come to the English-speaking world without Sir Frank Whittle, but it would probably have done so through belated copying of German achievement. For the British people and for the world, Whittle's efforts to develop his invention - almost completely vain throughout the 'thirties - had tremendous consequences. How many lives were saved because Florey innovated Fleming's discovery of Penicillin and the U.S. Government deployed vast resources to produce it, when they did, even if it, or its equivalent, might eventually have become available in some other way? Although less than in the case of the artist, the element of uniqueness in what the inventor or innovator does is important, and he is relatively, even if not absolutely irreplacable. Innovative activity is only possible at all because of individual human creativeness. It represents one way in which individuals imprint their personal stamp on the world, justifying in its own way Eric Gill's phrase: `The artist is not a different kind of man, but every man is a different kind of artist'. What will next be seen is that the exercise of creativity in innovation is a particular kind of learning process.

CHAPTER II

Innovation As Learning

In a lecture which John Constable delivered to the Royal Institution in 1836, he asserted that:

> Painting is a science, and should be pursued as an inquiry into the laws of nature. Why, then, may not landscape painting be considered as a branch of natural philosophy, of which pictures are but the experiments?[1]

Constable found that science enlarged his understanding of landscape; in particular he became fascinated by geology, which taught him the physical structure of what he painted with such feeling. `The sister arts', he wrote elsewhere, `have less hold on my mind in its occasional ramblings from my one pursuit than the sciences'.[2] In all this he was untypical of post-Renaissance artists, and the idea that artistic activity is an alternative to science as a means of exploring reality, is quite strange to the modern mind.

In a parallel way, we think of working in industry and `being an artist' as being mutually exclusive, and both artists and serious writers are characteristically antagonistic, not merely indifferent to business and technology. It was not so at the beginning of the industrial revolution which was welcomed with enthusiasm by both painters and poets, although disillusion was not long in coming.

Knowledge: `Delight' or `Power'?

Behind these antipathies there lies a much deeper and older conflict. This is between two ways of valuing knowledge, one of

---

[1] C.R. Leslie *Memoirs of the Life of John Constable, R.A.*, (Shirley edn. 1937) 403.
[2] ibid. xliv.

which considers knowledge as worth seeking for its own sake, in other words, it is valued as *delight,* whereas the other values knowledge for the practical benefits it can bestow, it seeks knowledge as *power.* The first is the Greek strand in our tradition, the second is rooted in the cultures of Islam and China. When, in the thirteenth century, Roger Bacon was advocating an experimental science which could create automobiles, flying machines and devices to destroy enemy armies, he was the intellectual heir of the Arabic scientists who had sought knowledge in order to discover the Elixir of Life and to change base metals into gold and silver.[3] Marco Polo is only the best known of a host of travellers from Europe who looked to the Orient as a source of advanced technology as well as riches, much as productivity teams from Europe flooded across to the United States in the 1950s.

Modern technology, applied science and business organisation have their origins in Arabic magic, Chinese empiricism and Roman practicality. Our intellectual and artistic traditions have other roots, and even at the peak of Western culture, the two approaches to knowledge were far from being reconciled. In recent centuries, the emphasis in the West has increasingly been on knowledge as power, with consequent divergence between the way of exploring reality by artistic activity and experience, and that of exploring it through science, because the dominant Western version of science is the one which has least in common with the artistic tradition. Beauty and immediate experience are the common language of the artist and the `pure' scientist, but the typical scientist of the West is an applied scientist, whose criterion is not `does this give delight?' but rather `what does it produce?' They have some access to the tradition of pure science, but none to that in which Art is equally a way of exploring and expropriating reality. Innovation bridges the gap, because it is a learning process in both dimensions, in Constable's way as well as Bacon's way. The joy, satisfaction or delight of individual innovators as they go through this particular learning experience, will be shown to be central to getting new things done, in which the power of knowledge is demonstrated.

[3] Christopher Dawson *Medieval Essays* (1953) 159.

Ignorance of Implications

Innovation must involve learning because it is concerned with drawing out the concrete implications of new things, and these implications cannot be known in advance.[4] The problem about every true discovery is that individuals neither know what they have discovered, nor how this relates to what they already know. `The trouble with most people who try to invent is that they do not know when they have got the thing they are looking for': Columbus, thinking he had found a new route to the East (with all that that implied) when in fact he had discovered America (with all that *that* implied) is the very type of all inventors. Sir Frank Whittle thought that the only use his jet engine would have would be in long-range mail planes. Sir Alexander Fleming `had no conception of the therapeutic possibilities of Penicillin'.[5] What the inventor does not know, the innovator has to find out. For innovators, the problem is a dual one. They stand between the new thing and the world of concrete realities for which this new thing has implications and possibilities, and into which it is to be integrated. The new thing is only partially known and understood, the world into which it is to be inserted is also known very imperfectly, so that the implications of one for the other are surrounded by very considerable uncertainty.

Sir Barnes Wallis, whose views are backed by outstanding achievement as inventor, innovator and practical engineer, has expressed very well this feeling on the part of an innovator of surrounding, all-pervading uncertainty, in which his own role often seems imprecise, and even the goal can be obscured:

> Research ... has a time element ... almost as inexorable as the time element in the playing of a great symphony; only, in this case the symphony one is conducting? composing? playing? is not only unfinished but *unknown*.[6]

[4] T. Marschak et al. *Strategy for R & D* (1967) 1.
[5] R. Hare *Birth of Penicillin* (1970) 108.
[6] Quoted in J.E. Morpurgo *Barnes Wallis* (1972) 351.

Amongst people with experience of innovation, there is always realisation that it is never known until the very end of the innovatory process, either what the true nature of the idea that is being turned into concrete form is, or where it fits into the world. This leads to procedures for matching new things (with all their potentiality) to markets (with all theirs). The list of such procedures includes analysis, evaluation of mathematical or paper models, focussed applied research, building and testing of physical models, similar work with full scale prototypes, and finally the testing of production items. The Creative Engineering Program of the U.S. General Electric Co. formalized these steps as: Recognize the Problem, Define, Search, Evaluate, Select and Follow-through.[7]

Information

It will be observed that every single one of these steps, except perhaps the last, is concerned only with *learning*; at every stage the knowledge gained in all earlier stages is used as a basis for further advance. What goes through this system, then, is information, not hardware. Ideally, hardware should only emerge at the very end, when completion of assembly of all the relevant information enables just the right embodiment of the original idea for a particular market to be manufactured. Of course, reality very rarely, if ever, allows this ideal to be realized in practice. At different points in the process of learning what is in the new idea, it may be necessary to embody it in hardware. The kind of learning which leads on to the next stage may only be obtainable in some sort of experimental way, and more can usually be learned from simple experiments than from mathematical models. This kind of learning is also the only one possible for a particular kind of mind, the kind which becomes especially important in the later stages of innovation, for which tangible reality is essential. Moving downwards (towards the activity of the trader) in the rectangle of Chapter I, the type of person suited to the activity increasingly becomes one for whom purely mental constructs have less meaning. The process of innovation is such a movement and follows the same pattern. At the very outset, what is needed is

[7] E.K. von Fange *Professional Creativity* (1959) 117.

someone who is highly sensitive to ideas as ideas, since otherwise the products of inventive brains would strike no chord in the minds and hearts of innovators. Later on, however, this requirement takes second place, especially as difficulties and obstacles multiply, to a desire to see the idea realized in concrete form, since only the strength of this desire can surmount the problems. The real innovator combines both qualities within himself, so that it is no wonder either that Schumpeter should have claimed that he represents a distinct sociological type, or that good innovators are quite scarce.

Imagination

The first requirement of innovation is therefore imagination. It is this which enables innovators, as they look towards the new idea, to visualize its possibilities, and then, by keeping both the partially formed idea and its ultimate possible embodiments in mind through the power of their imagination, they undertake to control the intermediate steps by which one becomes the other. All modern theory accepts that learning only takes place through activity. Moreover, if learning performance is to improve, the stimuli situations must themselves be evolving, otherwise diminishing returns quickly set in.[8] For the process of innovation considered as learning, analysis produces stimuli as well as data, leading to the making and evaluation of models on paper, then to applied research designed to throw light upon various dark corners, and so on. All the time, the process is controlled by the willpower of innovators, rooted in their imaginative grasp of the original idea, the present level of information relative to it, and the ultimate objective, all simultaneously. It is they who must decide the approximate performance attributes for each of the components or subsystems, the extent of their interrelatedness, the distribution of effort between uncertainty-reducing tasks, whether parallel approaches are to be tried for any component, and if so, how many.[9] Further indirect confirmation of the importance of the innovator's role in keeping the eyes of all intermediate ones, is given by the experience that response from the ultimate user should

[8] K.J. Arrow in *Review of Economic Studies* (1962) 115.
[9] T. Marschak op. cit. 29.

be built into the learning process at every stage, and from the earliest possible moment.

Inertia

The capacity of an innovator's imagination to grasp and hold on to the ultimate objective is vitally important for innovation, because there is a strong tendency for the process to generate its own inertia or to get sidetracked. One important reason for this in technological innovation, is that engineers are prone to the temptation to express the idea in hardware too early. Everything in the mentality and training of engineers causes them to prefer a detailed drawing to a disembodied idea, and a piece of hardware to either. The engineering mind much prefers perfected hardware to 'breadboard' models, and left to itself, it will try to move hardware, not information, through the innovatory system, so slowing it down and increasing its costs enormously. A prototype should always be regarded as a learning device, never merely as a proof of design.[10] Engineers cannot be blamed for wanting to see the idea on which they are working emerge into a physical embodiment as early as possible, but successful innovation depends upon there being a strong discipline which stresses throughout that the only hardware that is really wanted is the ultimate product that will be sold, that all that is needed up to that final point is information, and that if hardware is essential for generating needed information, it must be strictly limited by defining clearly the information it is intended to produce and ensuring that no elaboration of design or construction is allowed to go beyond what is justified by this objective.

Just how important this type of control may be, is suggested by one expert view that the overwhelming cause of American advantage over Britain in innovation can be found in shorter development times.[11] This is not only due to being able to bring greater resources to bear simultaneously, but also to better direction of the build-up of information in the light of the ultimate objective, especially through insisting upon intermediate hardware being a means, not an end. Another aspect of the innovatory process,

---

[10] cf. Marschak op. cit. 36.
[11] M.J. Peck in R.C. Caves (ed.) *Britain's Economic Prospects* (1968) 473.

considered as a flow of information, is the parallel function of the innovator in making sure that no more information is generated at any stage than is needed to enable the next stage to begin. Just as engineers like to see ideas expressed in hardware, scientists like to see promising lines of enquiry followed up, and above all, they like their data to be comprehensive.

Consequently, just as an innovation can be slowed down and its cost greatly increased, by too much hardware too early, the same can happen by elaborating information-collection at any stage, beyond what is strictly necessary. This is particularly apparent in large organisations, where in addition to elaborate resources for developing information, there is frequently a management structure which places a premium upon minimising risk in decisions from the point of view of the career-safety of the people concerned. There is little or no reward for reaching a decision which turns out to be right, quickly and cheaply, but the results of reaching a wrong decision can be disastrous. Everything therefore pushes towards the piling-up of information. It *may* contribute to more certainty, but in any event it postpones the time when a decision has to be taken.

An interesting example of this process is to be found in a pair of U.S. Government development contracts on searchlights which were given at the same time to the General Electric Co. and to Elmer Sperry's infant firm. Sperry produced far more for his money, and quicker, and it was generally considered that General Electric tried to assemble far more information from sophisticated tests than was justified by the state of the art at that time.[12] In other words, by letting the information-gathering process become out of proportion to the end in view, they did not act as innovators, whereas Sperry did.

Innovators' control

Against these powerful tendencies, of engineers to elaborate the intermediate hardware, and of scientists to elaborate the intermediate information, there is only one counterbalancing force. This is the imagination of the controlling innovators, holding both the idea and its ultimate embodiment together so that the steps

---

[12] T. P. Hughes *Elmer Sperry* (1971) 223.

between them can be seen in their proper sequence, and their determination not to let the people in charge of these steps give in to any temptation which would slow down the process. This capacity, to force people always to bear in mind the war to be won years ahead even in the heat of a battle to be won to-day, has always been characteristic of the best generals; yet again reality endorses Schumpeter's dictum that successful innovation is a question of leadership. The need for this capacity is one reason why product `champions' are always identifiable in the case of successful innovations. Without them, the process of turning an idea into reality becomes bogged down in intermediate hardware or in making the collection of data into an end in itself. `Ability to do research work' as Fessenden insisted, `and ability to make developments are absolutely distinct'.[13] As an important inventor in his own right, his comment carries weight.

None of this is to decry the importance of putting together a sound basis of information at every stage before moving on to the next, nor to pretend that in many cases this will not require the making of hardware so that this can be tested. `We advance', as Kelvin said, `according to the precision of our measures' - and very often it is only working with intermediate hardware that can provide the measure needed. The practical rules which successful innovators have developed for dealing with this problem amount to: Develop only the bare minimum to prove an idea, prove only one idea at a time, never develop what can be bought or modified, minimize the time to demonstration, insist on the highest standards of workmanship, and do all of this with the smallest possible team.[14]

Learning By Doing

Use of hardware in this way is an aspect of `learning by doing', which in itself is very characteristic of innovatory activity. Even in areas where there is an immense amount of scientific information, many innovations still only come about through tackling the uncertainties empirically, in the confidence that the programme required is within the resources of the organisation.

[13] R.A. Fessenden *The Deluged Civilization of the Caucasus Isthmus* (1923) 128.
[14] J.A. Kuecken *Creativity, Invention & Progress* (1969) 76.

Usually, this occurs in technical rather than technological innovation. The famous Boeing 727 and 737 wings, for example, were developed by an immense amount of pragmatic wind-tunnel testing, coupled with much courage in pitting great engineering resources against the problems involved, rather than by theoretical work. The results are important enough to justify calling such an innovation a technological one, even though the outcome may have been logically implicit in the situation as it was perceived at the start.

Why 'learning by doing' is so important to innovation is illustrated by the many attempts which have been made in the field known as industrial dynamics, to build models of business situations. These rarely have less than 150 components, and sometimes as many as 1500. By no means all of these components vary independently of one another, but the complexity is nevertheless far in excess of what the human mind can cope with - situations involving 6 or at most 7 variables. Consequently, interaction of the various components in a real life situation can only be dealt with if it is greatly simplified, and the greater the uncertainty, the more need there is for 'decision rules' to achieve this.[15]

Uncertainty

It will be clear from the Chapter I rectangle, for example, that technological innovation is even less predictable and involves more variables than any business or 'trading' situation, and therefore has all the more need for simplification. On the 'invention' side of innovation, almost everything is a matter of decision rules, since uncertainty is so high. On the 'entrepreneurial' side, uncertainty is less, but even here the characteristic role of the entrepreneur in 'filling gaps and completing inputs', directs his activity precisely to the areas for which least information is available. The human mind is able to work with two approaches to a problem simultaneously, but can only go beyond this with difficulty. The higher the level of technology, the harder it has been found for someone doing research to consider more than two approaches. Concentration also

[15] J.H. Hoskins in David Allison *The R & D Game* (1969) 270.

seems to be associated with quality, in that research groups which produce higher-rated solutions to problems, also tend to generate fewer new approaches.[16]

Another side to the limitation of the human mind as far as innovation is concerned is that new ideas do not emerge by an automatic process of feeding in old ones. Even if relationships between two pieces of information in the mind do exist in the abstract, they will not be perceived by individuals unless they are alert to both pieces simultaneously - and this alertness is at least as much a matter of emotion as of rational behaviour. The information received in the conscious mind is only a sample of the total amount of information input. Moreover, it is not a random sample, in which every item of new information arriving has as much chance of being taken up and considered consciously as any other. It is a *weighted* sample, and the weights attaching to individual pieces of information as received are *largely made up of feeling*: `Creative thinking is not a purely intellectual process; on the contrary, the thinker is dominated by his emotions from start to finish of the work'.[17]

Emotion Essential

The first reason for this is because creative thinking is always thinking in the face of uncertainty. In such a situation, rationality is defeated, and the individual who relies upon rational thinking exclusively, is paralysed, unable either to think constructively, or to act. Nothing except feeling can then come to the rescue, to make a leap forward into the unknown possible. And it is because emotion is individual that creative thinking is also individual, even at the level of innovation, so that innovation is invariably associated with some identifiable person. Even if accomplished by a group, it is always a group with very strong and identifiable individual leadership. The `leap' which Schumpeter held that hindsight would always find in innovation, begins as a leap in the dark on the part of some individual. There was a time when it was fashionable to say that

---

[16] T.J. Allen, Meadows & Marquis, Sloan School of Management, M.I.T. Working Paper 313-68.

[17] E. K. Von Fange *Professional Creativity* (1959) 79.

the day of the importance of the individual in technology and business was gone, and that progress now depended only upon large scale R & D, and the work of teams of people. This view has been exploded by empirical research: In a study of a dozen new materials, all of which would necessarily have involved large resources for research in their development, a U.S. Government Agency found that in almost every case it was possible to identify a single individual who had played a uniquely important part. [18] This he had done by becoming involved with the project in an unusually personal way, involving his own pride in it, committing himself totally to its success. Similar evidence was given to a U.S. Senate subcommittee.[19] In a study of a large number of recent innovations in Britain, it was also found that in almost every case the influence of one individual was of paramount importance.[20]

Importance of Individuals

None of this is surprising if the role emotion plays in innovation is given its proper weight. Business leaders, however, want to be able to assume that innovation is a fully rational process which can be departmentalised and fitted into the organisation like any other function of the firm, so that the importance of the individual and of their emotional response is played down. They want this more than anything else, because the alternative gives status to unpredictability within the firm. Risk, not uncertainty, is what a business is organized to cope with. Yet nothing except the emotional response to a situation on the part of individuals in positions of power within it can pit a firm against uncertainty with any hope of survival. This is why, as an early study in this field showed, for innovation, key personalities within a firm are more important than its structures.[21] Burns & Stalker also, in their well-known study, found that firms which were poor at innovating tended to have a mechanistic form of organization; that is, they had

---

[18] M. Goldsmith *Technological Innovation and the Economy* (1970) Ch. I.

[19] U.S. Senate, Committee on the Judiciary, Sub-Committee on Antitrust and Monopoly - 89th Congress, 1st Session (Hearings Pursuant to Sen. Res. 70) 1217.

[20] J. Langrish et al. *Wealth from Knowledge* (1971) 69.

[21] W.R. Maclaurin *American Economic Review* (1950) 110.

a hierarchic structure of control and communication, much insistence on loyalty and obedience, and they attributed greater importance to `local' than to `general' knowledge. Firms which were good innovators, however, were more likely to be organized in an organic form; that is, commitment to the concern as a whole had spread `beyond any technical definition'. In such firms, communication resembles consultation rather than command, but nevertheless they remain stratified and where the authority rests is more likely to be settled by consensus rather than by a predetermined order.[22] Indirect confirmation of the Burns & Stalker thesis is to be found in a U.S. study which found that the growth rate of knowledge within firms was directly related to *informal* contacts.[23] Innovation just cannot be turned into a kind of trading, however attractive the neatness of this may be to the business mind.

`Real' and `Notional' Knowledge

Just as it is only emotion which gives the courage to act in the face of uncertainty so as to produce new information, so it is only information which is associated with feeling that is available for doing innovative work. What this means has never been expressed better than by J.H. Newman, in the famous passage where he distinguishes between `real' knowledge (which we have made part of ourselves) and `notional' knowledge (which is there in our minds if we advert to it, but to which we do not attach any great importance)[24] Firms, too, have to make knowledge their own if it is to be applied successfully. Because of this, the apparent widespread duplication of research and independent generation of information by firms which it might have been thought they could simply extract from the general knowledge `pool', is not as economically wasteful as could at first appear. Knowledge which the key people in the firm have generated themselves may be `real' knowledge, whereas what is simply taken from the `pool' may remain `notional', and no cost saving,

[22] T. Burns & G.M. Stalker *The Management of Innovation* (1966 edn.) 120.

[23] Clearinghouse for Scientific and Technical Information. Hindsight Project No. AD 642-400.

[24] J.H. Newman *A Grammar of Assent* (1947 edn.) 59.

however great, can justify knowledge which does not call out the necessary emotional response that enables it to be used effectively. There is confirmatory evidence from experience with technical licensing: commercial success is rarely achieved by licensees who do no development work themselves with the information that comes with the license. Presumably it is partly through such development work that the purchased information becomes 'real' for the licensee firm. An aspect of this emotional response is pride, which should be engaged as early as possible. Sperry made a point of announcing his inventions publicly once he had reduced them to practice sufficiently to get a Patent, so as to engage his own pride as a stimulus to the often humdrum development work which had to follow.

Information Absorbtion

One of the innovator's main tasks is to see that information is not only received by his team but also *absorbed* by it. The evidence shows that organising a flow of externally generated information to a firm is not costly, but its absorption is.[25] This cost of absorbing information from outside has a bearing upon the balance of the whole R & D budget of a firm. It is very difficult to justify expenditure upon fundamental research in any but the very largest and most diversified companies, on the basis of products emerging that can be exploited by the company within a realistic time scale. There are, however, two alternative justifications for this activity in smaller firms. The first is what is known as the 'listening-post' function.[26] Basic research has been found to be necessary if the best monitoring of new developments outside the firm, involving applied research or potentially applicable findings, is to be maintained. Secondly, absorption of new information from outside into practical applications within the firm, has been found to be facilitated if basic research is also going on. One estimate puts the losses from inadequate searching of the existing knowledge pool at 3% of all research expenditure, but this is very probably low.[27]

---

[25] W.D. Nordhaus *Invention, Growth & Welfare* (1969) 37.
[26] M.J. Peck op. cit. 469.
[27] ASLIB *Accelerating Innovation* Nottingham Symposium (1969) 30.

Whatever the actual figure may be, the best searching is always done against a background of fundamental knowledge. It is also the level of existing basic knowledge which decides the lines along which applied research will go. Just as scientists operate on the principle. of 'Occam's Razor' - that the hypothesis which involves fewest assumptions is to be preferred - managements naturally prefer to fund research which relates to areas where prediction is least unreliable. These are the areas which are best understood as a result of basic research work. For example, radio began with semiconductors (crystals). However, 'work on the vacuum tube replaced that on semiconductors because the former was better understood at the time, and so development times could more easily be predicted'.[28] These two additional functions can justify expenditure on basic research in smaller firms than carry out this type of research at present.

Controlling Research

It is doubtful, however, if the potential returns in these ways from it are sufficiently widely recognized, since even in the U.S., basic research by industry amounts to no more than 4% of total research expenditure, and this is concentrated almost exclusively in the largest firms. 'Any new technological departure necessarily takes its rise in the workmanlike endeavours of given individuals, but it can do so only by force of their familiarity with the body of knowledge which the group already has in hand', said Thorstein Veblen.[29] However, it should be clear by now that innovation cannot simply be brought about by buying information on new things to be done, from an adjacent 'pool' of knowledge. The information has to be 'digested' by the firm in such a way as to be able to be used.[30] This generally requires further development work, and it is facilitated if there is R & D going on in any event, especially to the extent that this tends towards basic research. Frequently the required knowledge will not be in the 'pool' at all, so that investment in R & D will be essential. What are the factors that affect this?

---

[28] R.R. Nelson (ed.) *The Rate and Direction of Inventive Activity* (1962) 556
[29] T. Veblen *The Instinct of Workmanship* (1914) 104.
[30] Nordhaus op. cit. 60.

J.B. Conant, who was at one time Chairman of the U.S. National Defense Research Committee, held that there was only one proven method of assisting the advance of pure science: This was to pick men of genius, to back them heavily, and leave them to direct themselves. Equally, there was only one proven method of getting results in applied science: This was to pick men of genius, to back them heavily and to keep their aim on the target chosen.[31] C.K.. Mees, an Englishman who was the very well-known Director of Research for Kodak for many years, thought that `the best person to decide what research is to be done is the man doing it, and the next best is the department head. After that, there are only increasingly worse groups – the Research Director who is wrong more than half the time, a Committee, which is wrong most of the time, and finally a Committee of vice-presidents, which is wrong all the time'. [32]

`Loose' or `Tight' Control?

There is a sort of inherent instability about any research department because of the conflict in it between uncertainty and organisation. For good organisation, certainty is essential. It depends upon everyone knowing what there is to do, what each has to do, how to do it, and when it will have to be done, for a long time ahead. None of these factors is present when the work in hand is research, because the essence of research is moving into the unknown. Research laboratories cannot function properly if they are organized too tautly, and their loose control in practice reflects the uncertainty which is their environment. The closer the research comes to being fundamental, the looser the control has to be, precisely because the surrounding uncertainty is all the greater.

At the other end of the scale, where the type of applied research is really no more than development work along clearly definable lines, or even just trouble-shooting, control can have much of the tautness that characterizes the production side of a business. Some large firms, such as Kodak and Du Pont, allow these differences to be expressed in physical separation of the different kinds of laboratory. The production departments have

---

[31] J. B. Conant quoted by C. K. Mees *The Path of Science* (1947) 196-200.
[32] C. K. Mees *The Path of Science* (1947) 135.

their own facilities for the trouble-shooting and low-order applied research, whilst the higher-order applied research and any basic research which is done, are located elsewhere, so that there can be loose control where this is appropriate without adverse effects upon activity which is better kept upon a tighter rein. The productivity of research can only suffer if uncertainty is tackled as if it is a situation of measurable risk, and vice versa.

Parallel Approaches

In this process of uncertainty reduction, there is much to be said for pursuing several approaches at the same time if the resources are available to do so. One view is that, where money is no object, the more uncertainty there is at any decision point, the more alternative routes to the next decision point should be tried simultaneously. Perhaps the best known example of this was in the Manhattan project, when speed of obtaining the atomic bomb was essential and the cost did not matter. The isotope U^{235} was required to be developed from U^{238}. Five approaches to this were followed in parallel; the path that proved to be quickest was neither the most promising at the outset nor the most economical in the long term.[33] Apart from speeding up research results, attempting to solve problems from more than one angle at the same time introduces an element of competition into research, which can be of considerable help to the innovator in keeping the attention of the personnel involved on to the main target, as well as in stimulating them to achievement. Development of skill in handling parallel approaches while minimising the cost of doing so, is one of the most advantageous ways of improving performance in innovation.

The problem of controlling research budgets is one which no innovator has ever solved satisfactorily. U.S. studies show that projects regularly cost two to three times their original estimates, and take half to two-thirds longer.[34] In one British study, ratios of from 0.97 to 1.51 between estimated and actual costs were reported. The corresponding ratios for duration ranged

[33] R.R. Nelson in *Journal of Business* (1959) 117.
[34] Marshall & Meckling in R.R. Nelson (ed.) *The Rate & Direction of Inventive Activity* (1962) 474.

from 1.39 to 3.04.[35] If these studies are both reliable and typical, there is something to be learned from the contrast: In Britain, projects tend to escape from control more in terms of time than in terms of cost, whereas in the U.S., even if costs escalate, schedule slippage tends to be relatively less. Shorter development times, as mentioned earlier, have been authoritatively claimed to be a major source of American industrial advantage, and where lead-time is increasingly important as a source of the protection that is essential for innovation, this is quite plausible. There is, therefore, a hint here that U.S. industry's apparent preference for excess costs rather than excess time in research, may be justified by results. The inherent difficulty about controlling the time factor in research is that there is no automatic cut-off point, with a project that is going nowhere, as there is with one that is successful.[36] Once a new idea clearly looks like turning into a good product, pressure quickly builds up from the production and sales sides of a business, which are naturally anxious to get their hands on it. Even if the research people are reluctant to let it go because they wish to perfect it further, they are on weak ground compared with the others' ability to promise imminent sales and profits. An unsuccessful idea, however, has nothing at this level working against its continuance in the research department, to reinforce the will of top management to cut it out.

`Cut-Off' Arrangements

Paradoxically, then, the first question to be asked about any proposed expenditure on research is, what precise arrangements are there to *stop* it? In particular, *who* is to take that decision if there is need for it - since the necessity for a product champion for successful innovation is balanced by the equal importance of the personal factor in bringing R & D programmes to a halt. Second only to this in importance is the need to specify the objectives with absolute clarity, and in particular to insist that the people looking for finance should state without ambiguity by what criteria the results of their work are to be judged. The predictions made at the start of each stage of a project have to be

[35] K. P. Norris in *R & D Management 1* (1971) 25.
[36] Allen, Meadows & Marquis op. cit.

recorded in a formal way - too often they can get buried in paper so that nobody ever quite knows on what exact basis a project was initiated or continued. Any management that is serious about innovation has to insist that the answers to these questions appear on a research proposal ahead of any other information. If this requirement is met, and then acted upon when necessary, the result will be the cutting off of research projects that are heading for failure earlier rather than later, with much reduced losses. The savings are then available to reinforce the better projects.

Of course, the feeling will always remain that funding should have been kept on that little bit longer, and this feeling will occasionally receive powerful endorsement from the success of a competitor who apparently did just that. This feeling can be balanced by the knowledge that the chances of success in research projects are higher in laboratories where projects are regularly `axed' before they get out of hand, probably because of the effect this has in stimulating the people working there. In preventing energy being expended in useless and unwanted ways, this has exactly the same function as pruning any plant growth. Over a period of more than twenty years in Britain, one pharmaceutical firm produced a significantly better return for its investment in research than all the others. This is attributed to the quality of its Research Director, who was famous, not for any great ability to discern new lines of enquiry which would lead to successful products, but for a seemingly very highly developed sense of when a programme was leading nowhere. Cutting this off then enabled him to deploy his resources where they produced a better return.

In this area, the best people are not just twice as good as the second-best, they are incomparably better. This is because of the overwhelming importance of leadership in innovation, since wherever leadership matters, a few will invariably stand out from the crowd. Some reliable figures show how skew the distribution of leaders in any population is. In the first World War, 60% of sinkings were made by 5% of U-Boat commanders; in the second, operations research showed that the best U-boat-chasing captains were three times as good as the second-best .[37]

[37] J.H. Hoskins in Allison op. cit. 274; A.J. Marder *From the Dreadnought to Scapa Flow* (1970) v. 83.

Failure The Norm

Managing innovation must be a question of managing for failure, and cannot be other than this. In one U.S. study of research laboratories, the median failure rate was found to be 60% and the minimum rate 50%. A British study found a correlation of only 0.13 between projected and actual returns.[38] The great art in managing situations where failure has to be taken for granted in such a high proportion of cases, is in keeping a balance between   the human factors involved. This balance is between Kelvin's `one word characterizes my efforts over 55 years; that word is failure' on the one hand, and Pasteur's `my only strength lies in my tenacity' on the other. It probably consists in taking Kettering's advice `not to bruise too easily'. Knowing that there have to be mistakes, the objective of sound research management is to make them as fast and as cheaply as possible. Part of the difficulty of control of the intermediate stages between the idea and the ultimate product, is that breakthroughs have a low probability of occurrence, but' when they do occur, they make   a   large   and   immediate   demand   upon   resources. Consequently, it is not optimal to try to choose the best budget before development starts and then to allocate that budget as development proceeds.[39]

One means of coping with this is to make only an initial short-run plan for each stage of research. This is then adjusted in the light of experience, and after the adjustment, the firm takes up an explicit `posture' regarding the further commitment of resources in the light of further information as it emerges. Such a procedure   helps   to   avoid   under-   or   over-responses   to developments without reference to the impact of these interim decisions upon the future. Once again the innovator's imaginative grasp of the ultimate objective is the most important factor.[40]

It is also important that something should be kept in reserve to allow the unexpected breakthrough to be exploited. In research,

[38] R.R. Nelson op. cit. 114; P.M.S. Blackett *Technology, Industry & Economic Growth* (1966) 19.

[39] Marschak op. cit. 6.

[40] A. Cairnes & A. C. Stedry in *Research Program Effectiveness* - Conference of Naval Research, Washington D.C. (1966).

as elsewhere, it is true that `doing too much with too little, leaves no room for revolutions'.[41] Happy accidents do occur, but `only after a persistent and carefully conducted search for what is wanted'.[42] Fortune, as Pasteur said, favours only the prepared mind. Techniques such as Critical Path and PERT, so well established on the production side of business, are unsuitable for control of R & D because of the uncertainty factor. Attempts have been made to fill the gap by what are known as stochastic networks. In these, both tasks and events are probabilistic, that is, they are expressed not as a point estimate, but as a statement of the likelihood of particular estimates. Events (called nodes) are levels of knowledge, and activities (called arcs) are tasks which lead to knowledge.[43] There is no reason to think that in innovation, these or any other techniques will seriously reduce the need for the contribution of an identifiable individual.

Biassed Expectations

Good R & D control procedures require that members of the top management of a firm should conceal any enthusiasm they may feel for a particular project. This creates a special problem for innovation, since it has to be reconciled in some way with the need for a `champion' in the top echelons of the firm if the inevitable obstacles are to be overcome. If top management reveals that it favours a particular project on grounds other than the estimates and recommendations of its expert advisers, then imperceptibly perhaps, but nonetheless really, the figures and the recommendations will cease to be objective, and take on the tone which management is now known to want to hear. This biassing of results in the direction of expectations happens all the time in scientific research. There is similar need to guard against it in the learning process which is innovation.

Another major problem for top management in controlling R & D can only be defined, since there is as yet no established body of opinion about a solution to it.[44] This is the question of a `heavy'

---

[41] M.J. Peck op. cit. 448.

[42] J. Rossman *The Psychology of the Inventor* (1931) 118.

[43] B.V. Dean in Research Program Effectiveness - Conference of Naval Research, Washington D.C. (1966).

[44] Marschak op. cit. 139.

or a `light' approach to a situation of uncertainty. A `light'
approach proceeds slowly and cautiously, each step building on
the previous one. This is all very well until a situation is reached
where even a number of parallel approaches will be unsuccessful
as long as none of them is on a `heavy' level. Sometimes in such
cases the problem yields to a `heavy' approach, in which all
available resources are staked upon going in a single direction. In
other words, a policy of `hedging' research bets which is
appropriate in a risk situation, may not help at all in one of
uncertainty.

Getting Ideas Adopted

The `information absorbtion' task also includes the transfer of
information out of a laboratory into products that work and sell. As
in any other field, this takes place most effectively through people,
so the innovator has to take a great interest in the human qualities
of the personnel engaged in R & D, since it is these qualities which
will, above all, decide whether or not the information becomes
successfully `embodied'. An illustration of this can be found in the
history of Radar. No doubt partly because of the importance this
had for British survival during the second World War, it has been
subjected to a good deal of detailed sociological research. This has
shown that the reason why Radar became effective in Britain
earlier than in Germany was less because of any superiority in
British research and technology, than because of a quicker
acceptance by the RAF than by the Luftwaffe, especially through
better `feedback' from aircrew to research workers. It is not fanciful
to suggest that this could be due to the remarkably close links
between theory and practice in the tradition of the Royal Aircraft
Establishment at Farnborough. During the first World War, for
example, when by an interesting coincidence Tizard and Lindemann
(both later famous scientists) were on the Farnborough staff,
Lindemann made what was thought beforehand to be a suicidal
practical demonstration of the validity of his mathematical analysis
of the cause and cure of aircraft spinning. His solution was passed
on to the operational pilots, and saved many of their lives.[45]

---

[45]cf. P.B. Walker *Early Aviation at Farnborough* (1971); R. Harrod *The Prof.*
(1959).

In Bell Laboratories, which historically led the world in so many ways in both discovery and applications, there were specific arrangements to build up fruitful contacts between researchers and production people, which also helped to prevent research workers from being isolated in a world of their own. These started from the principle that wherever there is an intellectual barrier between activities, it should never be reinforced by a physical barrier. There is an evident intellectual barrier between research and production, so that it is considered a mistake to set the research activity apart in a separate establishment. Consequently, the Bell laboratories were scattered in location through the Western Electric production units.[46] How far this can be done with success obviously depends upon both groups of people having some form of language in common, but the principle it endorses is that concepts of efficiency taken from production experience cannot be applied to the carrying out of research. Note that there is no incompatibility between the Bell approach and that of firms such as Kodak and Du Pont, of physically separating different types of laboratory to permit differing degrees of control, referred to earlier.

Innovation and Imitation

Another aspect of innovation as learning is the way in which innovations are spread by *imitation*. There is little doubt that the most innovative firms, individuals and even nations are also the ones most ready to learn from others; Du Pont, which made two of its three really important inventions when its research budget was $5 million a year, a fraction of what it is today, went on to even more successful at improving the inventions of others.[47] Europe's head start in the industrial revolution has been attributed in part to the way in which it imported from the East over a period of centuries, a whole array of valuable and sometimes fundamental techniques, such as the use of the stirrup. The relationship between Japan on the one hand and Europe and the United States on the other, has followed just the same pattern: Having begun by imitation, Japan then went on to master Western

[46] D. Allison op. cit. 226.
[47] D. Hamberg *Essays in the Economics of R & D* (1966) 72.

technology in certain selected areas in a most comprehensive way, and has now emerged as an important source of innovations in its own right. For example, even if the A-phase of the semi-conductor revolution was American, the B-phase has been predominantly Japanese, especially from the aspect of developing mass-production and testing systems. It was Japanese shipbuilders who were responsible for innovating the giant specialized bulk carriers, beginning with the super-tankers. The same qualities as make good innovators make good imitators.[48]

It is equally true that no one can imitate successfully without grasping the inner core of the innovation being imitated in some way, which in turn means a type of sharing in the creative energy which brought it about. Even at the level where innovation shades off into entrepreneurship, the common ground of creativeness between imitation and innovation can be identified. In the U.S., the Thompson-Houston Co., which was a keen rival of Edison's firm in its early days, was noted for innovating nothing and imitating everything, whereas, of course, Edison's firm existed only to innovate. Yet in 1892, these two firms, based upon two apparently quite different philosophies, merged successfully. This could only have been possible because both their approaches had it in common that they were ways of learning.[49]

Innovation and Economic Growth

The relationship between the speed at which innovations spread, and economic growth, depends upon the better return which comes from imitating rapidly. New techniques are adopted more quickly in the faster growing industries and economies. The logic of this is that expansion means new capacity; this will be built to incorporate the newest techniques; firms with older equipment will be forced to match these techniques in order to maintain their competitive position; consequently, the faster an industry is expanding, the more readily innovations are adopted. There is also the social aspect. An expanding firm can the more easily introduce new ways of doing things because workers need not become redundant as a result - they can be transferred to some of

[48] D.S. Landes *The Unbound Prometheus* (1969) 27-8.
[49] W.P. Strassmann *Risk & Technological Innovation* (1959) 168.

the new jobs the expansion is creating. The opposite is the case in static or declining industry, where change generally results in 'technological unemployment'. Workers will naturally resist the cause of this - innovation - as much as they will resist any threat of unemployment, and so innovation is slowed down or made altogether impossible.

Numerous examples of these aspects of the spread (or the opposite) of innovations come to mind. In steel-making, the Carnegie plants in the U.S. were noted for the fastest rate of growth in the period 1870-1900. They also had the greatest number of innovations and the most important ones.[50] What is called the 'technological gap' between Europe and the United States must be attributed in part, at least, to a widespread readiness to accept innovation in a context where fast economic growth has been almost axiomatic. Conversely, when lack of innovation results in missed markets, leading to loss of jobs, strikes to protect what jobs remain and even less innovation in the next turn of the downward spiral, then catastrophe can come very quickly. The decline of shipbuilding in Scotland, from a level in the early 20th Century when almost half the tonnage afloat on the seas of the world had been built *on the Clyde alone*, shows what happens when an industry ceases to be able to innovate from its own resources, or by imitation.

The 'Sailing-Ship' Syndrome

One of the most interesting aspects of the way innovations spread - or in which learning about innovations becomes diffused - is their relationship with the previously existing technology. This has been called 'the sailing-ship syndrome', because paradoxically it was only *after* it began to be obvious that the steamship would sweep commercial sail from the seas, that the sailing ship reached its peak of efficiency. Faced with the challenge from steam, the average westward crossing of the Atlantic was brought down from 34 days in 1839 to 24.5 days in the 1860s by the American clippers.[51] In a similar way, more recently, the thermionic valve only reached its highest pitch of

---

[50] ibid, 43.
[51] S.C. Gilfillan *Inventing the Ship* (1935) 159, 168.

development when its makers were attempting to meet the challenge of the transistor. This phenomenon is fruitful for insights into the differences between invention and innovation, into the economic importance of the many small adjustments towards the optimum as compared with the big dramatic shifts in technology which gain the limelight, of the need creativeness has to be stimulated, and of the relationship between technology and art. Taking the ship as an example, the period 1840-1870 was one of great inventive effort directed towards the application of steam power, typified by Brunel's *Great Britain*, which was not alone the first large ship to be made of iron but the first to be screw-propelled, and his *Great Eastern*, which was equally far ahead of its time but which equally failed to make money. While this was going on, the sailing ship, without any invention, was in the last stage of a process in which

> it was transformed in appearance, transmuted into steel, doubled in speed, ten-folded in size, greatly bettered in seaworthiness, comfort and durability ... and all merely by little increments of change in size and proportions, and by adopting materials and machinery invented elsewhere ... all the marvellous perfection of the clippers, their speed, which quickly gave them the inter-oceanic passenger traffic of the world, and their famous beauty, were achieved with exactly the same rig and hull as their packet predecessors, only perfected, fined away and refined ... [52]

In other words, what was a period of invention for the steamship was one of innovation for the sailing ship. In the first case, creative energy was being expended to break quite new ground, to generate quite new information; in the second, the objective of the same kind of energy, working at a much lower level of uncertainty, was to turn existing information into concrete reality.

[52] ibid.

Leadership and Forecasting

In the spread of innovations, the importance of the `champion' is seen again through the effect of his leadership on the learning process. The amount or even the quality of the information available is secondary to this. Norman Borlaug won the Nobel Peace Prize for his work in developing dwarf varieties of wheat and rice which made countries such as Mexico and Pakistan self-sufficient in these products and caused `a breakthrough in food production on a scale the world hardly ever has seen' until it was undermined by energy price increases. In accepting the prize he stressed the need for scientific and organisational leadership: `This is not theory; this is reality, as illustrated by the fact that the leadership has been the determining factor in the relative success of parallel but different crop production programs within the same country'.[53]

The importance of the product champion can also be seen in relation to forecasting. Much effort has gone into the development and use of techniques which are supposedly objective, at least in the sense of being applicable by scientists who are not personally involved in any of the fields whose future is being plotted. The record is one of almost complete failure, which has done great harm. In contrast, there is too much evidence to be ignored, that a quite different approach almost always does better than those of the so-called `objective' techniques. When creative individuals are completely immersed in a particular area of life, they are recipient, repository and processor of a vast amount of information concerning it. Their interest in the area, even if it remains this side of obsession, discards information concerning other areas of life, so leaving more room for data relating to their own field to be stored and handled. For the same reason, information on their chosen field is `alive' for them, contributing to the building up of meaningful intellectual patterns, which they apply actively in turn to further information as it arrives. Most computer analogies with human mental activity are inadequate, but there is one which is helpful: Every computer up to the latest generation (which has what is called a `virtual memory')

---

[53] W. E. Borlaug *Nobel Lecture* (1970) 236.

has had a central processing unit, a fast-access store of information, and a remote store which is generally very many times larger than the fast access one. No matter how big the remote store is, the computer can only actually work with information that is in its fast-access store; consequently, the size of this primary store is a major limiting factor on its power.

`Self-Starters' and the future

What distinguishes creative people (the business variant of whom are known as `self-starters') from others, is that they have a bigger `fast-access store'. Everyone has met people who have a vast amount of knowledge, little of which ever seems to impinge upon what they think or do. Creative individuals often have far less knowledge, but they are able to make what they have, work. There is no such thing as information on its own, there is only information in relation to a mind. One mind, because of its active quality and the information in its `fast-access store', reacts to a new `fact' in a positive way, which inserts it into a developing pattern; another may have more information stored remotely. Since this is not brought to bear upon newly arrived data, such a mind allows the new `fact' to pass by without adverting to its possible significance. Consequently, an innovator tends to be above average both in the amount of information he has in his chosen area (he may well be correspondingly below average in other areas) and in the way he is alert to new information in this area.

Such a combination has enabled certain individuals to predict the future - within the limits of their field - quite accurately in too many recorded cases for it to be the result of chance. In 1892, Plessner forecast television. Easy enough, it may be said, to foretell that some day visual information might be transmitted by electrical impulses, since this was already being done with sound. Less easy, though, to say at that time, as Plessner did, that the key to it would be a selenium cell. Gilfillan himself forecast accurately in 1913, the way in which the growth in size of passenger ships would reach a peak in the 1930s.[54] Most remarkable, perhaps, is the prescience of Admiral `Jacky' Fisher,

[54] S.C. Gilfillan in J.R. Bright (ed.) *Technological Forecasting for Industry* (1968) 17.

which can only be explained in terms of the way his colossal energy enabled him to master the Navy, and politics insofar as they concerned the Navy, in the most fantastic detail: 'Fisher foretold in 1911 the date of the first War as the autumn of 1914; prophesied when flying was in its infancy the revolution that maritime aircraft would achieve; predicted years before the war the unrestricted submarine campaign on shipping (but not the antidote); and had a vision of an amphibious landing craft ('amphibious hippopotami crawling up the beaches') thirty years before D day in World War II!'[55] And there is a story told of his forecast at the end of 1918 that the next war would be in 20 years' time.

Business Predictions

Such a capacity to predict accurately is astonishing only in its range. Many business people anticipate equally correctly the out-turn of events within their own very restricted sphere, and it is indeed on this capacity, or lack of it, to predict rightly, that every business person is judged in the long run. These predictions are based upon being able to see the necessary relations between a large number of different factors which are 'felt' rather than completely understood. The number of factors to which Fisher's mind had to relate for him to be able to forecast with the sweep, on the time-scale, and with the accuracy he did, is unimaginable to ordinary experience. Nevertheless, there is no reason to think that it involves anything other than a more intense version of a common enough practice and achievement. Nor is it necessary to look to magic for an explanation of why forecasting by such creative individuals has a better record of success than anything that has been done so far by 'scientific' methods. In these methods, the mathematical and scientific content only represents a small part of the whole forecasting exercise. The mathematical techniques can only be set in motion on the basis of a set of assumptions on the part of the people who are using them, and these assumptions have to be subjective. Moreover, almost by definition, they are the subjective assumptions of people who are not totally immersed in the subject, emotionally as well as intellectually. Inevitably, they are

---

[55] Marder *From the Dreadnought to Scapa Flow* (1970) v. 365.

less sound assumptions than those of someone who lives and moves within a particular project, especially if this individual happens to be highly gifted to begin with.

`New' and `Old' Technologies

Ravenshear's distinction between `originative' and `intensive' invention also has a bearing upon innovation as learning. Using Gilfillan's ship examples, the use of the steam tug to bring ships in and out of harbour can be considered as `originative' innovation. It cannot be considered an invention as the content of new information in it is too low, yet it represented a dramatic change in the possibilities open to designers of sailing ships. From that time on, instead of trying to reconcile two conflicting sets of requirements, those of speed with those of manoeuvrability in harbours, they could concentrate on speed only. All the subsequent improvements can be regarded as `intensive' innovation, a process of drawing all the practical conclusions from this change. It is a matter for speculation how frequently a new technology has some element in it which can be used to improve the old, and which may postpone or fend off the replacement of the old by the new. What seems certain, however, is that it needs the challenge of a serious rival to bring out all the possibilities which were lying dormant in the old technology; there is always more information to hand than people will bestir themselves to put to practical use until they have to. Secondly, it is important not to be so obsessed with fighting off a threat from a new technology as to be unable to see whether that new technology may contain elements which could be useful to the older one. Only myopia of this type can explain, for example, the slowness with which the gas industry adopted electrical controls in domestic cooking and heating, which controls in the end opened up large new markets for gas.

Much depends, of course, on how long it takes from invention to innovation, and from innovation to the point where what was originally strange has become an accepted counter in entrepreneurial activity. A great deal of work has been done by sociologists on diffusion of innovations, much of it in fields that are not technological. This has enabled them to give precise meaning to terms such as 'early' and 'late' adopters, and 'laggards' as well as 'innovators'. Acceptance of any innovation over time by any population has been found to follow the normal curve, and different categories are defined by numbers of standard deviations either side of the mean, as in the following diagram:-[56]

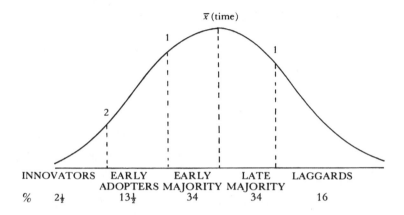

It will be noted how small is the percentage who can be classed as innovators, and that at the other end of the scale, the 'laggards' form a group more than six times as big. It is hardly surprising that research results show that relatively early adoption of innovation is associated with youth - both of individuals and organisations - and above-average education and social and economic status, with previous experience of innovation helping. It is also associated with multiple sources of innovation and upon personal rather than printed sources of information. Echoes of the product 'champion' are found in the particular need for a person-to-person channel of communication if adoption of an innovation involves changes in traditional values.

Innovation Time-scales

It is scarcely ever realized how long the period from conception of an idea to its common use in practice can be. The first observation of the detergent powers of enzymes was as long ago as 1919 (with the first use in a soap compound in 1932).

[56] From E.M. Rogers & Shoemaker *Communication of Innovations* (1971) 182.

Lionel Pilkington's 1957 British Patent for float glass was in fact significantly anticipated by a 1903 Patent to Heal, an American. When the Canadian developers of the vertical-axis windmill, in which there is currently so much interest, applied for a Patent, they found that the Frenchman, Darrieus, had been there before them in the 1920s. Researchers in this field generally try to measure the time lag from idea to prototype, then to practical use, then to commercial success and finally to important use. Such a procedure can hardly claim much precision, but in spite of all the limitations of the data, it does seem that the time lag between invention and innovation is shortening, which could also mean that innovations are being diffused more rapidly. One study shows the median time from idea to practical use as 37 years before 1900, but only 9½ years afterwards.[57] According to an even more important study, made of twenty major American innovations for the U.S. Commission on Technology, Automation and Economic Progress, there was an average span of 37 years from completion to commercialization between 1885-1919, 24 years between the two World Wars, and 14 years in the post second World War era.[58]

All these figures must be interpreted with the greatest caution, since extraneous social and economic factors may be decisive for the timing of innovation. The demands of War brought about a tremendous development of capacity to produce Penicillin in the U.S., which would hardly have taken place in peace-time at anything like the same rate, and the same was equally true of countless other inventions and discoveries from atomic energy, the jet engine and Radar to Scuba-diving equipment, D.D.T. (which had been first prepared as long ago as 1874) and synthetic rubber. Consequently, whether or not the time-lag between invention and innovation appears to be increasing or decreasing, may depend merely upon which periods are being compared. The interval is apparently shorter if the inventor is himself actively involved, which is to be expected, given the creative element in invention, innovation and imitation, and the importance of personal commitment to a

[57] S.C. Gilfillan *Invention and the Patent System* (1964) 107.
[58] Quoted in Landes op. cit. 519.

project if it is to succeed.[59] A striking example of this is the involvement of the original inventor, Dr. Edwin Land, in every aspect (from design to marketing) of the remarkable development of Polaroid instant photography.

`Personalized' Information

Just as the personal factor is of supreme importance in the carrying through of innovations, so it is in their diffusion. It is people who are the carriers of information in this context, typified by the way Samuel Slater went to America in 1789, having memorized the construction and operation of Arkwright's spinning frame, to introduce mechanical spinning there, or the way Woolwich Arsenal gained the skill of Jan Verbruggen from the Hague Foundry.[60] Just as invention and innovation do not happen unless there is an emotional as well as an intellectual response to a situation, so equally the learning process which is a key factor in diffusion of innovations has its emotional aspect. The growth of management consultancy is another confirmation that it is through people rather than paperwork that innovations tend to be spread. It is only rarely that the new information which the consultants bring with them to a firm would not be available to its management from published sources. What the consultants do is `personalize' this information, and render it concrete in a way that can be grasped by management.

It has been suggested that the process whereby innovations are diffused may be closer to entrepreneurship than it is to innovation itself; certainly, in the Chapter I diagram, this function is on the `entrepreneurship' side of innovation rather than on the `inventive' side. Consequently, the type of mind that is most important for decisions in this area is that of a business person. It is characteristic of a true business person's mind that they are not speculative, they are not excited by ideas in the abstract; the only reality they will take seriously is what they can touch, measure and use - ideas have little or no meaning for them unless they are *embodied.* Marconi, for example, was no scientist. His contribution to radio was not to invent anything, but to make apparatus of a laboratory type work

---

[59] R. R. Nelson *The Rate & Direction of Inventive Activity* (1962) 308.
[60] W. P. Strassman op. cit. 79; L.T.C. Rolt *Tools for the Job* (1965) 45.

commercially. He was an innovator - indeed in possessing a certain narrowness of outlook, he was even more of an entrepreneur.[61] It is things, not ideas, that interest business people.

The importance of the personal element, of course, is greatest at the outset of the diffusion process, in the transition from the stage of early practical use to that of commercial success. The Langrish study of Queen's Award innovations in Britain found clear evidence that the actual transfer of key personnel between firms could be an important element in this.[62] Economic history is full of examples. The spread of the industrial revolution from Britain owed much to the readiness of Britons to take their knowhow with them and go into business abroad on their own account: Brown of Brown-Boveri, the great Swiss engineering firm, is a typical case in point One of the greatest mines in the Ruhr is called the Hibernia mine, so testifying to the origin of its founder. The great Russian steel town of Donetsk was originally called Yuzovka after the Welshman, John Hughes. In Tzarist Russia, indeed, the adoption of industrial innovation was deliberately linked to a policy of tapping the external pool of entrepreneurship, knowledge and capital, so that foreign engineers, foremen and in some cases even skilled workers were the agents of industrial change.

Apprenticeship

Because the spread of innovations duplicates the creative activity involved in the innovations themselves, there is no escaping the personal and emotional element. Students can only learn from a teacher with whom they have some sort of mental affinity, and there is no substitute for actually sitting at the feet of the Master. The concept of apprenticeship is unfashionable at present, (except in Germany where the Meister remains a craftsman of training and proved achievement). However, its results, at every level of human activity, testify to its importance - an importance that quite transcends changes in theories of education.

[61] W. R. Maclaurin in *American Economic Review* (1950) 98.
[62] Langrish, J. et. al. *Wealth from Knowledge* (1971).

This is especially true in the case of innovation. People who break new ground are able to pass on to those who work with them something additional to the explicit information they generate, expressed in drawings or print, and it is this additional thing that makes these individuals either full innovators themselves, or active participators in the diffusion of innovations. What it is that passes by a sort of osmosis from the work of a master to that of an apprentice may be impossible to pin down, but the reality is undoubtedly there. It is most obvious in the arts and in science, but it exists in business too. The Cavendish laboratory in Cambridge has produced Nobel prize winners out of all proportion to its resources, and this has been attributed to the personal legacy of influence of Rutherford. In the history of machine tools, Bramah taught Maudslay and Clement; Maudslay taught Whitworth and Nasmyth. The brothers Krupp were trained by Matthew Murray's successors; so that the famous Round Foundry lives on today not in Leeds, but in Essen.[63]

Rejection of Innovations

The reason for rejection of innovations will more often than not be found to have the same source as those for their spread – the personal factor in the learning process. `The human mind' it has been said, `likes a strange idea as little as the body likes a strange protein and resists it with a similar energy'.[64] And `Boss' Kettering of General Motors, one of America's greatest innovators, held that the hardest substance in the world was that of the human skull, to judge by the force needed to drive any new idea through it. Nothing illustrates this better than the case of Semmelweis. It was accepted in his Vienna hospital that the death rate from puerpural fever in the wards where the medical students were taught was about five times higher than in those where the midwives received their instruction. Semmelweis, however, was not satisfied with the conventional explanation for the discrepancy (such as that women literally died from shame at having to give birth in the presence of men). When a colleague lost his life from an infected wound received in the dissecting room, with symptons

---

[63] cf. Rossman op. cit. 224; Rolt op. cit. 82.
[64] W.I. Beveridge *Art of Scientific Discovery* (1950).

very similar to those of puerpural fever, Semmelweis made the mental connection: Only the medical students performed dissections, and these merely washed their hands with soap and water between dissecting room and labour ward. By introducing a type of chlorine disinfection to replace this, he quickly got deaths down to the same rate as in the midwives' wards. What is extraordinary is that in spite of this incontrovertible evidence, he was unable to get his colleagues to accept his ideas. In fact, he was hounded back to his native Hungary, where, hardly surprisingly, he went mad.[65] So hard is it for new ideas to make their way that Fessenden developed the law that `there is less prospect of obtaining development in a given field from organisations engaged in that field than from any other conceivable source. No organisation engaged in any specific field of work ever invents any important development in that field; or adopts any important development in that field until forced to by outside competition'.[66]

`Not-Invented-Here' Syndrome

Another expression of this is what is called in America the N.I.H. (not invented here) syndrome. There is a long list of new things which - even at the stage of innovation rather than of invention - have been rejected by industry. It may be argued that domination of a particular field by one or a few large firms is beneficial to technological progress, since such firms are able to provide large resources for research and development. However, apart from so much Company-sponsored research being concerned with improvements that are trivial, this ignores important evidence to the contrary. The record of large firms in relation to invention is extremely mixed. Doubtless, the resources of Dupont were needed for the realisation of Nylon, just as those of the Bell Telephone Laboratories were necessary for Transistors and Lasers. But, incredible as it may seem to-day, computers were originally rejected out of hand by IBM, the Polaroid Camera by Kodak, and jet airliners for civilian passengers by Boeing, Douglas and Lockheed:

---

[65] W.J. Sinclair *Semmelweis – his Life and Doctrines* (1909) 29 ff.
[66] R.A. Fessenden, op. cit. 104, 103.

The big United States manufacturers... showed by massive theoretical and documentary evidence that such machines could never be economic. They showed that there would be no passenger demand for the high speeds that such machines would make possible. They showed that travel at altitudes above five or six thousand metres was `out of the question' for ordinary paying passengers.[67]

There is abundant evidence that firms which dominate their markets do not invest in innovations, however good in themselves, if these would upset their revenue pattern. This certainly occurred, for example, in stainless steel razor blades. We tend to be unaware of this inertia on the part of large firms in the matter of innovation, because they are frequently forced to react to the activity of smaller firms in their fields which are intent upon making progress in new directions. On the record, however, it is fair to ask what would happen to technological progress were the `gadfly' firms to disappear, leaving the field to the large ones. Steel-making in an oxygen furnace was invented and innovated in an Austrian firm which was tiny by the standards of the international industry in 1950. It was introduced into the U.S. by the small McLouth Steel in 1954, but not taken up by the giants for a further ten years. Although it saved $20 per ton in installed capacity, these same firms bought no less than 40 million tons of open-hearth capacity in the 1950s.[68] Watt was never able to accept that high pressure steam had advantages. Henry Ford could not see the point of the self-starter - long after this had been invented by Kettering and was installed in competitors' cars, and Edison was blind to the advantages alternating current had over direct current.

There are several points here; Rejection of an innovation by the people who have played a major role in the previous innovation is so common as to be almost automatic. If the earlier innovation has demanded unusual personal commitment, an individual's mind becomes so rigidly set in a particular pattern that it is unable to absorb something new. A tendency to fight old battles over again

---

[67] O. Stewart, *Aviation: The Creative Ideas* (1966) 205.
[68] W. Adams in E. Mansfield (ed.) *Monopoly Power & Economic Performance* (1969 ed.) 137.

is the price that must be paid for having won them in the first place. Since, considered in terms of everything that matters to innovation, firms are extensions of the personalities of creative individuals, the same tends to be true of them. A major effort in breaking new ground results in a type of exhaustion, so that the next advance is more likely to be made by another firm. In Britain, Metrovick & Cossor were deeply involved in Radar from the very start, but most of the post-war development came, not from them, but from Marconi and Decca.[69] General Electric (U.S.). and Westinghouse were not involved in aero-engines before the coming of the jets, and new firms such as Rocketdyne have in turn been more prominent in solid fuel propulsion.[70] Any mental rigidity on the part of management can be strongly reinforced by the existence of capital assets which will lose their value if the competing novelty turns out to be a success. In the Edison example, accepting alternating current meant not only that Edison had been wrong, but that his great rival, George Westinghouse, was right, and that the plant that Edison's firm already had in operation was obsolete. Incidentally, anyone who thinks that fierce competition in innovation only began yesterday, may find it worth reflecting on one ploy in this particular context. This consisted in the Edison forces lobbying the State of New York to bring in the electric chair as the means of carrying out the death penalty, so that Westinghouse would have an advantage in tendering for the supply of the equipment with alternating current and, in the public mind, would come to be associated with sudden death!

Protecting Markets

Protection of markets, as another aspect of protecting capital investment, may also be a factor in slowing down the spread of innovations. General Electric resisted neon type tubing for illumination and lagged badly in developing fluorescent lighting, so that it was a small firm, Sylvania, which effectively innovated

[69] C. Freeman, `R & D in Electronic Capital Goods' in *Nat. Inst. Econ. Rev.* (1965) 56.
[70] R.R. Nelson, Peck & Kalachek *Technology, Economic Growth & Public Policy* (1967) 50.

these European inventions in the U.S.[71] It has been suggested that this was partly because G. E. did not want to do anything which would reduce the demand for electric power, and therefore for generating equipment. These inertial forces operate mainly at the higher levels of management, where the important decisions regarding invention and innovation have to be made. At the lower, employee, levels, there is another factor operating. This is the relationship between risk and reward for middle management in accepting a new idea. What they gain in terms of job security and promotion prospects from an idea which is a success is frequently not outweighed by what they can lose if it fails, given the much higher probability of failure which can be attributed to them. 'Victory has many fathers; defeat is an orphan'. Consider, for example, ideas reaching the firm from outsiders. The odds are of the order of 2000 to 1 against any single one of these being useful to the firm, so that in endorsing it, managers are taking a great risk of being associated with a failure, with the consequences that will have for their careers. On the other hand, if they reject the one 'good' idea the chances are overwhelmingly that nobody will ever advert to the chance that was missed. Firms tend to look ahead rather than behind them, and a business climate of which post-mortems are a feature is not a good one. It will be clear that the balance of advantage therefore inclines sharply towards rejecting *everything*, as anyone who has ever tried to sell an idea to a large firm will learn with no surprise.

Ideas from `Outsiders'

The N.I.H. syndrome would be unimportant if all ideas which reach a firm from outside were from cranks or from people who cannot make a useful contribution because they do not know enough about the firm's technology or business. However, a tremendous complication is introduced by the abundant evidence that 'the things that make really big changes in the art are more likely to come from outside than from the inside'.[72] And 'the principles of overwhelming

---

[71] A.A. Bright Jr. *The Electric Lamp Industry* (1949) 456, 461.
[72] F.B. Jewett, Head of Bell Laboratories, in Evidence to U.S. National Economic Committee, quoted in W.B. Bennett *The American Patent System* (1941) 154-198.

numbers, and of freedom from custom, give most of the revolutionary inventions to outsiders'.[73] Not many major inventions, in fact, come from the R & D of large firms.[74] Almost all the major inventions in the oil industry have been made by individuals, generally close to the industry, but not in the most important firms. One, catalytic cracking, came from a man altogether outside the industry, the Frenchman Eugene Houdry, who, like a latter-day Duke of Bridgewater with his famous Canal, doggedly spent virtually all of a large private fortune until he eventually emerged victorious.[75] In dealing with this problem, the need for creativeness in imitation is again underlined: the firm which has an uncreative management will automatically reject everything from outside, or select ideas haphazardly, a process in which the odds are stacked against it. If there are creative people in the right positions of influence in the firm, however, they will respond to the creativity at the heart of others' innovations, and push for the firm to play a part in their diffusion.

Management Types

There has been much discussion as to whether innovation and the diffusion of innovations depends upon the kind of training of the people who make up management. Veblen, for example, thought that the control of capital by non-technical people brought with it a decline in the power to innovate. This over-simplifies the issue. For every case which can be quoted in support of this view, another could be found where, precisely because the people in charge were technical people and little else, attempts to innovate have failed. Such failures sometimes even bring about the downfall of the firm, or are the cause of its control passing to other hands. Schumpeter's insight is undoubtedly correct – innovators reflect a distinct psychological type. They have to have a feeling for the work of the technically qualified people they work with, yet at the same time their vision of the world must be broader, since their task is to see where their ideas fit into

---

[73] S.C. Gilfillan *The Sociology of Invention* (1935) 91.
[74] J.L. Hamberg in *Journal of Political Economy* (1963) 109.
[75] J.L. Enos in R.R. Nelson *The Rate & Direction of Inventive Activity* (1962) 302-4.

the world, and how they must be adapted if they are to serve practical human wants.

Management of innovation is not so much deciding between operating alternatives, as choosing between methods of dealing with information, and analysing the alternatives before events combine to dictate the selection of a particular one. The difference between an innovator and a line manager is then the relative size of their working vocabularies of management skills.[76]

For these reasons, if there is one characteristic which marks out innovators more than anything else, it is a capacity for and an enjoyment of learning. They learn from books, from calculations, from experience, from other people. This curiosity is vital, because without it there is none of that special kind of learning which results in ideas becoming embodied. Thus, innovators stand at the point of intersection between several areas of life, between art and technology, between invention and business, between ideas and artifacts. Most important of all, perhaps, their function involves reconciliation, at however humble a level, of the two different approaches to knowledge.

Their excitement in the learning process, their emotional response to an intellectual challenge, is indispensable to the achievement of mastery over nature. Knowledge as delight is always to be found at the core of knowledge as power.

[76] P.V. Norden, Schedule Recovery in *Research Program Effectiveness* - Conference of Office of Naval Research, Washington, D.C. (1966).

CHAPTER III

Antibiotics, Invention and Innovation

`The Antibiotic Revolution'

The antibiotic revolution (the `domestication' of micro-organisms) ranks in importance in human history with the domestication of wild animals. Its story is full of lessons for discovery, invention and innovation, not least because its two main components, penicillin and streptomycin, were found and developed in completely different ways, by quite different kinds of people. Because it all took place within a single generation, and is well documented, these lessons are very accessible. Amongst the topics on which they throw light are funding and protection of new ideas (as well as resistance to them), path dependence and research as an evolutionary process.

In 1939 and 1940, two research grants were made, whose results far exceeded any conceivable expectations for them, on the part either of the grantors or their beneficiaries. One of these was by the Rockefeller Foundation to Professor Howard Florey of the University of Oxford, and it led to the widespread availability of penicillin, the first antibiotic to be used on a large scale; the other was from Merck to Professor Selman Waksman of Rutgers University, NJ. To it we owe streptomycin, a drug which is powerful against infections with which penicillin cannot cope, notably tuberculosis. Between them, the researches thus funded brought about what we now call the antibiotic revolution, in which `good' bacteria are set to work to combat `bad' ones, and which has saved countless lives and alleviated immeasurable suffering. Even if it may not quite rank in importance for the human race with the transition from hunting and gathering to settled agriculture, it can certainly be spoken of in the same breath as a major aspect of the latter change, which was the domestication of wild animals. The `domestication of microorganisms for combating the microbial enemies of man and of his plants and animals[1] represents a radical shift in the pattern of human evolution, and has given untold millions a vastly better level of health than they could have dreamed of otherwise. A change as important as this could hardly fail to have important lessons for economic innovation, and many of these are readily accessible, partly because the events which brought about the antibiotic revolution are so well documented, but also because everything happened so quickly, within a single human generation. In order to be able to learn these lessons, it is first necessary to grasp the story of what happened in brief outline. This outline will be built up into a complete picture by adding in details from individual aspects of the antibiotic revolution, as these are matched against some theories about discovery, invention and innovation.

Bacterial Antagonism

The obvious starting point for the context within which the antibiotic revolution took place, is Louis Pasteur's discovery in 1877 that `common' bacteria (i.e., those that need air to live) could inhibit the growth of anthrax organisms. At that time, it was already recognized that there was a struggle for Spencerian survival of the fittest amongst bacteria as well as other living things. This struggle was especially notable between fungi, and, for example, in an 1874 *Royal Society Note,* William Roberts had written:

> I have repeatedly observed that liquids in which the *Penicillium Glaucum* was growing luxuriantly could with difficulty be artificially infected with bacteria; it seemed, in fact, as if this fungus played the part of the plants in an aquarium, and held in check the growth of bacteria, with their attendant putrefactive changes. On the other hand the *Penicillium Glaucum* seldom grows vigorously, if it grows at all, in liquids which are full of bacteria. It has further seemed to me that there was an antagonism between the growth of certain races of bacteria and certain other races of bacteria.[2]

[1] Waksman, S.A. *Scientific Monthly,* November (1940).
[2] Waksman, S.A. *The Antibiotic Era* (1975) 13.

Two years later, the physicist John Tyndall wrote to Thomas Huxley, `the most extraordinary cases of fighting and conquering between the bacteria and the penicillium have been revealed to me'.[3] However, Pasteur was the first to articulate the idea that perhaps there could be human intervention to take sides in these struggles. If this could be achieved, he wrote in 1877, it would offer `perhaps the greatest hopes for therapeutics'. This must surely be the beginning of the dream of controlled bacterial antagonism, out of which modern antibiotics eventually emerged.

Antiseptics and Vaccines

From then onwards, the concept of using antagonism between microbes for therapy was `in the air'. The word `antibiosis' was coined for it by Vuillemin in 1889,[4] although it was as late as 1941 and by one of the main players in the story, Selman Waksman, that the noun `antibiotic' was first used to describe compounds which acted in the way Pasteur had hoped for.[5] But bacterial antagonism remained marginal to medical development for many decades, mainly for three reasons. The first of these was growth in the use of antiseptics, very much associated with the work of Joseph Lister. He grasped the causal connection between infection and the ubiquity of bacteria in the air which Pasteur had discovered in 1865, and concluded that `decomposition in the injured part might be avoided without excluding the air, by applying as a dressing some material capable of destroying the life of the floating particles'. He called this the `antiseptic principle', and he reported his tests of it, using carbolic acid, in the *Lancet* between March and July, 1867.

The second reason why bacterial antagonism was not pursued more energetically was the growth of interest in immunotherapy. In this, the body's own natural defences are stimulated by injection of a mild version of a particular disease. This was how Pasteur had dealt with rabies, and by the end of the nineteenth century antitoxins against diphtheria and typhoid fever were also available.

---

[3] Friday, J. *Br. J. Hist. Sci. 7, 61-71.* (1974).
[4] Crellin, J. in Parascandola, J., (ed.) *The History of Antibiotics* (1980) 6.
[5] Woodruff, H.B., *A soil microbiologist's odyssey* (1981) 7.

Chemotherapy

Thirdly, there was the beginning of significant developments in chemotherapy. The first of these did not come from research with a specifically therapeutic focus, but was a by-product of quite different work. Throughout the nineteenth century industrial chemistry effectively meant dyestuffs, and German firms were the unchallenged world leaders in it. They developed dyes which selectively stained nerve tissue. Certain bacteria (such as diphtheria and tetanus) also attack specific parts of the body such as nerve cells or heart muscles. This led to the hope of finding a chemical that would selectively stain only harmful microbes and not the surrounding tissue, from which it might then be possible to take the further step of finding ways to attack the microbes thus identified. This would be all the more valuable because the antiseptics which were known at the time had the drawback of attacking both bacteria and body tissue indiscriminately.

Research along these lines by Ehrlich led in 1910 to Salvarsan, the first drug to be effective against syphilis, and enabled the basic principles of chemotherapy to be laid down. After a considerable delay, Prontosil emerged in 1935 out of Domagk's work, also on dyestuffs, in the great German chemical conglomerate of I. G. Farben (which grouped Bayer, BASF and Hoechst). This was the first of the general-purpose chemotherapeutic agents known as the sulphonomides. These were superior to antiseptics because they distinguished between bacteria and body cells and only attacked the former.[6] The sulfa drugs were particularly effective against streptococcal infections, so that for example, puerperal fever, which killed more than two mothers in every thousand childbirths in Britain even as recently as the 1930s, was quickly conquered by them.

Fleming and Penicillin

The story of antibiotics, which made bacterial antagonism a reality, begins in the era of chemotherapy, and is dominated by four scientific personalities, each of whom won a Nobel prize. The first of these was Alexander Fleming. He joined the staff of

---

[6] Wilson, D. *Penicillin In Perspective* (1976) 44, 121.

St. Mary's Hospital, Paddington, London, in 1906 as soon as he qualified as a doctor. There, he worked under Sir Almroth Wright, who was one of the great figures of immunisation therapy. (Wright was Bernard Shaw's model for the hero, Sir Colenso Ridgeon, of his play, 'The Doctor's Dilemma'.[7] He was so committed to vaccination and serum techniques that his important 1909 book on this topic made the claim that 'the physician of the future will be the immunisator'.[8] Indeed, St. Mary's had a lucrative sideline in the production of vaccines and Fleming eventually became responsible for this.

In spite of being under such strong influence favouring immunisation, Fleming shared in the hope of bacterial antagonism as an alternative to it. He did discover a substance in nasal mucus discharge which was interesting from this point of view. Since this was a product of the body itself, it could scarcely be harmful to it, as contemporary antiseptics were. He called it lysosyme and had hopes that it would be a useful therapeutic agent. To his disappointment, however, he found that its effect was very weak. He could not know to what it would eventually lead.

A Unique Mould

In the Summer of 1928, Fleming read a scientific Paper on unusual colours in cultures of staphlococcal bacteria.[9] This interested him, so he prepared a number of cultures of staphlococci on petri dishes to replicate the experiments. He then went away on holiday, and when he returned, he noticed that on one of these cultures there was a growth of mould, and that all round this growth, the colonies of germs had failed to develop. At the time, St. Mary's also had a mycologist (an expert on moulds) on the staff, who was investigating moulds as a possible cause of asthma. This was Dr. Charles La Touche, and he identified the mould as a strain of penicillin. In fact, although he was wrong about the actual strain, La Touche's contribution was much greater than he knew, because he had actually provided the all-important mould. For a long time, it

[7] McFarlane, G. *Alexander Fleming: The Man and the Myth* (1984) 76.
[8] Crellin in *Parascandola, J.,* (ed.) (1980) 11.
[9] Bigger et al. *J. Pathol. Bacteriol.* (1927) 30, 261-268.

was thought that this had come in through an open window in Fleming's laboratory, but it is now believed that it came up through a stairwell from the laboratory on the floor below where La Touche kept his unique collection of moulds from damp and cobwebbed basements all over London.[10] It is interesting that in the days before scientific medicine, a common remedy for an infected wound was to cover it with cobwebs. Those who treated wounds in this way may have been unwittingly administering penicillin.

Fleming studied scores of moulds, but found that none of them had any worthwhile antibacterial power except the one which had contaminated his experiment. He and his assistants tried to purify and stabilize the penicillin from this, but failed. They could only produce it in a very weak form, and were even unable to replicate Fleming's original experiment. Much later, it was discovered that this was because they kept applying the mould to full-grown bacteria: penicillin can only act on organisms during the very short phase in their life history when they are actually dividing.[11]

However, in the midst of these disadvantages, Fleming identified a valuable laboratory use for his discovery. When culturing swabs taken from patients' throats, other microbes over-grew those of influenza, allowing this disease to escape diagnosis. Penicillin was found to have no effect on influenza microbes, but it could inhibit the growth of other microbes from a swab, thus allowing those of *B. influenzae* to flourish and signal their presence. The importance of this was not alone that it was a means of diagnosing this disease, but that it might enable a vaccine against it to be prepared. Fleming consequently wrote a scientific paper to this effect for the *British Journal of Experimental Pathology*.[12] He took penicillin no further as a possible substance for the treatment of deep-seated infections. Fortunately, however, because of the value of his technique for identifying influenza, his virtually unique strain of penicillin was kept constantly in production, even if in tiny amounts. This availability was crucial for the eventual emergence of penicillin as the first large-scale antibiotic.

---

[10] Hare *The Birth of Penicillin* (1970) Chap. 3 and 4.
[11] Hare 'New light on the history of penicillin' *Medical History* 26, (1982) 3.
[12] Fleming *British Journal of Experimental Pathology* (1929) (10) 226 – 36.

Lysosyme Studies: Florey and Chain

Nearly two decades later, when Fleming received the Nobel prize in 1945 he had to share it with two other scientists. These were Howard Florey and Ernst Chain, to whom the credit for innovating his discovery, that is, turning it into practical reality, is primarily due. Florey had come to Oxford as a Rhodes scholar from Australia and then spent a year in the U.S. as a Rockefeller Fellow. He was later Professor of pathology at Sheffield before being invited to return to Oxford as Professor in 1935. Although not a biochemist himself, he was convinced that this comparatively new science had much to contribute to pathology, so in building up a research team, he recruited Ernest Chain, a biochemist who had been Professor in Berlin, but who had to flee from Hitler's persecution of Jewish people.

The Rockefeller Foundation provided a grant for 3 years from 1936, and the topic on which it was agreed that Chain would begin his research was lysosyme, which Fleming had discovered, and which had interested Florey even before he came to Oxford.[13] He thought at that time that lysosyme might possibly have some causal connection with duodenal ulcers.[14]

Since it was Fleming who had discovered lysosyme, it was inevitable that in his literature survey for this work, Chain would find his 1929 Paper on penicillin. This interested him enough to persuade Florey that they should address the problems which had defeated Fleming and his team. He felt sure that they could stabilize and purify the active substance. Some of Fleming's original mould was available in Oxford, where it was being used in the way Fleming had invented, for experiment preparation and calibration. Florey and Chain failed to get financial support from the British Medical Council for this work, so they applied again to the Rockefeller Foundation, explicitly to carry out `a chemical study of bacterial antagonism', supported by the claim that:

> The experience obtained in this Department during the prolonged studies on the mechanism of the action of lysosyme, is, of course, of

---

[13] Florey *Application to the Rockefeller Foundation* (1939) 3.
[14] Hobby *Penicillin: Meeting the Challenge* (1985) 16.

great value in the study of these problems which are so closely related to, and, in fact, emerged from the lysosyme studies.[15]

The Foundation granted them US$5000 for a year's work, which seemed to them `a sum of royal generosity'.[16] As Chain put it:

> So we started our work on the isolation and purification, not in the hope of finding some new antibacterial chemotherapeutic drug, but to isolate an enzyme which, we hoped, would hydrolyze a substrate common on the surface of many pathogenic bacteria. The motive for this work was, therefore, a general biological one. There was nothing in Fleming's paper which justified the hope that his penicillin was a substance or mixture of substances of extraordinarily high therapeutic power which, for some reason, was neglected by everyone for many years.[17]

The Famous Experiment

After toxicity tests showed that penicillin was promising from the point of view of chemotherapy, Chain did a crucial experiment on a day which is so important in the history of medicine that it is widely remembered (25 May 1940). 8 mice were given a lethal dose of streptococci, and then 2 of them were given a strong dose of penicillin and 2 a weak dose. Next day, the 4 mice which had not had penicillin were dead. The two which had been given the small dose of penicillin survived for a few days, and the two with the strong dose remained unaffected. Then, with great difficulty, enough penicillin was made to do clinical trials on a few human cases which had been given up for lost by the surgeons, all of which were very successful - `in some cases unbelievably so'.[18] The power of penicillin to deal with infection was thus clear immediately, and Chain and Florey reported it in the *Lancet* on August 24, 1940, but the problem was how was enough penicillin to be made to carry out full-scale clinical trials with humans?

---

[15] Florey *Application to the Rockefeller Foundation* (1939) 3.
[16] Chain *The History of Antibiotics* (1980) 21.
[17] ibid.
[18] ibid. 22.

Waksman, Merck and Streptomycin

Before going on to describe how the production problems were solved, the focus of attention needs to shift forward to the fourth individual (and Nobel prizewinner) who is crucial to the antibiotic story, Selman Waksman. Originally from Russia, he was not in the medical area at all, but a soil microbiologist. In his U.S. student days, he became interested in actinomycetes, which are fungus-like microorganisms which he found to be regularly distributed in the soil. Bacteria which are pathogenic for man and animals find their way to the soil, either in the excreta of the hosts or in their remains, but they do not survive for long there. Bacterial antagonism had been suggested as the reason, and indeed as early as 1881 von Pettenkofer had proposed that useful bacteria might be cultivated and domesticated in the soil under a house, so that they could starve out or destroy pathogens.[19]

In 1936, Waksman began serious study of 'the associative and antagonistic phenomena among microorganisms'.[20] Then, in 1939, a student of his, René Dubos, isolated a substance which he called tyrothricin.[21] He showed that this had the power to kill pathogenic bacteria both in the test tube and in infected mice. In fact, his experiment with mice antedated that of Chain, so justifying the claim that it was this which 'clearly showed for the first time in the history of experimental medicine the powerful effect of an antibiotic against bacterial infection'.[22]

Although tyrothrycin was far from being an ideal antibiotic, Waksman later said of it that 'it was the beginning of an epoch, it pointed a way'.[23] What it pointed a way to was undoubtedly the research programme of isolating and testing microbes from soils and other sources which Waksman began with funding from Merck in 1939.[24] This required testing of thousands of soil fungi (Waksman himself put the figure at over 10,000) from

---

[19] Crellin *The History of Antibiotics* (1980) 7.
[20] Waksman et al. *Associative and antagonistic effect of microorganisms* (1937).
[21] Dubos *J. Exp. Med.* (1939).
[22] Gause *The History of Antibiotics* (1980) 91.
[23] Waksman *My Life with the Microbes* (1958) 206.
[24] Waksman *A Most Fruitful Connection* (1963) 10.

which came only 22 results that had any use at all.[25] But one of these was streptomycin (Ferdinand Cohn had named an actinomycete *Streptothrix* in 1872) found in 1943 by Waksman's PhD. student, Albert Schatz. It filled the gap between penicillin and the sulfa drugs, and eventually proved to be amazingly effective against tuberculosis. This was all the more important because penicillin was largely ineffective against this disease. In a curious parallel with Fleming, both Waksman and Schatz were slow to grasp the full power of what they had discovered.

Antibiotic Innovation Problems

Reverting to penicillin, the mould could only be grown on the surface of a culture medium, so every effort was made to find shallow containers for maximising this surface area. Florey also tried to interest the British drug industry, but with intensifying problems of wartime shortages for making their existing product ranges, none of the firms in this could help in any worthwhile way. Eventually, Florey decided that production of penicillin would never match its therapeutic potential if it depended on the British effort. He therefore decided that he must try to bring the productive capacity of the United States to bear on it. Once again, the Rockefeller Institute provided him with funds, this time for a visit with his colleague Heatley to the U.S.[26]

In the United States, Drs. Dawson and Hobby of the New York College of Physicians and Surgeons had reacted immediately to Chain and Florey's *Lancet* paper. They were able to obtain some of Fleming's strain of penicillin from Roger Reid, who had published two papers on it in 1934 and 1935, but whose professor in Pennsylvania State University had seen no future in penicillin and would not allow him to do his doctoral dissertation on it.[27] They administered this to patients in September 1940 and published the results the following May, after which `interest in the drug was enormous'[28] Florey and Heatley, who arrived in July, could not have come at a better time.

[25] Waksman *The Antibiotic Era* (1975) 35.
[26] cf. Florey *Report to Dr. W. Weaver* (1941).
[27] Hobby *Penicillin: Meeting the Challenge* (1985) 46.
[28] ibid. 73.

U.S Productive Capacity

Although the United States was not yet in the war, it was at that time at the beginning of the process of putting its economy on to a war footing. It is no exaggeration to say that there has never been such an outburst of material production as the mobilisation by the United States of its innovative and manufacturing capacity (albeit for destructive ends) between 1941 and 1945. A unique aspect of this mobilisation was the high level of awareness of the importance of applied science, expressed in the establishment of the government Office of Scientific Research and Development. This in turn set up a Committee on Medical Research, and it was here that Florey found his first assistance. (It was only at this time, too (just after Dunkirk) that he fully adverted to how important penicillin could be in the context of the war). The CMR immediately introduced him to a U.S. Department of Agriculture research laboratory in Peoria, IL. For many years, this laboratory had been looking for an economic use for corn-steep liquor, which is what is left over after starch has been extracted from corn. This turned out to be an ideal culture medium for penicillin, so that within a few weeks of Florey's arrival in the U.S., ability to produce the drug had been improved by a factor of 12.[29]

The CMR then set about gaining the support for penicillin production of the U.S. drug industry, especially the leading firms such as Merck and Squibb. There were two main obstacles to this. Firstly, U.S. anti-trust policy outlawed cooperation between firms, even for research; secondly, the firms feared that if they invested in the production of natural penicillin and a rival discovered how to synthesize it, their factories would be made obsolete. The CMR dealt with the first problem by getting appropriate waivers from the Federal Trade Commission, and with the second by a subsidy of US$75 million - a huge sum at the time.[30]

Pfizer's `Submerged Fermentation'

Of the firms recruited by the CMR, it was the smallest, Pfizer, which made the crucial contribution. This was the technology

---

[29] Sheehan *The Enchanted Ring* (1982) Chap. 3.
[30] Williams *Penicillin and After* (1984) 142.

known as 'submerged fermentation', and it is not difficult to see how the possibility of using the volume of a culture medium rather than only its surface for growing the mould, transformed productivity. There was only enough penicillin to treat a single human case in March 1942, but 10 had been treated by June, 90 by the end of the year, and 500 by August, 1943.[31] By 1944, 21 firms were producing penicillin, output multiplied 70-fold in the following 2 years, and the yield per ml. of culture was improved more than 7000 times. As a result, enough penicillin was available for the needs of all the casualties of the Normandy invasion in 1944, by which time limited distribution to civilians in the U.S. had also commenced. The price came down correspondingly, from US$200 per million 'Oxford units' in August 1943 to US$50 in April of the following year and to only 50 cents in 1950.[32]

Medical Inertia

With the problem of production in quantity solved, another one faced Florey. In spite of the evidence from the U.S. clinical trials, the military doctors were reluctant to adopt penicillin treatment. He solved this by his own direct intervention, going to the battlefield in North Africa, telling the doctors to treat wounds with penicillin and then to sew them up, and insisting, against their protests that this was little short of murder, that this be done.[33] Eventually, Florey's persuasive powers, supported by the practical demonstrations of healing by the methods he was advocating, were enough to overcome the medical profession's conservatism. The adoption of penicillin and 'closed cavity surgery' as a result of Florey's efforts was later said by the Americans to have 'saved as many lives and mitigated as much suffering, as the war cost us'.[34]

Search for synthesis

A synthetic pharmaceutical product has many advantages over a natural one, including reliability, cheapness and the possibility of adding special features. Consequently, in 1943, the

[31] Richards *Nature* (1964) 442.
[32] Williams *Penicillin and After* (1984) 149.
[33] Wilson *Penicillin In Perspective* (1976) 142.
[34] Williams *Penicillin and After* (1984) 180.

U.S. Committee on Medical Research had sponsored an all-out effort (surpassed only in scale by the Manhattan Project which led to the development of the atomic bomb) to synthesize penicillin. Eventually, no fewer than 1000 scientists in 31 laboratories in Britain as well as the United States, worked on the problem, but with no success. U.S. public support for this research depended only upon the urgent need for penicillin resulting from the war, so that this work was finally closed down in 1947. The low price to which natural penicillin dropped also caused the commercial firms to lose interest in synthesising it, especially as this had now come to be widely regarded as impossible.[35]

Through research which may have been stimulated by the success of penicillin, Professor Jörgen Lehmann of Gothenburg found a synthetic product which could combat tuberculosis. This was *para*-aminosalicylic acid (PAS) which gave good results either alone or in combination with streptomycin, and had the advantage of being able to be administered orally.[36] Still more important was isoniazid (INH) which was even able to substitute for streptomycin. What was particularly remarkable about this was that it had been synthesized as long ago as 1912, but its power against tuberculosis had to wait to be demonstrated until Bayer, Hoffman-LaRoche and Squibb all did this independently in 1951.[37]

The Beecham Group and the Semi-Synthetics

For reasons which will be discussed below, Ernst Chain, although he shared the Nobel Prize for Medicine with Fleming and Florey in 1945, was unhappy with the way things had turned out. As a result, after the war, he left England and took a post in a Research Institute in Rome. He was sought out there by the Beecham Group. This British firm had begun in the mid-nineteenth century with the manufacture and sale of simple drug products (known as `patent medicines' long after the expiration of any patent protection they may have had). It had grown to be one of the biggest British firms in this field and in that of low-technology products with high

[35] Galdston *Nature* (1958).
[36] Lehmann *Lancet* (1946).
[37] Waksman *The Conquest of Tuberculosis* (1964) 184.

psychological ingredient, such as mineral water, hair cream, toothpaste and shampoo. Even before the war ended, Beecham's dynamic Managing Director, H. G. Lazell, had grasped that the antibiotic revolution had begun, and that big profits were to be made by joining in what was clearly the wave of the future in the pharmaceutical business.[38] Lazell succeeded in recruiting Chain as Consultant for this development in 1955 by offering to put large-scale resources for research at his disposal. This imaginative move led to the semi-synthetic penicillins, which came on the market in 1959, just as bacteria were beginning to develop resistance to the first type. These also had the considerable additional advantage of being able to be administered effectively by the oral route.[39] Beechams marketed them internationally in association with the U.S. firm, Bristol-Myers. As a result, the British firm became such a significant player in the international pharmaceutical game that within recent years it was able to negotiate a merger with Smith Kline Beckman in the U.S., to make a group that is now one of the biggest pharmaceutical firms in the world.

The Cephalosporins and Streptomycin Development

As will be seen, the discovery of the cephalosporins, a new type of antibiotic closely related to penicillin, was just as dramatic and `personal' in its way as Fleming's had been. It was offered to Florey, and his team overcame a number of difficulties before taking the cephalosporins on to great success, with firms such as Glaxo and Eli Lilly licensed to market an entirely new range of antibiotics throughout the world.

In the case of streptomycin, Waksman did not have to face any of the problems in getting his and Schatz's discovery into widespread production and use, which Florey had to overcome for penicillin. He did not have to persuade any public authority or commercial firm that streptomycin was worth producing, because penicillin was already demonstrating the beneficial effects of antibiotics for all to see. Also, the research programme from which streptomycin had emerged was a commercial initiative by

[38] Wilson *Penicillin In Perspective* (1976) 258-259.
[39] Hobby *Penicillin: Meeting the Challenge* (1985) 230.

one of the most advanced pharmaceutical firms in the world. Consequently, when in November 1943, Waksman and Schatz were able to advise Merck formally of their discovery of Streptomycin, some of the best resources in the world were ready to innovate it.[40]

Fifty Merck scientists were assigned to this task, and within 2 years, Merck had completed a large programme of clinical trials from pilot plant production. The results from these gave them enough confidence to commission the building of a full-scale plant to come on stream in 1946.[41] By then, largely because of work at the Mayo clinic, it was becoming increasingly clear that streptomycin was the answer to tuberculosis, so its future was assured.[42] By 1954, 9 firms were producing it in the U.S., and there was also production overseas. Its price followed a parallel downward path to that of penicillin: from US$25 a gram in 1947 to 25 cents in 1953 to 3 cents by the 1970s.[43] In only 9 years from 1950, death rates of children under 15 years of age from tuberculosis dropped by an amazing 90% in several Western countries.[44]

The success of penicillin and streptomycin inaugurated a huge wave of activity in searching for organisms with antibiotic properties, so that by 1950, in addition to the two original drugs and their derivatives, the important tetracyclines and chloramphenicol were beginning to be used. This wave continued until about 1960, so that by that date the antibiotic revolution, which had begun with Fleming's observation in 1928, reached substantial completion. From then onwards, new antibiotics tended to emerge from the routine incidental testing of products which had been isolated for some other reason.[45] Attention may therefore now be turned to the lessons for discovery, invention and innovation which the story of controlled bacterial antagonism teaches.

[40] Gruber *M.I.T. Technology Review* (1947).
[41] Porter *Chemical Engineering* (1946).
[42] Waksman *The Conquest of Tuberculosis* (1964) 123-132.
[43] Waksman *The Antibiotic Era* (1975).
[44] Kiple *Cambridge World History of Human Disease* (1993).
[45] Lechevalier in Parascandola, *The History of Antibiotics* (1980) 118.

Schumpeter's Insights

Schumpeter is such a key figure in the history of innovation studies that it is interesting to examine how his theories stand up to testing against the antibiotics case. In his early writings, the active agent in innovation is the heroic individual; in his later ones, it is the large firm.[46] Rather surprisingly, the case provides support for both sets of views. What fascinated `early' Schumpeter was the dynamic of `incessant rise and decay' in economic life. For him then, new ways of doing things `do not and generally cannot, evolve out of the old firms, but place themselves side by side with them and attack them... '. In the process whereby new things emerge, as noted in Chapter I, he made a clear distinction between invention and innovation:

> The inventor produces ideas, the entrepreneur `gets things done' ... and as different as the functions are the two sociological and psychological types. It is in most cases only one man or a few men who see the new possibility and are able to cope with the resistances and difficulties which action always meets with outside of the ruts of established practice.[47]

And for such an entrepreneur or innovator, he insisted,

> It is not the knowledge that matters, but the successful solution of the task *sui generis* of putting an untried method into practice ... Successful innovation ... is a feat not of intellect, but of will. It is a special case of the social phenomenon of leadership.[48]

Fleming and Florey Contrasted

It is hard to imagine a better illustration of these differences than the contrast between what was done by Fleming and by Florey. Fleming did indeed discover penicillin, but he only realized the least important part of its potential. It was due to Florey that penicillin was *innovated*, that is, turned into the concrete reality that was of benefit to the whole of humanity, and

---

[46] cf. Schumpeter *Capitalism, Socialism and Democracy* (1943).
[47] Schumpeter *Journal of Economic History* (1947) 152.
[48] Schumpeter *Economic Journal* (1928) 64.

not just to sufferers from influenza. Just as their activities were different, so were their personalities; once he had written his scientific paper describing the use of penicillin for identifying influenza, Fleming decided not to try to take it any further and went on to other things. He was a very model of the inventor as described by Schumpeter. Hobby, herself a scientist who was deeply involved in later developments, wrote of Fleming that

> as an academician of the 1920s and 1930s...he could have had no understanding of the necessarily close relationship between those who observe microbiological phenomena and those who `develop drugs'.[49]

Fleming later laid partial blame on the lack of cooperation from the surgeons in his hospital for his failure to grasp the therapeutic value of penicillin. But even his colleague, Hare, has to admit that he `failed to exhibit the fire and energy in his dealings with the surgeons required of someone with a passionate faith in his discovery'.[50] In contrast, `fire and energy' was precisely what characterized Florey's performance. When he was shown the therapeutic potential of the rediscovered invention by Chain, his immediate concern was how to obtain enough penicillin for proper clinical trials. Later on. his objective shifted to having it produced in quantity and used as widely as possible in the various theatres of war. The scientific aims with which the original study had started out, necessarily became secondary in importance to the achievement of penicillin's therapeutic potential. Both in setting these goals for himself, and in achieving them, Florey showed the personal commitment to a project that is so characteristic of innovators.

This determination is first evident in the speed and determination with which he focussed all the resources of his small Department on penicillin development the moment Chain's experiment with mice revealed its potential. It becomes even clearer in his reaction to the failure of the British pharmaceutical firms to provide him with the penicillin he needed for clinical trials. He decided to turn his university department into a factory,

---

[49] Hobby *Penicillin: Meeting the Challenge* (1985) 57.
[50] Hare *New light on the history of penicillin* (1982) 23.

and as one of his biographers observed:

> If the venture had failed, it would have been seen as an outrageous misuse of University property, staff, equipment and time, and Florey, as he well knew, would have been severely censured.[51]

He showed himself to be an innovator once more when continued slow British progress in producing penicillin led him to insist on the radical step of seeking help in the United States. The subsequent speed of development there was due, not just to the favourable circumstances of the U.S. war effort, but also to Florey's own tireless travelling and advocacy of the cause of penicillin production all over the country. In this, he suffered the pioneer's usual lot of being, as he recorded, `made to feel like a carpet-bag salesman trying to promote a crazy idea for some ulterior motive'.[52] When the army doctors refused to use penicillin, Florey showed his qualities as an innovator yet again by going to the battlefields himself to ensure that the new drug was widely used. Later on, it was also his determination which brought the difficult task of innovating the cephalosporins to success.

Importance of the Product Champion

Florey is by no means the only individual in the antibiotics case who corresponds to `early' Schumpeter's definition of an innovator, whose role within large firms is often that of `product champion'. A feature of Pfizer's involvement in penicillin, which was the crucial factor in making that firm into a modern pharmaceutical giant, was the personal interest of the firm's President, John L. Smith, and of John J. McKeen, its Chief Chemical Engineer. Smith was personally involved in some of the early clinical trials, and he and McKeen were so impressed by the potential of penicillin that they decided to go from a pilot plant to full-scale production without any intermediate scaling-up. This involved the same sort of risk with their careers as Florey's earlier decisions had in respect of his. Chain later wrote of McKeen that

[51] MacFarlane, *Alexander Fleming: The Man and the Myth* (1984) 182.
[52] ibid. 190.

he was `one of the best chemical engineers that I ever encountered' and that without Smith `the history of penicillin production in the United States might have been very different'.[53]

H.G. Lazell's leadership in moving the Beecham Group decisively into the newly-emerging field of antibiotics, in a firm with a relatively low-technology base, was of similar calibre. These examples illustrate Schumpeter's point quoted above, that `successful innovation is a feat, not of intellect, but of will. It is a special case of the social phenomenon of leadership'. His later thinking, when he saw the large firm taking over the leadership role in innovation, will be discussed further below.

`Radical' and `Incremental' Change

Schumpeter had also called attention to the difference between radical and incremental innovation. An aspect of this difference is that once a fundamental change has been made, incremental innovation along the line of the earlier production system becomes increasingly irrelevant - `there is no bridge back to the earlier situation'[54]

This is perfectly illustrated in the case of penicillin. The surface fermentation method used by the British producers was made obsolete by submerged fermentation, and even though the British firms had made some incremental progress during the war with surface techniques, they had no option eventually but to licence the new technology from the U.S. patentees. Naturally enough, this caused considerable resentment in Britain at what looked like American monopolisation of a great British discovery, especially when the British had originally refused to preserve their advantage by patenting it.[55] (This view was probably wrong, since, as will be discussed below, a valid patent was unlikely to be obtainable, but few would have been aware of this point).

One result was the establishment of the National Research Development Corporation, (NRDC), to which for many years all inventions in Britain which had been made with any form of public subvention (e.g., in University laboratories) had to be offered

[53] Chain *The History of Antibiotics* (1980) 24.
[54] Schumpeter *Journal of Economic History* (1947) 150.
[55] cf. Bud R. (1998) *British Journal for the History of Science* 31, 305-333

in the first instance. The NRDC built up exceptional expertise in innovation of patented products, and was privatized in 1990. As will be seen below, during the time it was State-owned, its biggest success was the world-wide patenting and licensing of the cephalosporins. These brought large royalties to Florey's laboratory in Oxford.

Psychological Aspects

The antibiotics case is particularly illuminating on the psychological aspect of the nature of scientific knowledge, and the way in which this progresses. It contains two remarkable 'what-might-have-beens'. Chain's famous experiment with penicillin on mice could have been done a decade earlier. Even if they did not have the resources to do it themselves, Fleming's team could have found a laboratory to do it for them. Waksman and Curtis isolated *Streptomyces griseus* as early as 1915, but did not test it for antibacterial properties.[56] Both Waksman and Fleming won Nobel prizes for making their discoveries when they did, but, lay people will ask, how could Fleming have missed the therapeutic value of penicillin? And why did it take nearly 30 years for a student working under Waksman's direction to discover streptomycin? Experienced scientists do not ask questions like these, because they know that research is normally an activity of failure or qualified success. Their usual hope from an experiment is that they will find something of a little value, rather than nothing at all; they certainly do not expect that their work will bring about something of world-shattering importance. Hopes and expectations of this undramatic kind played their part in the successes and failures of the antibiotic revolution.

Psychological Path Dependence

'Path-dependence', describing the way in which each step of technological development is conditioned by the steps which have been taken previously, is well-known in the innovation literature.[57] It also has a psychological dimension, which is well illustrated by the antibiotics story. The dictum of the great Pasteur, that 'fortune

[56] Waksman *My Life with the Microbes* (1958) 183.
[57] e.g., David *Technical Choice, Innovation and Economic Growth* (1975).

favours only the prepared mind', clearly applies to Fleming, and to Chain also. Fleming's sensitivity to what was going on in his experiments seems to have been altogether exceptional - indeed, to a degree noted and recorded by his colleagues. He had a delight in actual experimentation.[58] The extraordinary set of chance happenings which led to his discovery of penicillin will be referred to further below, but their number is enough to rule out any possibility that he could have had any expectation of what he saw on the petri dish. Many scientists might simply have noted that one of the cultures had become contaminated by a mould, and thrown it out. Fleming did not, because a vital spark leapt across his prepared mind when he noted that the bacteria had been prevented from developing. Fleming did not altogether miss the therapeutic potential of penicillin. In his 1929 paper, he suggested that `it might be an efficient antiseptic for application to, or injection into, areas infected with penicillin-sensitive microbes'. He lost hope about this aspect of his discovery because of the difficulty of handling the mould. Waksman noted that Fleming never mentioned penicillin in a session he had chaired on antiseptics at an international congress on microbiology in New York in 1939.[59] But once some of the practical obstacles has been overcome by Florey's team, his interest revived quickly. Chain records how very shortly after his and Florey's article appeared in the *Lancet* on August 24, 1940, Fleming arrived in Oxford, saying that `he had come to see what we were doing with *his* penicillin'.

Fleming was probably quite right to shelve it in 1930, given the limitations on the techniques for purifying and stabilising it which were available to him and his colleagues. Hobby pointed out that he

> was caught in a circular situation. Without enough penicillin of adequate purity to prove its chemotherapeutic efficacy, he was unable to arouse interest in studies on methods for its isolation and purification. Without the methodology, there was no possibility of obtaining penicillin suitable for clinical use.[60]

[58] Hare *The Birth of Penicillin* (1970) 61.
[59] Waksman *The Antibiotic Era* (1975) 25.
[60] Hobby *Penicillin: Meeting the Challenge* (1985) 50.

Chain's retrospective view was that the lack of sufficiently sensitive preparation techniques such as partition chromatography, caused the delay in isolating and studying the antibiotics.[61] This of course reflects path dependence in the more usual sense in which this is discussed in the innovation literature.

Scientists deploy scarce resources, in terms of laboratory manpower and equipment, and they have to be economical with both in the sense of directing them towards ends which are at least believed to be achievable. The starting point of the activity of innovation has been well described as `the imagined, deemed possible'.[62] The imagined can also be deemed `impossible, given our available resources'. Against such a background, apparent failure to see the potential in any situation may simply reflect a deliberate turning away from it because of a rational assessment that it is not the most promising way of using whatever resources are to hand, in a context of other urgent tasks. In Fleming's case, his colleague Hare wrote that

> soon after the discovery, what seemed to be good scientific evidence had been found that penicillin was unlikely to be of much value as a therapeutic substance. This may well have generated doubts in his mind about the feasibility of spending a great deal of time and energy on further research with nothing of any value at the end of it. Rather than take this risk, he allowed penicillin to lie fallow while he pursued what seemed more profitable lines of research.[63]

The `Masking Effect' of Partial Success

It is even likely that an element in Fleming's failure to follow up the therapeutic potential of penicillin, was that he did *not* miss its usefulness as a means of isolating influenza infection. The fact that he saw an immediate opportunity to put this aspect of his discovery to work in vaccine development could well have deflected him from exploring penicillin's potential further. Nevertheless, it was precisely because of this particular perception on his part, and the subsequent use of penicillin for laboratory

---

[61] Chain *The History of Antibiotics* (1980) 26.
[62] Loasby *In: Helmstadter* (1996).
[63] Hare *Medical History 26* (1) (1982) 24.

discrimination between different bacteria, that strains of his unique mould were available later when and where they were needed for the work of learning how to produce penicillin in quantity for administering to patients. It was in Oxford for Chain, and it was in the U.S. in the hands of Reid, from whom Dawson and Hobby were able to obtain it. The clinical research of these two was very likely a factor in stimulating Merck's interest in bacterial antagonism. Not alone must it have pointed them towards involvement in penicillin production, it must also have helped their decision to provide Waksman with the financial and other resources which led to streptomycin.

The records of both penicillin and streptomycin also teach the important lesson that every experiment has the potential to yield more information than the researcher carrying it out will be able to extract from it. How easily important aspects of an experiment can be missed, and how long it can take for the full implications of any result to be grasped, has been well expressed by Lechevalier (who, incidentally, was a student of Waksman's):

> Waksman and Woodruff (1940) did not guess that actinomycin could be used as an antitumor agent and as a laboratory reagent capable of inhibiting DNA-dependent RNA synthesis;[64] Schatz et al. did not seem to be very concerned about the potential role of streptomycin in the treatment of tuberculosis when they wrote their first paper on this compound;[65] likewise, Dr. Waksman and I did not guess that neomycin would be used for the prevention of hepatic precoma;[66] and I and my colleagues would never have thought that candicidin would ever be used to reduce the size of prostates.[67]

Another illustration, of course, is the antibiotic potential of INH against tuberculosis, which was unnoticed from 1912 to 1951. There is every reason to think that it would have remained so were it not for the research activity stimulated by the discoveries of penicillin and streptomycin.

[64] Schatz et al. *Proc. Soc. Exp. Biol. Med.* (1944).
[65] Comroe *Am. Rev. Resp. Dis.* (1978).
[66] Lechevalier *CRC Crit. Rev. Microbiol* (1975).
[67] Orkin *Urology* 1974; Lechevalier *The History of Antibiotics* (1980).

Unconscious Influences

Previous successes and failures have a cumulative effect on researchers' expectations from experiments, and consequently on how much of the range of implications of their results they will be able to grasp. In the antibiotics case, the story of Dr. Paine, a pathologist in Sheffield Royal Infirmary, is intriguing from this point of view. Shortly after Fleming published his Paper, Dr. Paine (who had been a pupil of his) wrote to him for some of the penicillin mould, which Fleming provided. He tried to culture it himself, but ran into the same difficulties as Fleming and his team had done. But with what penicillin he could grow, he saved the sight of an injured miner, the first cure to be recorded. It was so remarkable that he told the Professor of pathology in the University, who happened to be Howard Florey. Florey forgot all about it, but it is at least an interesting speculation that some residual memory of this cure played a part in the speed with which he was able to take the decision to throw all his resources behind the innovation of penicillin after Chain's experiment with mice.[68] Whether or not this is so, his mind was certainly `prepared', because he was able to take that decision within 26 hours of the start of that famous experiment.[69]

Unconscious influences can also have a *negative* effect on the power to invent or discover, as well as to innovate. During the first world war, all of Almroth Wright's team worked in a casualty clearing centre in Boulogne in France. Here, Fleming's experience with wounds convinced him that the antiseptics of the time did more harm than good, because they did so much damage to the body's own power to overcome infection. It is an interesting speculation that Fleming might have taken the therapeutic potential of penicillin more seriously, and made a greater effort to move his discovery towards clinical trials, were it not for these earlier experiences. It is not impossible that when reinforced by his disappointment with lysosyme, they may have left him subconsciously sceptical about the very possibility of achieving controlled bacterial antagonism. It is plausible that if he was looking out for

[68] Wilson *Penicillin In Perspective* (1976) 112-115.
[69] Williams *Howard Florey: Penicillin and After* (1984) 112.

anything, it would have been something like lysosyme, only stronger. If that was so, he cannot have been helped by the fact that penicillin acted in a quite different way to lysosyme.[70] Factors such as these help to explain why his grasp that he had actually come face to face with a uniquely important version of bacterial antagonism on his own laboratory bench was so incomplete.

Mental Rigidity

Path dependence at the psychological level often takes the form of mental rigidity. Ideas which have been proved to be successes or failures in the past remain in the mind with a strong influence. This can blind individuals completely to the possibilities of alternatives, which is one reason why the progress of knowledge is erratic and slower than it apparently needs to be. As in so much else, the antibiotics story provides illustrations of this phenomenon.

German scientists were not ignorant of what was happening in penicillin research in both Britain and the U.S., and were even able to pass information on it to their Japanese ally, via Switzerland. However, they made almost no progress in production during the war, and it has been plausibly suggested that this was due to their prevailing approach to pharmaceutical research. The German chemical industry dominated world markets up to the first world war, primarily because of their success in synthesising dyestuffs to replace products such as natural indigo. As has been noted, they had produced the first effective chemotherapeutic drugs in Salvarsan and Prontosil, which were triumphs of chemical analysis and subsequent synthesis, as were the later sulphonomides.

Not surprisingly, with such a record of success in synthesising drugs behind them, they applied the same approach to penicillin, expecting to understand and to be able to synthesize it, too. Penicillin defeated them, just as it defeated the massive effort to synthesize it in the United States. The crucial difference was that in the U.S. there was a parallel microbiological approach which was successful in producing natural penicillin in quantity.

[70] Gardner in *Nature* (1940) and see Hare, (1982) 3.

It is significant that countries like Holland. France and Austria, because of their knowledge of industrial microbiology, including fermentation technology, were able to make more progress with penicillin under wartime conditions than Germany did.[71] Mental rigidity also held back British penicillin production. Boon, the head of Imperial Chemical Industries, and Jephcott, the head of Glaxo, visited the U.S. together in 1944, where they saw everything the Americans had achieved, including Pfizer's submerged fermentation. Jephcott was convinced that this was the technique to pursue, but Boon could not be shifted from his belief in surface fermentation, because I.C.I. engineers had produced a design for a continuous version of this. Not alone did they build a useless plant to this design, their opposition prevented Jephcott from getting government support for the submerged fermentation plant that was so urgently needed.[72]

Waksman's Reflections

Waksman left us, not just an autobiography, but also several other writings which are autobiographical to a significant extent. These provide an extraordinarily valuable insight into the thought processes involved in scientific research. In particular, they make it clear just how much what researchers see or fail to see in their experimental results is affected by a range of factors which are only very partially under their control. Waksman, for example, is extremely frank about reporting how slow he was to advert to the therapeutic potential of the microbes which had been his life's work - the actinomycetes. The seed of the research for which he became world-famous was sown nearly 30 years earlier by his Professor in Rutgers University, Jacob G. Lipman. Waksman had done so well as an undergraduate that in his final year Lipman allowed him to join a group of graduates who were investigating soil microbes. This resulted in a Paper by Waksman on `Bacteria, Actinomycetes, and Fungi in the soil', which was read for him by Lipman at the Society of American Bacteriologists in 1915. His full report on this research, shared

---

[71] Hobby *Penicillin: Meeting the Challenge* (1985) 202-208.
[72] ibid. 135-136.

with Curtis, was published in 1916.[73] It was a very long time, however, before he adverted to bacterial antagonism in this context, even though, as he recorded, when

> making agar plates, I was frequently struck by the fact that very often certain colonies, usually actinomycetes, developing on the plate were surrounded by halos or clear zones, in which no other microbes developed, or produced only very small pin-point colonies ... I paid only little attention to the significance of this phenomenon. Some impression remained, however, and I frequently thought about it. Certain experiences that I had during the years 1918-1920, while working in an industrial laboratory ... tended to give me another slant on the possibility of utilising antimicrobial agents for the treatment of infectious diseases. These two unrelated experiences simply did not at that time tie up together in my mind, but the impression remained to be taken advantage of later.[74]

The last sentence of this contains an interesting echo of Florey's forgetfulness of Dr. Paine's remarkable cure with penicillin.

Anticipation of Fleming?

In his last book, Waksman records that Müller in 1908 and Lieske in 1921, had both showed the power of the actinomycetes, and Professor Gratia of Liége (who, incidentally, had been working on penicillin at the same time as Fleming) had actually used them to treat patients suffering from streptococcal infection. Moreover, in 1923 Waksman and his assistant, Starkey, had observed that

> certain actinomycetes produce substances toxic to bacteria [as illustrated by the fact that] around an actinomycetes colony upon a plate a zone is found free from fungus and bacterial growth.[75]

Although no reference is given to a report on this, which of course is a clear anticipation of Fleming's experience 5 years later, Waksman can scarcely be doubted, since his honesty about

[73] Waksman *My Life with the Microbes* (1958) 3.
[74] Waksman ibid. 18.
[75] Waksman *The Antibiotic Era* (1975) 10.

the number of times he missed bacterial antagonism is so patent. In another book, for instance, he confesses that:

> I was not prepared to investigate the problem of antagonism among microorganisms even when W. H. White of the National Tuberculosis Association urged me, early in the thirties, to study the destruction of the tuberculosis organism in the soil, and the role of soil microbes responsible for such destruction. Although I accepted a grant from the Council in 1932 ... I turned it over to one of my graduate students ... I also failed to pursue further the phenomenon of microbial antagonisms when a colleague drew my attention to a culture of avian TB which had been killed by a growing mold ... My failure to devote special attention to these important observations was due not to insufficient appreciation of the processes involved but rather to the fact that I was too busy with ... a study which resulted in two monumental treatises ... There also was undoubtedly some mental unpreparedness on my part ... The time appeared to be ripe in 1936, when I published (January, 1937) a series of papers on `The associative and antagonistic phenomena among microorganisms'...[76]

Penicillin The Stimulus for Streptomycin?

Even if the time was ripe, it took the advent of penicillin in the end to make Waksman concentrate on the therapeutic possibilities of the actinomycetes. One of his students recalls how

> Dr. Waksman appeared in the laboratory one day. He was highly agitated. `Woodruff', he said, `drop everything. See what these Englishmen have discovered a mold can do. I know the actinomycetes will do better!' ... Thus was initiated the first search in Waksman's laboratory for antibiotics from actinomycetes.[77]

When reading these accounts, it is only fair to bear in mind the great differences there were between Fleming, Chain and Florey, on the one hand, and Waksman on the other, both in terms of professional orientation and the milieux in which they were working. Fleming was a doctor, working in a hospital, whose specific concerns all related to the control of disease, since he was in charge of the vaccine `factory' in St. Mary's. As an academic pathologist,

[76] Waskman *My Life with the Microbes* (1958) 11.
[77] Woodruff *Annu. Rev. Microbiol.* (1981) 7.

Florey would also have had contact with practitioners. Chain's background was in medically-related biochemistry. In contrast, as Waksman wrote of himself:

> I was primarily a soil microbiologist... concerned with products of microbes that are used in green plants . . . or with products of microbes ... used in a variety of industries. Prior to 1939, I scarcely dreamed of becoming profoundly involved in problems dealing with human and animal diseases.[78]

Resistance to New Ideas

The antibiotics story provides several striking examples of the rejection of novelty. `The human mind' it has been said, `likes a strange idea as little as the body likes a strange protein and resists it with a similar energy'. Charles Kettering, the inventor amongst other things of the self-starter for automobiles and later a great innovator in General Motors, held that the hardest substance in the world must be that of the human skull, to judge by the force needed to drive any new idea through it. The case of Ignaz Semmelweis, not long before the work of Pasteur which started off the antibiotic revolution, has already been referred to.[79] In the United States, Oliver Wendell Holmes, like Semmelweis, noted in 1847 that puerperal fever was caused by `conveyance to the pregnant woman of putrid particles derived from living organisms, through the agency of the examining fingers'.[80] He, too, met with such opposition to his theories that he abandoned medicine and devoted his energies to literature instead. Indeed, rejection of a new idea was the very reason why there was an immunisation centre in St. Mary's hospital for Fleming to work in. Almroth Wright had been Professor of pathology in the British Army Medical School, where he produced the first effective vaccine against typhoid fever. When the military authorities would not adopt it, he resigned and went to St. Mary's. There is an interesting parallel between this rejection of something new, in the face of clear evidence, and the

---

[78] Waksman *My Life with the Microbes* (1958) 182.
[79] In Chapter II. See also Carter and Carter, *Childbed Fever: a scientific biography of Ignaz Semmelweis* (1994).
[80] Rosen *A History of Public Health* (1993), 294.

later refusal of the Army doctors to use penicillin, which caused Florey to travel to the battlefields to convince them personally.

Brotzu's Ploy

The great success of the cephalasporins in dealing with penicillin-resistant microbes has already been noted, and the origin of these drugs not alone displays resistance to new ideas, but also how resourceful those who have them need to be if they are to gain acceptance. Dr. Brotzu, a public health biochemist in Cagliari, a small town in Sardinia, noticed that raw sewage has some power to purify itself and concluded that some form of antibiosis was going on. He produced a culture of what turned out to be the first of the cephalosporins, and tried to interest the Italian pharmaceutical industry in it. He had no success, nor could he even get a journal article published on his findings. Eventually, his highly original method of promoting his ideas was to found his own scientific journal with an impressive title, *Lavori dell' Istituto d'Igiene di Cagliari.* He then printed a single issue of it which contained only his own Paper, and sent a copy of this to Florey with a culture of his antibiotic.[81] Both were taken seriously by the Oxford scientists, the National Research Development Corporation provided funding for development, and the cephalosporins reached the market. By the 1970s, these outsold the semi-synthetic penicillins.[82]

Brotzu succeeded in eventually getting his ideas accepted because he was exceptionally skilful in promoting them. Many discoverers and inventors lack such skills, and their natural frustration at repeated rejection of their ideas does not help them to overcome the apparent stupidity and blindness they encounter. Part of the problem with Semmelweis, for example, was his obsession that there was only a single cause of puerpural fever, which was decaying organic matter. In this he was wrong, because it was later discovered that the cause was microorganisms, especially streptococci, and these of course could also have other sources. If Semmelweis had been less intransigent with his critics who considered that they had good

---

[81] Williams *Howard Florey: Penicillin and After* (1984) 302.
[82] Wilson *Penicillin In Perspective* (1976) 251-256.

grounds for rejecting a monocausal explanation, he might have found it easier to get his proposals accepted.

In this, it is possible to see a classical dilemma of innovation. This requires individuals to have a strong commitment to whatever has been imagined and deemed possible, since without such a commitment it will never get turned into concrete reality in the face of scepticism and resistance. But reaching such a level of commitment can mean tunnel vision on their part which may exclude other, related, and sometimes even better ways of achieving the desired end. In particular, it explains the many cases where innovators fail to repeat an earlier success, by approaching the new problem with the mental approach that had been successful with the earlier one. Or where some technique is not used when it is appropriate, simply because it has failed before in a different context.

The Role of `Outsiders'

Path dependence of both kinds, in relation to both the techniques and equipment available on the one hand, and to mental rigidity on the other, means that much progress depends on those who are outside the previously existing technology, though ideally they should be close to it. Why was it Pfizer, the smallest of the firms which were originally approached by the U.S. Committee on Medical Research, that made the breakthrough which made penicillin widely available? One part of the answer must be in the special nature of its business. By far the biggest part of this was the production of products *by fermentation* for the confectionery, brewing and similar industries. Its subsidiary in London had in fact been a supplier of material to Florey's laboratory in Oxford in the very earliest days of penicillin research there. Pfizer had been working on submerged fermentation techniques for several years, and it was this which gave them more understanding of how to solve the problems of producing penicillin in quantity than any of the other firms had. They had enough presence in pharmaceuticals to understand these problems, but it was their special expertise from *outside* the field that launched them into the new and highly profitable world of antibiotics.

Note that in a sense this `outside but close' phenomenon as a positive factor in innovation may be the other side of the coin of the `not-invented-here' and `sailing-ship' syndromes which are so negative for it. The value of scientific education in saving redundant research is of course very great. Inevitably, however, because the body of knowledge in the possession of any scientific community is both imperfect and incomplete, it can *prevent* experts from following up particular lines of enquiry. The corollary of this is that on occasions advances will be made by individuals who lack the formal knowledge which would tell them that what they are trying cannot possibly work. The `not-invented-here' syndrome reflects how such a discovery or invention by an outsider is of course felt as an insult by members of a technological community. How could such a person possibly tell us something that we (who have devoted our lives to mastering this body of knowledge) do not already know? If it could have been invented, we would certainly have invented it, so what is now being proposed simply cannot work. We can therefore ignore it.

When others prove us wrong by innovating the invention, and we are forced to pay attention to it, frantic work to meet the challenge frequently finds possibilities in the older technology which had not been adverted to when it was dominant. The reason why this is called `the sailing-ship syndrome' is because paradoxically it was only after it began to be obvious that the steamship would sweep commercial sail from the seas, that the sailing ship reached the peak of its efficiency. In a similar way, more recently, the thermionic valve only reached its highest pitch of development when its makers were attempting to meet the challenge of the transistor - which of course replaced it in virtually all amplifying applications. Significantly, too, *not one* of the thermionic valve manufacturers was successful in making the change to transistors, presumably because of mental rigidity.

In his study of the turbojet revolution, Edward Constant (1980) stresses that this was brought about by a `new technological community' which had not been associated previously with aero-engines. The contributions to the antibiotic revolution of firms like the Beecham Group (not previously involved in the pharmaceutical industry at all) and Pfizer (whose main business was elsewhere) illustrate the same point, which is how much major changes owe to `outsiders'.

Illustrations of Creativity

The human creative energy which is expressed in discovery, invention and innovation is just the same creativity as can be expressed in other ways, such as intellectual activity and the arts of all kinds.[83] Chain illustrates this, in that he was as exceptional a musician as he was a scientist. In fact, in his days in Germany he had had to decide whether or not to make his career as a professional musician; instead, he opted for biochemistry.[84] Ehrlich's achievement in discovering Salvarsan, Domagk's with Prontosil and Sheehan's in synthesising penicillin, also confirm the point that where creativity is concerned, the best are not just ahead of the rest, they are incomparably better. And how long might the Beecham Group have taken to see a return on their investment in the pharmaceutical field if they had not been able to have the benefit of Chain's quite exceptional vision? In terms of creativity in business, how many lives were saved by John L. Smith's ability to decide to `bet the farm' by ordering that Pfizer would go from a pilot plant to mass production of penicillin in a single move?[85]

Patent Aspects – Germany

The antibiotic revolution teaches a number of lessons about the patent system which are helpful in understanding how it works, and which also illustrate some of its deficiencies as well as its advantages.

The German chemical industry was the first to use the international patent system systematically, and this enabled its firms to dominate world markets until their foreign patents were expropriated as a result of World War 1. Just how important they considered patents to be is illustrated by an incident from the early history of chemotherapy. Although the Bayer work on Prontosil was

---

[83] As discussed in Chapter I.
[84] Williams *Howard Florey: Penicillin and After* (1984) 53.
   Hobby *Penicillin: Meeting the Challenge* (1985) 60.
[85] ibid. 187-190.

completed in 1932, it was not revealed until 1935. It is believed that the delay was due to Bayer's attempts to obtain a version of the new drug on which they could get a patent.[86] This is quite plausible, since Prontosil had two components which were broken down in the body, and the active one, sulfanilamide, was already known and therefore unpatentable. Bayer's protection for Prontosil was therefore weak, and other firms were quickly able to develop and manufacture new sulfa drugs, of which May and Baker's M&B 693 became one of the most widely used.

Patent Aspects – Penicillin

When he realized how valuable penicillin might be, Chain was very anxious that it should be patented. This was because as a refugee who had arrived in England from Germany virtually penniless, one of his only ways of restoring his fortunes was to share in royalties from it. However, the British medical establishment refused to consider this, on the ground that it was wrong for anything which was for the general benefit of mankind to be allowed to produce monopoly profits. Resentment at the failure even to try to patent penicillin was a factor in Chain's decision to leave England for Italy after the war, although friction with Florey and the resources for research which were offered to him in Rome of course had a major bearing on this also.

This element in Chain's resentment was probably misplaced, since it is unlikely that penicillin as originally discovered could ever have been patented. Even if it escaped being ruled to be `a product found in nature' and if Fleming's 1929 scientific Paper had not destroyed patentable novelty by releasing the information into the public domain, later disclosures such as Chain and Florey's paper,[87] and those to the U.S. pharmaecutical firms by Florey and Heatley on their tour there, would almost certainly have precluded the grant of a valid patent.

Even so, Florey was concerned lest a U.S. pharmaceutical firm might try to patent penicillin. During the tour, he reported to Dr. Weaver of the Rockefeller Institute:

---

[86] MacFarlane *Howard Florey: the Making of a Great Scientist* (1979) 149.
[87] Chain and Florey The *Lancet* (1940).

> While Heatley was working at Peoria, I made numerous enquiries
> from the various people I met, and concluded that it would be safe
> to approach the main pharmaceutical houses individually; it seemed
> unlikely that any one firm could patent the mould and process of
> extraction, and so block the field.[88]

He was right about this, but of course the technology for
producing penicillin, especially that of submerged fermentation,
later became the subject of numerous patents.[89]

In the 1950s, the Beecham Group in England was close
behind Sheehan in synthesising penicillin, and this led to a long
drawn-out patent battle between them in the U.S., which Sheehan
won, but only as late as 1979. An interesting aspect of this
conflict is the reluctance of M.I.T. to patent any discovery in the
public health area, just as had happened with penicillin in Britain
originally, and on similar grounds. M.I.T. in fact only took action
when Sheehan told them that if they did not apply for a patent for
synthetic penicillin, he would do so on his own account.[90]

Patent Aspects – Streptomycin

In contrast to penicillin, because the discovery of
streptomycin was effectively under the control of Merck, the
research on it was *intended* to lead to patents. A condition of
Waksman's appointment as Consultant to Merck in 1938, with
funding for work on fermentation, mainly in relation to citric
acid, was that the firm would patent any invention that might be
made, paying a 2.5% royalty to his University on any resulting
sales. This condition also applied to Merck's funding of research
into bacterial antagonism by Waksman and his team, which began
the following year. The agreement in respect of this also specified
that Waksman and his assistants would handle the microbiology,
and Merck scientists would look after the chemistry and
pharmacology as well as any subsequent laboratory or clinical
testing that might be justified for any discovery.[91] Consequently,
when Waksman was able to report the discovery of streptomycin

---

[88] Florey *Report to Dr. W. Weaver* (1941).
[89] cf. Hobby *Penicillin: Meeting the Challenge* (1985) 284.
[90] Sheehan *The Enchanted Ring* (1982) 166.
[91] Lechevalier *The History of Antibiotics* (1980) 118.

to Merck, they applied for a patent for it, as they were entitled to do under their Agreement. Although by that time they were heavily involved in producing penicillin, the prospect of a patent monopoly gave them more incentive to put their innovatory resources behind streptomycin. The contrasting cooperative arrangements for the production of penicillin were explicitly designed by the Committee for Medical Research to avoid `giving any manufacturer a monopoly derived from government support'.[92]

The decision of the United States Patent Office on this application was a landmark one, and was in fact the basis of the entire subsequent development of the antibiotics industry, and indeed of the patent system. If they had considered that streptomycin was nothing more than the *streptomyces griseus* which Waksman and Curtis had first isolated in 1915, then, as a product found in nature, it could not be granted a patent. Instead, they appear to have held that the modifications carried out to purify and stabilize it amounted to the production of `a new composition of matter' as required by the Patent Act, and so approved the issue of patent No. 2,449,866 to Merck on September 21, 1948.

Patent Aspects – Crisis for Law

Coming after the success of penicillin, this patent was the start of a deluge of antibiotic inventions which caused a crisis for the U.S. Patent Office. This was because the Courts had always required evidence of a `flash of creative genius' for a patent grant to be valid. The words are from a 1941 case (*Cuno Engineering v. Automatic Devices*) but the standard had been set nearly a century earlier in *Hotchkiss v. Greenwood* (1850). This distinguished the work of an inventor from that of `the skillful mechanic'. Penicillin had undoubtedly been discovered through a `flash of creative genius', but the massive, indeed mechanical screening processes such as those from which Ehrlich and Domagk had obtained Salvarsan and Prontosil, had nothing of such a `spark' about it. Salvarsan was No. 606 in the sequence of compounds containing arsenic which Ehrlich tested, and its improvement,

---

[92] Richards *Nature* (1964) 442.

Neosalvarsan, was number 914.[93] These laborious analytical techniques had indeed aroused the contempt of Almroth Wright as a way of doing science: `To Wright, who believed that the human reason was the only light that could show the way forward in research, such groping in the dark was a form of sacrilege'.[94]

Similarly, streptomycin emerged from the painstaking examination and testing of thousands of different soil microbes for antibiotic activity by Waksman's team. It was Albert Schatz who actually first isolated streptomycin, and his name is on the patent for it with Waksman's, but it could just as easily have been any of Waksman's other graduate students who were working on his program of research into the actinomycetes. After streptomycin, the way in which virtually all valuable new drugs were discovered was by massive screening processes carried on by `skillful mechanics'. There was no longer any point in looking for a `flash of genius' from an identifiable individual's mind as their source, since this source was now large-scale investment instead. The pharmaceutical industry became one of programmed, large-scale, routine activity which is anything but inspired. This new way of `inventing' faced the authorities with a dilemma, because they could hardly refuse to grant these pharmaceutical patents, yet the way in which the antibiotics were being found could not be reconciled with even the most liberal definition of individual `flash of creative genius'. A new law which would frankly recognize the change from individuals to investment as the source of what is to be protected, would have needed an amendment to the Constitution. Since this was of out of the question, change could only be made in a way that forced the reality of invention by investment into the pretence of invention by individuals.

Patent Aspects – New Criterion

The United States 1952 Patent Act achieved this by providing that `patentability shall not be denied because of the way in which the invention was made', and by changing the Office's operating definition of invention. This change was made by formally replacing

---

[93] Hare *The Birth of Penicillin* (1970) 51.
[94] MacFarlane *Alexander Fleming: The Man and the Myth* (1984) 148.

the `flash of creative genius' requirement by the `inventive step' or `non-obviousness' test. According to this, a patent can only be granted for something which, in addition to being new, is `not obvious to one skilled in the relevant Art'. Because of the strong influence of the United States on the Conventions which govern patents internationally, this requirement was soon adopted world-wide.

The new criterion is particularly suitable for industries such as chemicals, in which inventions result from having a portfolio of research topics (such as Waksman's 10,000 soil microbes). It is virtually certain that something patentable will be discovered somewhere within the portfolio (which makes it rational to make even a very large investment in the research) yet it will not be `obvious' to try any particular component of it, so that valid patents can be obtained. In industries such as mechanical and electrical engineering, where inventions are not made by the portfolio approach, it is much harder to meet the `non-obviousness' criterion. It is scarcely an exaggeration to say that the international patent system is now largely run for the international pharmaceutical firms, which are amongst the biggest users of it.

I.G. Farben and Prontosil

As well as its bias towards chemical inventions, another question mark in relation to the patent system in its present form, is raised by I.G. Farben's reported patent procedure in respect of Prontosil, referred to earlier. This drug was of enormous importance because `never before had it been possible to cure a bacterial infection by administering a chemical agent'.[95] The number of deaths in childbirth alone which might have been saved if Prontosil had been available all during the 3-year delay in putting it on the market, must have been very considerable indeed. This can be verified from the work of Leonard Colebrook, a colleague of Fleming's at St. Mary's. In the face of scepticism from both Fleming and Wright, he treated 64 cases of severe puerperal fever with Prontosil, and found that it brought the death rate down from the usual 25% to 4.6%. He was then criticized for not carrying out a proper clinical trial by treating half his patients

---

[95] Hobby *Penicillin: Meeting the Challenge* (1985) 31.

with only a placebo, but he defended what he had done on the ground that the alternative would have condemned 8 of them to death.[96]

One of the classical arguments in favour of a patent system is that it encourages early disclosure of inventions to the public by offering the inventor a better alternative than keeping them secret. If it does not do this or, even worse, if it actually *encourages* delay in disclosure (as the Prontosil case suggests, however rarely this may occur) the case for having patents in their present form is that much weaker.

Change in Industry Structure

Not alone did the antibiotic revolution transform the operation of the patent system, thus providing the institutional basis for a huge increase in investment in the search for new drugs, it also brought about a radical change in the way the drug industry was organized. Before it, pharmaceutical firms were primarily manufacturers, with their products being distributed through wholesalers. Once it was clear that antibiotics would obtain strong patent protection, the emphasis shifted from production to research, and firms built up their own sales forces to market their products, mainly through influencing doctors to prescribe them.[97] In a modern pharmaceutical firm, R&D can cost 20% of sales, but marketing costs can be even higher. The entry of a firm like the Beecham Group, which had long experience of selling products with very high marketing to sales ratios, may well have contributed to the escalation of marketing costs in the pharmaceutical industry after the second World War.

Support for Basic Research

Amongst the reasons why German firms dominated the world chemicals markets up to the second World War was the availability of funds for research from the State. These supported basic research in the Universities, and each chemical firm had a close link with one or more of these, such as Bayer with Munich, Hoechst with Frankfurt

---

[96] MacFarlane *Alexander Fleming: The Man and the Myth* (1984) 149
[97] Schwartzman *Innovation in the Pharmaceutical Industry* (1976) passim; Temin *Taking Your Medicine: Drug Regulation in the United States* (1980) 67.

and AGFA with Berlin. There was no comparable support for research in the English-speaking world, except in relation to agriculture in the United States. There, by the Morrill Act of 1862, lands were dedicated to the funding of Land Grant Colleges, and funds for agricultural research were made available by the Hatch Act of 1887. The result of both has been the remarkable productivity of U.S. agriculture. Waksman's University, Rutgers, had been a Land Grant College originally, which is why he had been able to carry on his research into the actinomycetes there.

Until the establishment of the great charitable Foundations towards the end of the last century, therefore, little money was available for medical research in Britain and America. Researchers who had medical practices were able to fund their research from their fees, or, if they were persuasive like Almroth Wright, they might get donations from rich friends. St. Mary's hospital was unusual in having quite a lucrative source of research funding from its vaccine `factory'.

Rockefeller Foundation's Vision

Consequently, the role of the Foundations in funding medical research before the advent of large-scale public funding (itself a permanent legacy of the success of the U.S. Office of Scientific Research and Development in World War 2) was crucial. The Rockefeller Foundation was amongst the best endowed of these, and has a claim also to be the best, by the criterion of the ability of its staff to `pick winners'. Penicillin is not by any means the only case which illustrates this. The research which led to the dwarf varieties of wheat and rice which made countries like Mexico and Pakistan self-sufficient in food for the first time[98] was also funded by them. The Foundation did not operate simply by responding to applications for funding, but actively followed up how its funds were used, and the potential for new projects. According to its own view of its mission, as reported by its chronicler:

Projects were not espoused according to the degree to which they

[98] cf. Borlaug *Nobel Lecture* (1970).

promised an immediate practical result. The test was ... the increase of fundamental knowledge ... That was the faith in which, in the early 1930s, the Foundation entered upon its plan to advance experimental pathology.[99]

In the antibiotics case, the amount for which Florey asked the Rockefeller Foundation in May 1936 for laboratory equipment to get Chain started on research into lysosyme, was £250. This was granted in July, and as a later Foundation internal report put it

seldom has so small a contribution led to results so momentous. For it was this laboratory, this equipment and this group under Dr. Florey that pioneered the clinical use of the new drug penicillin.[100]

In the autumn of 1939, Dr. Miller from the Foundation visited Florey's group in Oxford to see how the work on lysosyme was coming along, and Florey told him that they had been preparing a submission for additional funding. This was sent on November 20, and the covering letter stresses `the growing importance of biochemistry to Pathology and Bacteriology' and the value of having Chain in charge of this aspect of the research, listing no fewer than 14 Papers in which he was an author. It concludes that `the work proposed, in addition to its theoretical importance, may have practical value for therapeutic purposes'.[101] Although the proposal described six lines of investigation which were being pursued in Florey's laboratory, the application was for funding for only two, of which the first was for the study of bacterial antagonism. Florey claimed that lysosyme, of which the Oxford group had achieved a good knowledge, could be regarded as a model for the process involved in this. He was aware of Dubos' discovery of tyrothricin (published at the beginning of the year) and quoted this in support of the claim that the proposed work had `great potentialities for therapeutic application'. The amount sought was £1,670 a year for 3 years, plus an equipment grant of £1,000. The budget item for `a fully qualified Biochemist' (presumably Chain) was £600 a year. The Foundation responded with a grant of US$5000 for 1 year in February, 1940 and provided

[99] Fosdick *The Story of the Rockefeller Foundation* (1953) 274.

[100] Rockefeller Foundation *Extract from Trustees' Bulletin* (1943).

[101] Florey *Application to the Rockefeller Foundation* (1939).

a further US$5000 in December of the same year. It continued to support Florey's work, for example with US$6500 in 1942 and US$4860 in 1943, and onwards into the 1950s. In addition, they paid the expenses of the visit of Florey and Heatley to the U.S. in 1941, described in their President's report of that year as a grant `of emergency origin but of obvious long-range value', and which indeed did have such important consequences.

In spite of the danger of wartime travel, Dr. Warren Weaver, Dr. Miller's superior in the Foundation, visited Oxford in April 1941, and his report on this urged their full commitment to the work on penicillin in terms which must have given him and his colleagues much satisfaction later on:

> This project, if it were indeed successful, would be more revolutionary than the discovery of sulfanilamide or a sulphocyanogen (?) (sic), and must be recognized as a project of the very highest potential importance. We certainly ought to do all we can to accelerate its progress.[102]

An aspect of their success in this must surely be their awareness of the importance of individual creativity. Behind their involvement in penicillin was their contribution to the lysosyme research; and behind that was their much earlier award which had enabled Florey to study in the United States. This aspect of their work is recognized in a later internal paper, which ends with the comment that `Those earlier efforts at developing research men and equipping them for work, no less than the direct grants to Oxford ... are part of the penicillin story'.[103] When Florey was in the U.S., he regarded it as his duty to keep the Foundation, which had provided the funds for his visit, well-informed about his progress with penicillin. For example, after his tour of 7 of the main pharmaceutical firms in the U.S. and one in Canada, he provided a list of comments on each of these to Dr. Weaver, with the conclusion that `the only firm likely to make a significant amount of penicillin is Merck'.[104] In considering the role of Foundations, it should also be noted that both the Commonwealth

---

[102] Rockefeller Foundation *Report by Dr. W. Weaver* (1941).
[103] Rockefeller Foundation *Extract from Trustees' Bulletin* (1943).
[104] Florey *Report to Dr. W. Weaver* (1941).

Fund Foundation and the Lasker Foundation provided funds to Waksman. for his work on the actinomycetes.

Bureaucracy and Innovation

As noted earlier, in his later writings, Schumpeter saw the modern large firm as the vehicle for innovation. He was a disciple of Max Weber's in several ways, and amongst the many views of Weber's that he shared was that bureaucratic organisations are the most effective way to carry out tasks which are definable and measurable. He was also sensitive to the increasing role played by science in the development and manufacture of new products. The combination of both these ideas led him to exaggerate the value of scientific research and development, and to downgrade the importance of leadership, in industrial organisations. His thinking thus went well beyond Weber's, by asserting that the bureaucratic firm, by incorporating growing scientific knowledge, is also able to break out of established routines, that is, to innovate.

He was wrong to lay this down as a general rule, because there is an intrinsic incompatibility between bureaucracy and innovation.[105] It should be noted, however, that innovation in the modern pharmaceutical industry does take place largely in the way of his later model. This industry depends more on R&D for its growth and development than any other, and its discoveries come from routine mechanical screening of huge numbers of compounds for possible therapeutic value. As Lechevalier pointed out, by about 1960 every newly-isolated chemical substance was being routinely tested for antibiotic activity.[106] Waksman described the systematic search for antibiotics in 1945-1950 in the following way:

> The extensive screening programs were in charge of large numbers of workers, who did not rely solely on chance observation for the isolation of antibiotics ... well-equipped laboratories ... whole teams of microbiologists and pharmacologists.[107]

---

[105] cf. Kingston *Innovation or bureaucracy* (1995).
[106] Lechevalier *The History of Antibiotics* (1980) 116.
[107] Waksman *The Antibiotic Era* (1975) 57.

The pharmaceutical industry can operate a portfolio approach to its investments in R&D, but other industries cannot. For them, innovation cannot escape being a venture into the unknown. Bureaucratic organisation, in contrast, requires complete information if it is to operate, and it is also this, as Max Weber was the first to recognize, which gives it its strength in carrying out routine and fully understood tasks. Conversely, the lack of information is precisely what makes innovation difficult for it. Moreover, the older any bureaucracy gets, the less tolerant of uncertainty - and therefore of innovation - it becomes.[108] This is why Schumpeter was wrong to think that even privately owned bureaucratic organisations could ever take the place of individual entrepreneurship. As Langlois has observed

> for reasons that have to do with the nature of cognition and the structure of knowledge in organized society, some essential part of capitalism must always remain personal... whether Schumpeterian entrepreneurship operates from the top of an existing organisation or in the creation of new ones, the same conclusion seems unavoidable. The charismatic authority and coherent vision of such entrepreneurship remains an inevitable part of capitalism, however modern.[109]

It is virtually a defining element of entrepreneurs (and all the more, of innovators) to be able to make decisions on the basis of limited information. Common observation, again, testifies that there are some people who are unusually capable of extracting meaning from signals which have no effect on the majority. For such individuals, these kinds of `pre-quantitative, pre-semantic' information can act as a stimulus to action. Indeed, it has been perceptively observed how much the world owes to

> a limited number of industrial entrepreneurs ... [who] ... have possessed the sanguine outlook which enables a man to reach a policy decision even when a good deal of information theoretically necessary is not available.[110]

---

[108] cf. Olson *The Rise and Decline of Nations* (1982).

[109] Langlois *Microfoundations of Economic Growth* (1998) 77.

[110] Jewkes *Public and Private Enterprise* (1965) 48.

It is impossible not to think of Florey and the Rockefeller people, in the world of scientific entrepreneurship, and of people like Smith, McKeen and Lazell on the borders of it, in the light of such observations.

Government as Patron

The limiting case of bureaucracy is the public service, and there is no shortage of evidence in the innovation and public choice literature that Government intervention is not productive of successful economic innovation. In remarkable and unexpected contrast, the antibiotics case provides evidence of government intervention in innovation which was highly successful. Penicillin simply could not have been innovated as quickly and on the same scale as it actually was, without the direct actions of U.S. Government agencies such as the Department of Agriculture, and, above all, of the Committee on Medical Research. These agencies operated very efficiently indeed. In particular, their arrangements for free transfer of information between the firms concerned speeded up the innovation of penicillin greatly.[111] One line of possible reconciliation between anti- and pro-interventionist views is that the sustained levels of creativity, motivation and readiness to take risks on which all innovation depends may indeed be capable of achievement by the public sector at times such as those of war, when entire populations are bound together in ways that are absent in peacetime. An illustration of this is that after the first meeting convened by Richards, the head of the Committee on Medical Research, to try to get research on penicillin going in the interest of the U.S. as it faced into the war, R.T. Major, the head of Merck, sent him a simple message: `Command me'.

At such times, too, necessity justifies risk-taking, and there is less time and energy for apportioning blame, so that bureaucrats need not be so fearful of damage to their careers through being associated with failure. In particular, war conditions decouple financial risk from technical risk. The premium placed on success also forces quality change in leadership positions in public bureaucracies. This is especially visible in the U.S., where the highest levels are filled by political appointees.

---

[111] Hobby *Penicillin: Meeting the Challenge* (1985) 213.

In relation to penicillin production, for example, Sheehan commented from first-hand experience that:

> The cooperative arrangements were not easy to make. Richards complained over and over again of the difficulty of bringing the companies together. However the cooperative research and development program was finally arranged, it is a tribute to the strong personalities of the men leading the program. Richards himself was a powerful and persuasive man. Vannevar Bush was a giant, Chester Keefer could play the role of `God' because he was endowed by his colleagues with godlike qualities. The leaders of the penicillin research and production program took on heroic dimensions equal to the magic of the compound they worked with.[112]

Similar levels of motivation and performance are likely to be quite impossible to reach in peacetime, when the natural antagonism between bureaucrats and innovators is not tempered by necessity on the part of the bureaucracy to become innovative, and there is no national peril to impose changes which would enable it to do so.

Yet, good as the U.S. wartime bureaucracy was, there are indications from the antibiotics case that even this had difficulty in handling diversity, which is an essential condition for successful innovation. When Waksman began to look at the therapeutic possibilities of the actinomycetes, he naturally approached the Committee for Medical Research for funding. He was refused on the ground that his project was `too theoretical'. `But', he was told, `if you want to work on penicillin, you can have all the funds you require'.[113] Richards did send on his request to the Commonwealth Fund Foundation, which helped him quickly, but of course it was the backing of Merck which was decisive for his discovery of streptomycin.

University–Industry Collaboration

As noted above, it was the German chemical industry in the mid-nineteenth century which pioneered formal links between industrial and university laboratories. The contemporary importance

---

[112] Sheenan *The Enchanted Ring* (1982) 202.
[113] Waksman *The Antibiotic Era* (1975) 33.

of biotechnology has made this type of cooperative research into an important issue world-wide. The antibiotics case throws much light on this also, in the first instance because of the relationship built up by Florey between the Sir William Dunn laboratory in Oxford and several U.S. pharmaceutical firms, with the Committee on Medical Research acting as intermediary.

For example, Merck invited Florey's colleague Heatley, who had come with him to the U.S., to join their staff, which he did (with Florey's encouragement) for the crucial period of the first half of 1942.[114] There was also fruitful interaction between Waksman's Department at Rutgers University and Merck in relation to penicillin as well to the actinomycetes. In 1940, in spite of the Chain-Florey paper of that year, almost nothing was generally known about penicillin in the United States. Waksman recalls a meeting of the Society of American Bacteriologists in late December with Dubos talking about tyrothricin, and Waksman himself discussing actinomycin. Only one question was asked about penicillin - and nobody present could answer it.

When Merck were shown a culture of Fleming's strain of the penicillin mould (almost certainly by Dawson and Hobby) in 1940, they were not greatly impressed by its antibacterial properties. At that time, they shared other expert medical opinion that the most promising products would come from derivatives of Dubos' tyrothricin[115] and Waksman was urging them to do development work on this. However, they were at least sufficiently interested to ask Waksman for advice on penicillin and to go back to the papers Fleming and his colleagues had produced in 1929 and 1932. Waksman promised to obtain more of Fleming's mould for them, and with his encouragement, they recruited three researchers from early in 1940 'to prepare useful chemicals by fermentation and to study isolation of therapeutic substances from microorganisms'.

It was because of these early steps that Merck was the only firm which raised Florey's hopes of having penicillin produced in quantity, when he did his tour of U.S. establishments, as he reported to Dr. Weaver of the Rockefeller Foundation. Further, when

---

[114] Helfland *The History of Antibiotics* (1980) 38.
[115] ibid. 32.

the CMR was negotiating with the main pharmaceutical firms to bring about a cooperative effort for penicillin production, they found that it was Merck which `had shown the most serious interest and had made the most progress' and it was the only firm ready to commit itself `to proceed with production and to share information as far as was legally permissible'.[116] In September of 1941, Pfizer joined Merck and Squibb in an agreement which included full exchange of research and production information. Since, as noted earlier, Pfizer had solved the production problems, this would have given Merck access to all the information on submerged fermentation technology it needed for quantity production, not just of penicillin but eventually of streptomycin also.[117]

Need for Patent Strategies

Two lessons from the antibiotics story stress the need for Universities to have well-developed patent strategies if they are to benefit from cooperation with industry in research. The first of these lessons relates to licencing. The Waksman patent was originally assigned exclusively to Merck and both the firm and the University profited handsomely from it. In Merck's case, the lead time which the patent gave them in constructing large-scale production facilities for streptomycin led to dominance of the market for it. So much was this so, that as early as 1946 they were willing to agree with a proposal from Waksman to yield their patent rights to a new Research Foundation in Rutgers University.[118] It has been estimated that by 1978 Rutgers had received no less than US$12 million in royalties from this arrangement. However, the University then gave seven *non-exclusive* licences of the patent rights, and according to Lechevalier, these

> were to have a devastating effect on its abilities to pursue the search for new chemotherapeutic agents ... What was good for streptomycin in 1945 was not necessarily suitable for chemotherapeutic agents discovered 10 or 20 years later ... by 1953 it became obvious that with the plethora of antibiotics then available, new antibiotics could not be developed and marketed

[116] Richards *Nature* (1964) 442.
[117] Lechevalier *The History of Antibiotics* (1980) 119.
[118] Waksman *The Antibiotic Era* (1975) 52.

competitively without an *exclusive* lead time. The search for new chemotherapeutic agents came practically to a halt at Rutgers, and it was only in 1976 that the agreements guaranteeing non-exclusivity were terminated.[119] (Emphasis added).

Schatz–Waksman Litigation

The second lesson is the need for clear rules regarding ownership of any intellectual property rights that may arise from University research. Lack of these in Rutgers led to complications which caused much pain to Waksman, as Schatz initiated Court proceedings against him in 1950. Streptomycin was the subject of Schatz's PhD dissertation (which he had defended in 1945). He had performed most of the basic laboratory manipulations involved in the discovery, his name was on the original paper reporting it, as well as on several later papers referring to it, and he was named as a co-inventor in the patent application. Even though his work had been directed by Waksman, it would have been hard for him not to think of himself as the discoverer of the new and valuable drug.

On the other hand, Waksman equally naturally considered that he was chiefly responsible for the discovery. It had come about because of his life-long devotion to the study of soil bacteria, from which interesting antibiotics such as actinomycin, streptothricin and tyrothricin (the latter discovered by Dubos) had already emerged. The opportunity to discover streptomycin depended specifically on the research program he had started in 1939 with funding from Merck. Schatz was the lucky one of the group of graduate students who were working on this program, so Waksman thought that his contribution was `only a small one'. Schatz's charge against Waksman, according to the latter's own description, was that

> by virtue of my power, position, and influence in the field of microbiology and in the world of science, as contrasted with the student's youth and inexperience, I would see to it that he would be refused employment in the scientific and professional field for which he was trained, that no reputable institution would employ him, if he should embarrass me by refusing to sign an assignment to

[119] Lechevalier in Parascandola, J., (ed.) (1980) 118-119.

the Rutgers Foundation of a patent on which his name appeared; that if he should refuse to sign such assignment, I would cause his name to be withdrawn from the patent application. The complaint contained these and other claims and included demands for a share of the streptomycin royalties and for an order restraining me from representing myself as the sole discoverer of streptomycin.[120]

The case was settled out of Court on the basis that Schatz would receive 3% of the royalties, plus a lump sum of $125,000 in respect of the foreign patents. Waksman then generously arranged for a substantial part of his own royalties to be distributed between 26 of his research assistants and former students.

Waksman's Research Methods

As noted in Chapter II, J.B. Conant, who was at one time. Chairman of the U.S. National Defense Research Committee, held that there was only one proven method of assisting the advance of pure science: This was to pick men of genius, to back them heavily, and leave them to direct themselves. Equally, there was only one proven method of getting results in applied science: This was to pick men of genius, to back them heavily, and to keep their aim on the target chosen.[121] The antibiotics case bears him out, not only because its protagonists were clearly men of genius, but their approaches to research were so different. This is especially evident in the contrast between Waksman and Chain.

It is clear from his writings that Waksman's approach to research was to set himself objectives which could be clearly defined, and which had good chances of being reached with whatever resources were available to him. `Aim-directed' research was just where Waksman was at home. He told a U.S. Congress Sub-Committee in 1945 that `the discovery of streptomycin is another illustration of the importance of planning biological research in the solution of a given scientific problem'.[122] Later, in his autobiography, he wrote that

---

[120] Waksman *My Life with the Microbes* (1958) 250.
[121] Quoted in Mees *The Path of Science* (1946) 196.
[122] Waksman *The Conquest of Tuberculosis* (1964) 118.

we discovered streptomycin, because we were looking for it, because we had studied previously this type of compound, because streptothricin that preceded it had similar chemical and biological properties, and because we had already worked out detailed procedures for the production and isolation of this type of compound.[123]

His book on `The Conquest of Tuberculosis' also contains a perfectly logical explanation of why he did not take the results of the research by his student which was funded by the National Tuberculosis Association in 1932-1935 `to its logical conclusion'. These are just the same grounds as were suggested to explain why Fleming missed the therapeutic value of penicillin.

As the Director of the research programme on the actinomycetes from which streptomycin emerged, Waksman undoubtedly deserves the credit and the Nobel prize which he received. But he does not add to the quotation above what a complete account requires, which is that `we were looking for it because we already knew about penicillin'. It is relevant that whereas Fleming discovered both lysosyme and penicillin and Chain discovered the semi-synthetics, Waksman himself discovered nothing important. Dubos found tyrothrycin (`which', as Waksman said, `pointed the way') and Schatz found streptomycin, one as a former student and the other as an actual student of Waksman's, working under his direction. With hindsight, Fleming's lysosyme seems to be the most important discovery of all because everything which followed stemmed from this.[124] Moreover, it should be noted that Schatz's discovery of streptomycin was no less than 28 years after Waksman with Curtis had first isolated *Streptomyces griseus*.

Aim-directed research encounters the problems of handling information in a bureaucratic context, which has been touched upon earlier. Because members of a bureaucracy must be concerned to minimize the risk to their careers, the aims of this type of research will tend to be narrow and as safe as possible. Further, because bureaucracy stifles creativity, unexpected results which emerge may go unnoticed.

[123] Waksman *My Life with the Microbes* (1958) 184.
[124] cf. Hobby *Penicillin: Meeting the Challenge* (1985) 3.

Chain's Suspicion of `Targets'

In contrast to that of Waksman, Chain's preferred way of doing research, like Fleming's own, stressed autonomy. From this standpoint, research also needs the `charismatic authority and coherent vision' which Langlois claimed was essential for entrepreneurship. Chain had to be left to direct himself by Florey, since he was bringing an entirely new discipline (biochemistry) to Oxford. Florey stressed Chain's `very great flair for the elucidation of enzyme as well as other biochemical problems' in the 1939 application to the Rockefeller Foundation. In any event, it is quite clear from the following comments of Chain's that any other arrangement would not have suited him:

> In actual practice, I do not know of a single case of a major disease for which a cure has been found because the research worker *wanted to* find one ... I became interested immediately in penicillin after seeing Fleming's paper, not because I hoped to discover a miraculous drug for the treatment of infection which, for some reason, had been overlooked, but because I thought it had great scientific interest. *In fact, if I had been working, at that time, in aim-directed scientific surroundings, say in the laboratory of a pharmaceutical firm, it is my belief that I would never have obtained the agreement of my bosses to proceed with my project* ... we obtained a result of great practical importance without setting out with the aim of achieving it. Many successful cases in the pharmaceutical field have a similar historic pattern, and it would generally help if those responsible for the financing of medical research familiarized themselves with the histories of these discoveries.[125] (Emphasis added).

In the antibiotics revolution, both approaches produced remarkable results, leaving the question of which is better an open one. Perhaps, in spite of his comments, Chain's work was *both* autonomous and aim-directed, because he certainly had the aim of learning all about lysozyme, and it was in the course of this that he came to Fleming's 1929 paper, with everything that followed from it.

---

[125] Chain *The History of Antibiotics* (1980) 23.

How Inevitable was the Antibiotic Revolution?

When discovery, invention and innovation themselves became the subject of study and reflection, it was not long before the question arose of how far these were individual or social processes. As discussed above, in Schumpeter's early writings, for example, he attributed achievement in these areas to heroic individuals; in his later ones, he went close to claiming that invention and innovation had become routine matters, because of the modern large firm's ability to carry out R&D continuously and on a large scale.

It is possible that this mental evolution towards emphasising the social dimension was influenced by writers of the 1930s like Rossman and Gilfillan, who played down the contribution of the individual discoverer or inventor. As noted in Chapter I, the former held that our inventions are the result of social accretions to prior inventions,[126] and Gilfillan was led to conclude from his study of cases of simultaneous invention, that `[Invention] is a sociological phenomenon, a complex of folkways ... the inner culture sets the goals, for which the inventor contrives the appropriate tools of civilisation ..'.[127]

Jãnos Wolf's Evolutionary Theory

A modern version of this line of thinking can be found in a doctoral Dissertation, in which Jãnos Wolf has plotted many of the factors in the antibiotic revolution, and used them to illustrate an evolutionary approach to innovation. In a paper which summarizes this dissertation, he claims that the story of bacterial antagonism reflects the existence of a `macrostructural order', which is:

> a pattern of a spatiotemporal series of converging discoveries and discrete research sequences. Not until a certain degree of macrostructural order was reached in science was it possible for an integrative question with a high degree of feedback to arise. This question was, in a certain sense, prepared by a decades-long, convergent drifting of various research sequences.... all pursuing

---

[126] Rossman *The Psychology of the Inventor* (1931) 3.
[127] Gilfillan *The Sociology of Invention* [1935] (1970) 10, 151.

different aims. The macrostructural order, however, was 'searching for' its own goal and one day 'drove' one of the persons involved to adopt this goal.[128]

A single quotation does not do justice to the subtlety of Wolf's thought, but nevertheless this is a good example of a view of research as an activity that tends in some sort of linear fashion towards ends that are inevitable. It is highly deterministic, although Wolf attempts to evade this by locating his argument in theories of complexity and of 'spontaneous self-organisation'.[129] The many twists and turns of the story of bacterial antagonism, however, do not leave one anything like as sure as he is of the inevitability of discoveries and innovations.

To begin with, how far do we have to delimit the concept of a 'macrostructural order' to a particular time-bound development before it can have the dynamic quality (the power to 'drive' individuals to adopt its goal) which Wolf attributes to it? Hero of Alexandria invented a heat-powered device to open temple doors. Was this posing what Wolf calls an 'integrative question with a high degree of feedback' in relation to steam power? Are we to believe that a 'macrostructural order' was thus established, and that this eventually 'drove' Newcomen (and, later, Watt) to adopt its goal? Similar questions arise in relation to the inability of the Chinese to take their knowledge of gunpowder as far as the making of cannon. From Wolf's standpoint, it would be a reasonable answer to claim that his complexity theory relates only to the period after applied science became important, roughly since the middle of the last century. As has been discussed, steam power was innovated without the benefit of any usable theory of thermodynamics, which was only developed subsequently by thinkers such as Clausius.[130]

But there is evidence against his view from the era of applied science, too. It will be recalled that chemotherapy emerged from dyestuffs research. Perkin had invented the first synthetic dye in 1857 and set up his plant near London, so Britain was first with the technology. It also had by far the largest textile industry in the

---

[128] Wolf *Publications series of the Research Unit* (1996) 15.
[129] ibid. 47-49.
[130] cf. Cardwell *From Watt to Clausius* (1971).

world to use such dyes and by far the biggest source of their raw material (coal tar). This combination surely adds up to a 'macrostructural order' in Wolf's terms, whose goal could hardly be other than the development of this industry *in Britain*. Yet, by the end of the century, and primarily through more and better scientific research, and a better patent system, Germany had achieved 85% of the world market for such dyes, and British firms only 5%.

Doubts about `Self-Organisation'

It seems reasonable to think that within any area of scientific enquiry every unit of knowledge exercises a pressure on researchers to use it, and that the strength of this pressure can be affected by competition from other units. Within the antibiotic revolution itself, the 'integrative question' is clearly the dream of controlled bacterial antagonism. Yet it has been seen above that research directed towards this was held back for decades by successive waves of interest in antiseptics, immunisation and chemotherapy. There seems to be no intrinsic reason why further new waves of therapeutic advance could not have postponed achievement of the related 'macrostructural goal' indefinitely.

Wolf quotes Chain to illustrate the way in which pressure from the 'macrostructural order' works:

> Microbial antagonism had become ripe for study in 1938... we would have started our research programme on these substances even if Fleming's paper had not been published, and if we had not done so, someone else in some other laboratory in the world would have taken the initiative.[131]

He goes on to argue that antibiotics would then have emerged from a combination of Chain's and Florey's research in Oxford, with Waksman's 'long-term and systematic' study of the actinomycetes. Streptomycin would have been the first antibiotic, and penicillin would have been arrived at through subsequent programmatic research.[132] All of this, of course (including Chain's observation) is based on hindsight, and conveniently begs many

---

[131] Chain *Thirty years of penicillin therapy* (1971) 302.
[132] Wolf *op, cit.* 18.

questions. As noted earlier, isoniazid (INH), so good an antibiotic that it could substitute for streptomycin, had been synthesized as early as 1912. Why, if `the macrostructural order was seeking its own goal' of controlled bacterial antagonism, did it miss such an opportunity of `driving' someone to research its clinical potential before Bayer, Hoffmann La Roche and Squibb did so simultaneously, but only after they had seen the success of penicillin and streptomycin? It seems that when the history of science gets down to details, it drives us away from belief in self-reproducing systems, towards acceptance of the importance of individual personalities and chance - in other words, towards seeing science as another expression of human creativity with all its quirks.

Basalla, Mokyr and Technology Evolution

Two historians of technology whose ideas appear to be capable of taking both types of change into account are Basalla[133] and Mokyr[134]. The common element in both is the concept of evolution by `punctuated equilibrium', involving long periods when incremental changes are all that can be observed, but also times when major discontinuous changes take place. These changes parallel macromutations in biology, although the parallel cannot be pushed too far. Basalla observes that:

> Modern theorists of technological evolution indeed face the same dilemma that confronted the Darwinists in 1859. The latter could point to reproductive variability as a fact of nature but were unable to explain precisely how and why variants arose because they did not possess a knowledge of modern genetics. We who postulate theories of technological evolution likewise have our Darwins but not our Mendels.[135]

Nevertheless, the punctuated equilibrium approach that is common to both authors looks as though it could accommodate Wolf's theory as well as one which stresses genius and luck. Mokyr, for example sees new techniques evolving in two different ways:

[133] Basalla *The Evolution of Technology* (1988).
[134] Mokyr *The Lever of Riches* (1990).
[135] Basalla *op, cit.* 210.

One is through a sudden macroinvention, followed by a series of microinventions that modify and improve it to make it functional without altering its content. The other is through a sequence of microinventions that eventually lead to a technique sufficiently different from the original one as to classify it as a novel technique rather than an improved version of the original one.[136]

He stresses that this distinction is important because the two kinds of invention or discovery `appear to be governed by different laws'. Microinventions result from an intentional search for improvements, but:

> Macroinventions are more difficult to understand, and seem to be governed by individual genius and luck as much as by economic forces. Often they are based upon some fortunate event, in which an inventor stumbles on one thing while looking for another, arrives at the right conclusion for the wrong reason, or brings to bear a seemingly unrelated body of knowledge that just happens to hold the clue to the right solution. The timing of these inventions is consequently hard to explain.[137]

Mokyr quotes the discovery of coke smelting and Gutenberg's invention of moveable type as examples of such `fortunate events', but penicillin - in which both genius and luck are so evident - must be amongst the most remarkable of all.

If the application of Wolf's theory is restricted to the microinventions which realize the full potential of a macroinvention, that is, to incremental changes as referred to above, the theory becomes much more persuasive. A macroinvention (or equally of course a macrodiscovery) would then establish a particular `macrostructural order', because it would be `an integrative question with a high degree of feedback'. That is, it would define a trajectory for a set of incremental changes to exploit its own practical potential. Awareness of this trajectory would exert pressure on inventors and innovators to adopt the macroinvention's `goal', which is of course to have all its potential realized in practice. From this standpoint, the cephalosporins, the semi-synthetics, streptomycin and the synthetic

---

[136] Mokyr *The Lever of Riches* (1990) 294.
[137] ibid. 295.

penicillins can be seen as microdiscoveries along the trajectory established by a macrodiscovery, which was penicillin. Or, as noted by Hobby, lysosyme, and not penicillin, may be the macrodiscovery. In either case, such a trajectory is clearly visible in the post-penicillin rush to investigate all possible sources of antibiotics.

Might Waksman have discovered Penicillin?

Further light is thrown on these issues by pursuing the relationship between penicillin and streptomycin. Waksman's search for an antibiotic in the actinomycetes followed the penicillin development closely in time, and also had the same objective, that of achieving controlled bacterial antagonism. Indeed, it was Waksman who coined the term `antibiotic'. Wolf's argument is that penicillin and streptomycin might have emerged in reverse order, i.e., if the Fleming-Chain-Florey sequence had somehow never happened, the antibiotic revolution would have started with streptomycin. In practical, historical terms, this question is therefore, if Fleming had not discovered penicillin, would Waxman have done it? There are two assumptions here. The first is that Waksman would have discovered streptomycin without the stimulation he got from learning about penicillin – `Woodruff, see what these Englishmen have discovered a mold can do!' The second assumption is that he would then have gone on to discover penicillin. The evidence does not suggest that either outcome was likely. On his own admission, he had come into close contact with bacterial antagonism in the actinomycetes several times in his life, and missed *every single one* of the opportunities. His student Lechevalier[138] confirms this point. As Waksman wrote of himself, he was a soil microbiologist, who never showed any inclination to move outside his field - and indeed his achievements show that there was plenty for him to do within it.

If we accept Waksman's recollection of the 1923 incident (and there is every reason to accept it) then within 5 years of each other, both he and Fleming observed potentially controllable bacterial antagonism in action on their laboratory benches. But

---

[138] Lechevalier *The History of Antibiotics* (1980).

whereas Waksman did nothing at all about it, Fleming did everything he could with the limited resources at his disposal and at least got as far as a means of identifying influenza. The comparison does not suggest that Waksman would ever have discovered anything outside the expectations of an aim-directed research programme. It seems clear from Woodruff's testimony that it was indeed what Waksman learned about penicillin that finally directed him towards the goal of obtaining an antibiotic from the actinomycetes, which he had been studying all his academic life. This intellectual stimulus was reinforced by Merck's practical support for research directed towards that particular goal, probably in turn as a result of their awareness of Dawson and Hobby's clinical work with penicillin. Without these external influences, it seems very likely that Waksman would have continued with the broad spread of other projects which he had in hand at the time, and would consequently not even have discovered streptomycin.

Was Mass Screening the `Macro-Invention'?

A scenario that does seem plausible is extension of the screening techniques that had produced Salvarsan and Prontosil. If these techniques are considered to amount to a macro-invention in Mokyr's sense, then, sooner or later, they would have been applied to the actinomycetes. We can be fairly sure that streptomycin would have emerged as a result because in his patent litigation testimony, Waksman claimed that Schatz isolated it in less than two months from starting work under his direction.[139] But would penicillin have been discovered by use of the same techniques? There is reason to doubt it, and to think that it would have escaped from discovery for a considerable time, *because screening techniques were actually applied to it, and failed.*

When the Committee on Medical Research became energetically involved in the development of penicillin, Dr. Raper of the Department of Agriculture's laboratory in Peoria recruited the United States Air Force to collect samples of fungi as sources of moulds from around every foreign station, and to send these

---

[139] Waksman *My Life with the Microbes* (1958) 251.

back to the U.S. for testing. Some of the samples collected in this way were able to produce penicillin, but none of them was as good as the penicillin mould which Fleming had originally noticed on his bacterial culture. MacFarlane observes that

> Fleming's strain had the ability to produce penicillin at a level that put it in a class of its own, and it was one so rare that it would have been most unlikely to be rediscovered.[140]

Failure and Chance

The most humbling of the many lessons which can be learned about research from the antibiotics case, therefore, is how much it is an activity which is carried on under uncertainty, not even risk (which is uncertainty quantified). And central to this pattern of normal failure and rare success is the factor which researchers and innovators cannot control at all, i.e., luck. The case drives home just how important `Chance' is for those whose lives are devoted to basic research.

The odds against the one strain of penicillin that worked so well in man being amongst the moulds which La Touche collected for his asthma research are astonishingly high in themselves. So also are the odds against Fleming and La Touche both working at the same time in St. Mary's, with a physical connection between their laboratories which allowed the mould to contaminate Fleming's experiment. But these events are only the start of this astounding lottery. It was chance that focussed Fleming's interest particularly on *staphlococci* in 1927: he had been invited to write the relevant Chapter in the Medical Research Council's *System of Bacteriology*. Chance, too, that an experiment on *staphlococcus aureus* had been done the year before in Trinity College, Dublin; that when Fleming was replicating this, no doubt with a view to discussing it in his Chapter, he went on holiday for long enough to enable the mould effect to develop; and that the temperatures in his laboratory during this period were unusual. It is now known that the weather then was exceptionally cool for the time of year; because of penicillin's sensitivity to heat, if the temperature had been normal,

---

[140] MacFarlane *Alexander Fleming: The Man and the Myth* (1984) 138.

there probably would have been nothing to observe. Indeed, in a more generously staffed laboratory, the petri dish might already have been cleaned.[141] There was bad luck too: Fleming and his colleagues came very close to purifying penicillin and learned much about it that had to be re-discovered by later workers.

Taking everything into account, and bearing in mind that individual factor probabilities have to be multiplied together to arrive at the aggregate chance of an event's occurring, the ultimate odds against the antibiotic revolution coming about in the way it did, test even the wildest imagination to the limit. Yet this is the real-world context in which discovery, invention and innovation, that is, `finding new things' and `getting new things *done*', have to be carried on.

---

[141] Hare *The Birth of Penicillin* (1970) 64.

CHAPTER IV

Innovation and Money

In a 'Memorandum concerning Mr. Boulton', which is in the Birmingham Assay Office, James Watt says of his partner that he

> was not only an ingenious mechanick well skilled in all the practices of the Birmingham manufactures, but possessed in a high degree the faculty of rendering any new invention of his own or others useful to the public, by organising and arranging the processes by which it could be carried on as well as by promoting the sale by his own correspondents. His conception of the nature of any invention was quick and he was not less quick in perceiving the uses to which it might be applied and the profits which might accrue from it.

This is a perfect description of an innovator, including the eye to profit which must be possessed by anyone who seeks to get new things done in the economic field. As Boulton said himself in a letter to Watt, he had backed the famous steam engine 'through love of you, and love of a money-getting, ingenious project'.[1] The typical technological innovator links the world of ideas with the world of which money is the measure, and is interested in a project because it is ingenious as well as because it is money-making.

[1] L.T.C. Rolt *Tools for the Job* (1965) 67.

Once again, the rectangle of Chapter I can illuminate innovation:-

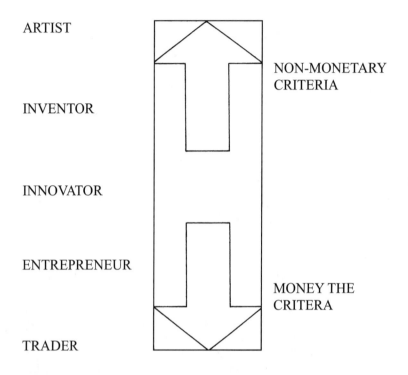

ARTIST

NON-MONETARY
CRITERIA

INVENTOR

INNOVATOR

ENTREPRENEUR

MONEY THE
CRITERA

TRADER

Moving upwards, money becomes progressively a less adequate measure of the activity in question; downwards, it becomes increasingly appropriate. It is no measure of art, and only a poor measure of the quality of invention, but it is the *only* measure appropriate to trading. A novelist's vision of a great comic character need have nothing at all to do with money, at least at the time when he conceives it. In contrast, traders are judged only by whether or not what they do, makes money. We do not praise traders for their *style*. Money, which is the only measure at one end of this spectrum, is totally inadequate at the other.

   This, of course, is because money is no more than a measure of exchange. It describes what people are prepared to give in terms of their own activity, for the activity of others. Consequently, it only comes into the picture in so far as such mutual evaluations and exchanges can take place, and do in fact do so.

What Money Measures

Money reflects the extent that any activity is public, conditioned by an external world of verifiable facts and concrete realities, rather than personal and private, concerned with an inner world of imagination and with things as they might be rather than as they are. Again, the innovator straddles both activities. Some innovation, such as that in technology, is better judged by its money-making capacity than by anything else; some, such as Semmelweis's nearly hopeless battle for hygiene as a means of combatting puerpural fever in the Vienna maternity hospital, has an importance for humanity which money cannot measure. Money is at highest risk in the case of invention, where nothing at all of the inventor's vision has yet been realized in the concrete, and at lowest (which may be virtually zero) in that of trading, where everything, except possibly one last element of stockholding or physical movement, has had to be rendered into concrete reality before traders will concern themselves with it at all. The risks, for example in modern property development, are so low that they are acceptable even to institutions which are dealing not with their own money, but with other peoples' which has been entrusted to them. Nor can the role of money be considered as a measure without bringing in the element of time.

As has been seen, creativeness is involved in different degrees in all the activities listed, but it is never possible to say how much creativeness there is in any particular activity, simply by what people are prepared to pay for it in the short term. Only during eras of high culture is there any correspondence between the evaluation of artists by their contemporary world and by posterity, and there is almost always much misunderstanding between artists and business people because of the difference in the measures they apply to what they do. Although by no means every artist would accept it as the only criterion to be applied to his work, nevertheless, being valued by a significant number of people with developed taste in the particular medium, has in practice been accepted by a high enough proportion of artists to be considered their typical measure. Almost certainly some of this recognition will be in the future; probably, though regrettably, some of it will be posthumous. Now clearly this is a criterion

[handwritten margin note: what about Linux Ubuntu?]

which, however readily a business person may recognize relevance to artistic activity in it, simply cannot be applied to business itself. Goods have to be acceptable now, not in the long-term future, certainly not in a posthumous one.

Time, Success and Failure

As a matter of fact, a frequent cause of business failure is that the time scale of the transactions which are being engaged in is too long for the firm's capital resources to stand. Until the early 1930s André Citroen ran a motor car factory which was renowned for advanced technical design, not only in France, but throughout the world. He had completed the design and virtually all the preparations for a new car which was to be much further ahead of its time than anything he had yet built (in fact, it had many features which other manufacturers only adopted in their post - World War II cars). His money ran out just before the car reached the market, and the Michelin tyre firm took the Citroen firm over. His design proved to be an outstanding success, but the time scale of the innovation had been just that bit too long for the capital of the independent Citroen firm to be able to stand.

There can be analogous failures in artistic activity, too, when the artist's ambitions remain unfulfilled because his physical or emotional powers are inadequate to them. However, they happen less frequently than in the case of innovation for two reasons: Firstly, an artist's creative energy is in itself a powerful aid to his physical survival even in the most adverse circumstances until his task is finished; secondly, he is generally dependent only upon himself - he is frequently his own innovator. There is no large team of variously endowed and motivated aides without whom the work, whatever it is, simply cannot be done, as there is in business. Consequently, a business person's apparent rejection of art frequently involves misunderstanding of the criteria by which art is measured. Equally, the artist rejects the standards of measurement which are appropriate to business activity, mainly on the grounds of their being too short-term and too restricted in time and place. Money on a short time-scale is a poor measure of creativeness and of artistic activity, but as the time scale is lengthened, it progressively improves. *In the long run* it is the classics that are also the biggest box-office draws. Business people may regard artists as impractical, but all artists know in their heart that if they were so inclined, and not preoccupied with more important things, they could do anything that business people do with the greatest of ease. If the amount and intensity of creative energy, rather than the way in which it is directed, is considered, there has never been a great artist for whom outstanding success in business could not be forecast in the unlikely event of this becoming the objective. Wagner, for example, was a financial genius, but happily he could never take money seriously.[2] By the highest standards of human activity, business is little more than child's play.

Innovation and Trading

Innovation shares the characteristics of the two worlds. Looked at from one side, it is intelligible in artistic terms; from another, it makes sense in terms of business. It has become fashionable in recent years for some firms to claim that their identifying characteristic is that they are innovative, but this can never be more than partially true. No business can be concerned with innovation only. It may be concerned with innovating and then with trading the results of the innovation, but that is not the same thing. The innovation stage of business can never be other than a cost. It is trading that produces more revenue than costs and which therefore permits a firm to stay in business and to grow. A firm which takes its 'innovative' role excessively seriously, so that it neglects to trade properly with what it has innovated, is in danger of getting out of its economic depth. This is another aspect of the need to keep innovation in line with the scale of the available resources illustrated by the Citroen example. Many component firms in the post Second World War spate of mergers in Britain found themselves taken over for this reason. Firms with their eyes fixed on the long-term future, trying to break new ground where the risks - when they could be measured retrospectively - were found to be higher than anything which had been contemplated, fell victims to rivals where much greater care was taken to see that risks were always matched by liquid reserves and that the areas of highest uncertainty were avoided.

---

[2] Ernest Newman refers to both these points repeatedly in his biography.

It is not only sentimentality which causes the firms which were taken over in this way to be mourned. There is widespread suspicion that the new conglomerates have the power to produce more short-term profits, and so earn the favour of stock market investors, but may not have the future on their side because of their short-term approach to innovation. The firms which failed in this race did so because they lived too much in the future for the demands which were being made of them in the present, but the firms which took them over may be living too much in the present to have much of a future. A big element in this situation is lack of understanding of the innovation process. It is for lack of this knowledge that firms get involved more deeply in innovation than they can afford, as they eventually discover to their cost. It is also for lack of it that the firms which take them over are firms whose present success is merely a prelude to being eventually taken over themselves, through having eaten the seed-corn which contains the creative germ.

The Function of Capital

Some innovation is brought about through the raising of fresh capital to found a new firm, but more comes from existing firms on the basis of successful trading to-day. In either case, the firms must be able to count upon being able to trade in the future with what they innovate. Only in this way can there be a proper relationship between the inputs and outputs of innovative activity over time. There has to be some factor which binds together innovation, entrepreneurship and trading. This connection is capital, which is either freshly raised for a new firm, or partially self-generated in a continuing firm. In the latter case, it is the cash flow from trading to-day which provides the resources which can be placed at the disposal of innovators within the firm so as to enable them to move forward into areas where much is uncertainty; it is their success in reducing uncertainty to risk in some few cases that will provide the cash flows of the future. Without innovation, there will be nothing to trade with in days to come when the present sources of cash flows have been superseded; but if too much innovation for the current resources of the firm is attempted, it will not stay in business long enough to enjoy trading on the results and others will reap where it has sown.

This question of maintaining a proper balance between innovation and trading in any firm is a particularly important one, since it can only be done at the very highest level of control, and inevitably the personalities of the chief executives are a major factor. Unless at least one of them is personally committed to getting some new thing done, it will not be done in that firm. A certain danger goes with this. There is, as was seen in earlier chapters, a psychological bias in the innovation process towards activities in which the personal element is stronger - the `natural' movement is upwards rather than downwards in the rectangle which illustrates the process. It is easy to see, then, how firms whose top management is innovative frequently become vulnerable to rivals which have kept to trading. The fact that the leaders of these innovative firms are generally more attractive as human types should not be allowed to obscure the fact that they can fail in their first duty to the firm, which is to see that its attempts to innovate and thus to be great in the future do not impair its capability to survive in the present.

Creative Energy

All of this, of course, applies only to the kind of innovation which requires commitment of resources which go beyond those of a single individual. As long as the innovation demands a personal commitment and little else, to that extent it can escape from being dominated by economic laws. The abolition of slavery in Britain was undoubtedly an innovation, and was due to the personal commitment of Wilberforce; Ghandi innovated passive resistance as a political force; the most influential innovator (as well as inventor) in modern economics was Keynes; but all of these, although they left large marks in the world, either did not make them through any institutional means or, if they did, did not do so through an institution which can be compared in any way with a continuing business. Their contributions were too personal for that and to this extent the element of artistic activity in them is strong. In contrast, although the transfer of jet propulsion of aircraft from the military to the civilian spheres owed much to the commitment to this task of one identifiable man, Sir Geoffrey de Havilland, the vehicle for this change was necessarily a large and existing aircraft business. Unfortunately, when it turned out that there was even more uncertainty in the situation than de Havilland realized, economic forces too strong for him to control caused his great firm, deeply rooted in aviation history, to lose its identity in a Government-stimulated merger.[3]

One great advantage of seeing innovation in terms of creative energy expressing itself in the direction of getting new things done, is that it enables management to see when this energy should more properly be directed towards an `artistic' outlet rather than deployed in an area where the appropriate measurement is money, and the relevant timescale is fairly short. A large part of the fascination of higher level management in an innovating company is to be found precisely in this. On the one hand, the personal element is all-important, since without `champions' there can be no successful innovation, and the firm relies more on what happens in the minds and wills of certain key individuals for success in innovating, than it does on all its other resources, such as laboratories and workshops for R & D, put together. On the other hand, this personal element has to be prevented from taking up challenges with the unknown on behalf of the firm which are beyond its strength.

Danger of Obsession

The emotional involvement of innovators does not stop at *response* to a need. At every subsequent step their identification with the concrete realization of the new ideas as these emerge is also charged with feeling, and dependent upon feeling. It is because they feel for the idea that they are under compulsion to discover what is in it, which they can only learn by innovating it. As the hidden possibilities and implications of the idea become clear, the innovator becomes still more closely identified with it. Here, there is a trap for inventors who are innovating their own ideas. It has been a common experience of those who have put up capital to back such people in the past, that the venture has failed because of too much emphasis upon technical development and too little upon commercializing the invention.

[3] O. Stewart *Aviation, The Creative Ideas* (1966) 200 ff.

The National Research Development Corporation's experience is explicit: `An inventor is seldom the best person to develop his invention beyond a certain rudimentary stage'.[4] Innovators who are working upon an idea which is not their own are less likely to be led by their feelings into areas which, however technically interesting, are also an evasion of the *social* test of invention.

It is, of course, in the very nature of an innovatory challenge that the demands it will make are unknown at the outset. It is also impossible to predict the behaviour of a presumptive `champion' reliably from their previous record. True, an individual who has achieved success as an innovator before has the prime characteristic for doing so again, which is the power to respond emotionally to a situation and thus take action in the face of uncertainty. But action may diverge from what the situation really requires in two main directions: Innovators' interest may be moving away from innovation in the direction of invention, that is, they may insist that the project in which they are involved will contain their own ideas and will bear their personal stamp explicitly reflecting their own creative energy, to a greater extent than the economics of the challenge and the firm can justify. If the firm allows them to go ahead with innovation on this basis, damage certainly, and disaster possibly, will follow.

The other side of the coin is that it frequently happens that successful innovators get `stuck' at a particular stage of a development, and this is most likely in cases where the successful achievement of the previous stage has demanded an unusually high degree of doggedness and persistence from them. Innovators' necessary personal commitment to bringing about one particular change has been so great that they have thereby disqualified themselves from being the right people for the next one. Few innovators could match Henry Ford's contribution to, and involvement in one series of great industrial changes, but few mandarins could match the rigidity with which he outlawed subsequent ones. The length of time it took for Edison to grasp that the future lay with alternating current can only be explained in terms of how deeply he had involved himself in founding the

---

[4] N.R.D.C. Leaflet No. 4, 12.

electricity supply industry on a basis of direct current. Charles Parsons, who not alone invented the steam turbine but innovated it, later went on record that the gas turbine was intrinsically impossible. And how many artists and writers find it altogether beyond them to avoid repeating the patterns and techniques of early success?

Law, Firms and Innovation

The continuing link between innovation and trading is the firm. Any firm, however, is what it is in the first place because of a particular system of positive law, and this is the first clear link between positive law and innovation. There are many other links, and it is necessary to explore them, because - in the Western world - it has been positive law which decides in which areas of life there is to be innovation and in which there is to be even less human creative energy expended than would otherwise be the case, since energy directed to one objective is generally energy withdrawn from another. Because innovation is a learning process, investment in innovation cannot escape being investment in the production of information which did not exist before. This is always risky, but it is doubly so when the new information is being generated in a competitive situation, as it is in the case of any economic system that relies even partially upon individual freedom to take investment decisions, because information travels so easily and cheaply. It is expensive to produce, but cheap to re-produce, and therefore difficult to profit by.[5]

Information is the classic case of what economists call `externality'. Briefly, whenever some economic activity is being carried on and it has an effect upon third parties who have nothing to do with the actual economic transactions, then there is externality. This can be positive, as when farmers who employ a contractor to cut their weeds, automatically eliminate the seedbed of their neighbours' weed problem at the same time, or negative, as when a paper mill discharges effluent into a river and so destroys the fishing downstream. Once information that can be put to practical effect by anyone who gains access to it, has been produced, there is real `positive externality'. Thus, before an investment in the production of

[5] W.D. Nordhaus *Invention, Growth & Welfare* (1969) 8.

new information can be justified, something has to happen to make it possible for the firm which had done the research to limit this effect - otherwise it is acting as a benefactor not only to the public, but also to its competitors.

Capturing `Externalities'

There are numerous devices for this - Gilfillan lists eighteen ways in which spending money by private individuals or firms on generating information can be protected. Most of these ways however, only provide a partial justification for such spending. Some of them do not cover basic research - work intended not for immediate expression in tangible ways but for use in developing further information which is what will result in hardware - at all, whereas others are even inadequate in relation to applied research. A useful illustration of this was the establishment by Bell Laboratories of a biophysical laboratory after the discovery by Watson and Crick of the way in which genetic patterns are `programmed' in DNA. The thinking behind this was that Bell was in the communications business; molecular biology was a new field where communication of information was now seen to be important; therefore Bell must have a stake in it. At that time, it was impossible to see where the applications in terms of new products would eventually emerge, but the range of Bell and Western Electric's interest in the communications field was so wide that no matter where the practical results emerged, they expected to be able to make use of them. Note that Bell's capacity to `internalize the externality' was the result of the firm's size and diversity; a smaller firm with less wide-ranging interests would not be able to count on doing the same thing because the practical applications of the basic research might all turn out to be in areas which it is not equipped to exploit.

If a competitive firm gains access to new and useful information which has been produced as a result of the R & D of another firm, it benefits twice over. It can use the information advantageously, and it also has the return on the money it has saved on R & D. In a situation where new information can circulate freely, then, no sane management would invest in innovation, since to do so would only be to give actual advantage to their competitors. Consequently, if there is to be innovation in any field where money is a measure, there is no escape from one fundamental principle: There must be some way in which the firm which invests in the production of new information can prevent its competitors from putting products on the market which use the results of its R & D. *In so far as a firm goes into any situation as a lone investor, it must emerge as a lone seller;* and the technical term for a market in which there is but a single seller is monopoly.

Now whether, and in what way an individual, a firm, or a public authority will be a lone seller, is the result of political decisions and consequently different legal and economic environments set limits to the amount, and strongly influence the kind of innovation there will be at any given time or place. Monopolies can be granted by the State, and in fact laws doing just this in respect of ideas and new information have been passed in all the economically advanced countries in the world. The link between monopoly and innovation even makes it possible to say that it is because they have these laws that these countries *are* advanced. The connection between the positive law of industrial and intellectual property and the industrial revolution has not yet received the full attention it deserves.

Three Industrial Revolutions

The industrial revolution is widely thought of as the application of scientific knowledge to the satisfying of human wants, because this is the form it takes at present, and has done for several generations past. However, it was quite different at the outset and three distinct stages (some would say three distinct revolutions) can be recognized. In the first of these, the characteristically important events, such as the building of the Canals, Watt's steam engine and George Stephenson's railway locomotive, came about on a basis of scientific knowledge that was so slender as to be virtually zero. It is of outstanding interest that the science of thermodynamics, as developed by Carnot, Joule, Rankine and Clausius, *followed* the development of effective steam power, and that by quite a long way, instead of preceding it.[6]

[6] D.S.L. Cardwell *From Watt to Clausius* (1971).

The roots of this went far back into European history. In terms of empirical technology, Europe was ahead of the rest of the world long before the industrial revolution - perhaps as much as a thousand years earlier, water power was being used for purposes other than milling grain, to the amazement of travellers from the more aesthetically sophisticated culture of Byzantium.[7] Moreover, as mentioned earlier, the Europeans were voracious learners. The keynotes of this first industrial revolution were empiricism and ingenuity, not knowledge:

> The emergence in widespread practice of the Baconian creed that scientific knowledge means technological power over nature can scarcely be dated before about 1850, save in the chemical industries, where it is anticipated in the eighteenth century.[8]

The history of technology is quite clear on the point:

> It was only during the last two decades of the nineteenth century that the methods of scientific research were intensively applied under commercial sponsorship to the study of such processes as the cutting of metals.[9]

In the second revolution, applied science and a generally more analytical and scientific approach are increasingly the characteristics of innovatory activity, from roughly the mid-nineteenth century to the first World War. A significant early example of the change in approach is Robert Stephenson's rail bridge across the Menai Straits to Anglesey. This was preceded by a comprehensive programme of deliberate testing to destruction, samples of the wrought iron it was intended to use, and models of the tubular design which Stephenson had in mind. Moreover, his bridge across the Dee at Conway was specifically designed as a prototype for the much longer crossing at Menai. The scientific approach of the second industrial revolution did not of course replace pragmatism and ingenuity. Major inventions and innovations continued to take place on an empirical basis; the voltaic

[7] L. White Jr. `The Historical Roots of our Ecologic Crisis' in R.M. Irving (ed.) *Crisis* (1971) 9.
[8] ibid. 7
[9] Rolt op. cit. 193.

pile, vulcanisation of rubber, aniline dyes and making aluminium are examples in which the `new thing' came first, with the scientific explanation only afterwards. The science of hydrodynamics came after many of the practical improvements in ships which it explained.[10]

Nevertheless, as the nineteenth century progressed, the extent to which innovations were based upon science increased. A particularly good example is the way in which the great German chemical industry developed in close connection with, and reliance on, both applied and basic research in certain German universities (foreshadowing a later, most fruitful link between German aircraft-builders and the University of Göttingen).[11] Yet another illustration of a new approach to innovation is the commercial development of electricity in the last decades of the century. This was based upon the experimental work of men like Faraday, Kelvin and Clerk Maxwell, and there was a rough balance between the content of applied science and practical engineering capability in the results.

Market Research

The difference between invention or discovery on the one hand and innovation on the other is underlined by the fact that all this important experimental work was done in England, whereas none of the successful applications of it were made there in the first instance. It was not only scientific research that underlay the commercial development of electricity. This was also associated with the beginnings of systematic study of markets, which has developed into the substantial market and marketing research and survey industry of today. For example, before building his famous Pearl Street plant in New York in 1882, Edison surveyed the number of gas jets which were burning every hour, and plotted the likely power requirements accordingly.[12] Such sophistication was a big advance on the simple

---

[10] R.R. Nelson in *Journal of Business* (1959) 106. S.C. Gilfillan *The Sociology of Invention* (1935) 18, 131, J. Rossman *The Psychology of the Inventor* (1931) 18.
[11] T.S. Kuhn in R. R. Nelson (ed.) *The Rate & Direction of Inventive Activity* (1962) 453, A.N. Whitehead *Science and the Modern World* (1947) 141.
[12] W.P. Strassmann *Risk & Technological Innovation* (1959) 177.

census of road traffic at Colnbrook and Uxbridge which the Directors of the Great Western Railway had commissioned before building their first line.

Just as making some use of science did not replace the pragmatism and ingenuity of earlier days but added its own contribution, so no sharp dividing line can be drawn between the second and the third revolutions. What characterizes the third revolution, however, is that science, from being largely absent in the first, and being on a basis of rough equality in the second, moved into the dominant role. The growth of `organized' inventing, it has been claimed, had been very rapid even before the Depression of 1929-31, but certainly between 1931 and 1961, there was an increase of no less than 2,000% in expenditures by firms in the U.S. on research and development. Equally revealing, the ratio of R & D expenditures to gross national product there, was 0.13 in 1927, 0.41-0.52 in 1941 and 1.26 in 1958.[13]

The growth of R & D laboratories within firms, the fact that the research in these laboratories can go beyond applied research in the direction of fundamental research (and even reach it in some cases) has accelerated the growth of technological innovation enormously. It should not be thought that this new pattern for organising business and technological innovation completely replaced the previous one, any more than that in turn had completely replaced the first. As late as 1923 Reginald Fessenden, who had quite unusual opportunities for understanding invention, was able to write that `the statement that inventions are derived from scientific work is seldom correct, and more often the reverse is the case'.[14] What seems to have happened in each instance was that the newer system took up the running, as it were, and opened up whole new areas of potential for innovation. The older areas continued to grow in absolute terms, but at a slower rate.

Each of the three industrial revolutions thus had its particular pattern of innovation, which in turn reflected the way industry was organized. In the first, practical capability was the keynote,

[13] S.C. Gilfillan *The Sociology of Invention* (1935) 52; E.F. Denison *The Sources of Economic Growth in the U.S.* (1962) 241; D. Hamberg *Essays in the Economics of R & D* (1966) 6; Y. Brozen in Nelson op. cit. 273.
[14] R. Fessenden *The Deluged Civilization of the Caucasus Isthmus* (1923) 127.

invention and innovation were generally the work of the same person, and capital requirements were small. In the second, the characteristic vehicle of innovation was a newly founded firm. More capital was involved than in the first stage (and the innovation of the Limited Liability Company was at hand to help provide it) and the widespread emergence of the innovator who was not also an inventor, can be seen. In the third stage, or third revolution, the typical innovating unit is not a new firm, but an established one - very probably operating internationally. Innovations are increasingly based upon large-scale R & D, and the capital resources of the firms which own the laboratories where this research is carried on are vastly larger than anything seen in earlier times.

Types of Market Power

What is also interesting about these three stages of the industrial revolution (or three industrial revolutions) is that each stage has a clearly identifiable type of market power that is characteristic of it. Originally, market power - uniqueness of advantage - came simply from having the resources and capacity to make something, in a world where these were at a premium. This persists under modern conditions also, and since it arises from ability to satisfy some objective requirements of the market, it is most accurately described as the market power of capability. This type of market power supports a pattern of innovation which takes place within existing firms rather than one which leads to the establishment of new firms. Capacity to satisfy objectively defined requirements of the market is something which builds upon what is there already in terms of organisation, skills and plant. A firm which has been manufacturing particular things for a time, has possibilities in terms of both material and human resources, especially the human ones, to make the next steps which emerge logically out of what has gone before. It is the ideal vehicle for B-phase innovation and it can innovate successfully at this level on a more or less continuous basis, and in this way generate its own growth, apart altogether from any revolutionary changes in technology.

What if there had been effective patents at the time of the steam engine's invention? Would this not have pulled back developing countries progression?

Little use of Patents

The characteristic firms of the first industrial revolution (the single major exception being Boulton & Watt, which depended upon the famous Patent) were all built upon market power of this type. John Wilkinson was the first man who could bore cylinders of the size and to the accuracy that Watt required; as long as his firm lasted, it had a monopoly of Boulton and Watt's orders, and he never bothered to patent his boring machine. Moreover, it is easy to be misled by Watt's Patent. This is the one that is always quoted, but it is hard to avoid suspecting that this is because it is the only one of the great innovations of the first industrial revolution to which the system of granting Patent monopolies for invention contributed much. Stephenson did not invent the steam locomotive, as is commonly believed. What he did primarily was to direct the steam blast up the funnel, so getting forced draught burning - and this overwhelmingly important idea was not patentable. It was Robert Mushet who made Bessemer's steel-making process work, but Mushet protected his idea by secrecy, experimenting in his retreat in the Forest of Dean. In fact, the strong impression that remains from a look at the British Patents granted during at least the first half of the nineteenth century, in Woodcroft's comprehensive Index, is that so many of the great names of technology are represented, *yet almost nothing of their important work.* It is almost as if the Patent system existed at the time only to record by-products, and generally unimportant by-products at that.

However, in the last third of the century, the Patent system was improved greatly and made effectively international, and this introduced a new factor, even though the market power of capability continued to be important. With Patents as the monopoly means, it was possible for technological changes to take place in a way which added to productive capacity alongside, and not only in existing firms. In the hey-day of Patents, roughly from 1880 to the First World War, the turning of a new idea into concrete reality frequently resulted in the foundation of a completely new firm, and growth thus took place by an increase in the number of firms as well as in the size of some of the firms already existing. It will be obvious that as long as the Patent system was the characteristic form of monopoly, this pattern would tend to persist, since any sound Patent can form a basis for a new and independent manufacturing unit for the device it covers. It must be stressed, however, that although monopoly through Patents was responsible for an important shift in the tempo of change and for an extension of the front along which advances could be and were made, it only replaced `capability' market power very partially. Perhaps it is best to see it as diverting some resources into revolutionary developments, resulting in the formation of new firms, which otherwise might have been directed to evolutionary developments within existing firms. Many businesses used both market power systems at the same time. There can hardly ever have been a firm which was more Patent-conscious than Edison's, yet in 1882, it decided to allow infringement of its electricity Patents to occur, on the ground that `the business ascendancy we have acquired is of itself sufficient to give us a practical monopoly'.[15]

Marketing plus Secrecy

Next, generally around the last third of the nineteenth century, came scientific marketing, seen for the first time in the career of W. H. Lever, whose use of advertising on a massive scale, coupled with pre-packaging and standard weights and prices in the British soap industry, was the prototype of all today's consumer goods industries. These operate on what may be called 'persuasive market power', and it has been a powerful reinforcement to capability market power in bringing about innovation. In fact, this combination, with secrecy added, has for some time been outstripping the Patent system in importance.

Taking Great Britain as a typical case, the rapid growth in Patenting during the nineteenth century, levelled off in the decade before the First World War, and never afterwards reached the pre-War level. Patents can therefore hardly have been the market power underwriting the growth in expenditures for organized R & D by firms, touched upon above. These were extremely modest before the slump of 1929, but have had an explosive growth since then. (That great trade recession, in fact, may mark the watershed

[15] H.C. Passer *The Electrical Manufacturers 1875-1900* (1953) 100.

between the second and third industrial revolutions in the same way as the major deflation of 1873-96 marked that between the first and second). Government support of R & D is one cause. Before the 1929 slump, it was meagre, but afterwards it grew very rapidly, both absolutely and relatively, until to-day it accounts for more than half of all R & D expenditures in the U.S. Persuasive power is the most likely candidate to provide an explanation for the rest of the increase for the following reasons:

The grant of a Patent is one side of a bargain between an inventor and the State in which the inventor's side is to divulge what he has discovered. He is under no compulsion to patent, and can, of course, try to protect his discovery by keeping it secret. This secret is 'out' once the product is launched on the market, except where it relates to a way of making the product, and even the secret of a process can often be broken by experts once they have free access to whatever emerges from it. The value of secrecy thus depends in most cases upon what it contributes to getting a head start on competitors, or gaining 'lead time' over them, and it is here that persuasive power becomes so important. Through this barrier to entry, knowledge of and interest in an innovation, as well as preference for a particular brand of it, can be built up much more rapidly than otherwise. Coupled with secrecy and, of course, 'capability', persuasive market power offers an effective alternative to the Patent system as a means of producing the above-average return that is essential to justify the above-average risk of innovation.

The 'uniqueness of advantage' of a Patent consists in that the Patentee can legally prevent others from using his innovation for a period of years. But what precisely is it in persuasive power? The answer is - speed in getting money from the market for the new product. This is not only the result of being able to use advertising. It also comes from having a sales force which can get the product into effective distribution, and the power to use other methods of sales promotion which cause it to move out quickly to consumers. All of this depends upon having a brand, so that protection begins once the brand name is registered, and sales can be built up quickly by the use of the techniques of modern marketing. Persuasive power therefore gives the advantage of 'lead-time' over competitors, just as Patents do, but often in a more effective way. The more rapidly change occurs, the more the balance of advantage lies with secrecy plus the market power of persuasion over Patenting.

Importance of Lead Time

Consider as an example, a product where the development time, from idea to first commercial use, is three years, and the life cycle in commercial use is seven years. If this is patented, competitors may be able to see what is coming, through the publication provisions of the Patent system, well before the first fullydeveloped product comes on the market, and will be able to rival it. Worse, the originator will still have several years' unused legal protection left in his Patent grant when the product comes to the end of its life-cycle. In contrast, using persuasive power, the first that competitors may learn about the new product may be when it floods the market. By the time they have been able to copy it, it can have established a commanding position in consumer preferences through reputation quickly built up by promotion and other techniques. The effective protection can be matched quite well to the life-cycle of the product through expenditure on promoting the product in these ways, instead of being for a fixed number of years, in the later of which protection may no longer be needed at all. It is obvious, then, why power to persuade has been increasingly becoming a favourite market power system with business people. 'Native' use of Patents has been largely static during much of the present century, so that the vast upsurge of innovation that has taken place has been attributable in roughly equal parts to the two factors of marketing resources and Government development contracts. This has meant a radical shift in the relationship between innovation and firm size and growth, as compared with the earlier stages of the industrial revolution.

When marketing capacity came into widespread use as a means of protecting investment in information, it did not eliminate the other two means, but rather repeated, on a very much larger scale, the Patent system's increase in the speed of change, and its extension of the field in which investments in innovation could prudently be made. Even if marketing monopoly may be the most characteristic form of monopoly of the last half-century, Patents remain important, as does the market power of capability. All firms use capability with one of the other two; some firms use all three. A modern pharmaceutical firm has market power from controlling one or more of the relatively few plants with the capability of producing drugs under carefully monitored, sterile conditions. It also uses Patent monopoly in a very highly developed form, and has persuasive power as well through its extensive use of advertising and sales promotion to doctors on behalf of its brands. This trebly-strong market power is the reason why, year after year, the pharmaceutical firms head the indices of rate of return on capital. In every field, innovative firms are well aware of the importance of market power. As one of Du Pont's Vice-Presidents has put it: `I would be less than frank if I did not say that we try by all legitimate means, to lessen the impact of competition. The usual tool for this is to try to achieve an exclusive patent position. If one cannot get a patent position, one tries to get a dominant market position so that most people are buying the company's product'.[16]

This can be summed up as the Market Power Paradigm:-

TYPE	CAUSE	LAW
Capability	Investment in productive assets	Corporation: (Joint stock, Ltd. liability)
Persuasive	Investment in *psychological* assets (brands)	Trademark *Registration* Law
Specific	Entry barriers set up by Public Authorities	Licences, tariffs, Intellectual property
Above are *Primary* market powers (Every firm uses all three, in varying ratios)		
Derived market power	Specialisation; solidarity	Trades Union etc. laws
Every kind of market power has its own particular type of innovation		

[16] R.L. Hershey in D. Morse and A.N. Warner *Technological Innovation and Society* (1966) 46.

Economic Growth

Unless Patents are the characteristic protection means, the tendency is for growth to take place less through the establishment of new firms than through extension of existing ones; this is inevitable as long as capability or marketing resources are the means by which firms most often protect their investment in information production. The bigger the firm based upon this entry barrier, the larger the sales force it can deploy to get goods into distribution quickly, and the higher the advertising appropriation it can bring to bear, all at once, to accelerate growth in demand for a new product, and so gain lead time over competitors. Moreover, as well as production economies of scale, there are also scale economies on the marketing side of a business, and these are virtually limitless, e.g. the cost of making a TV commercial is independent of the time cost of showing it. Most important of all, marketing resources combined with secrecy, especially when used to reinforce capability, are so much better a protector of investment in information production than the Patent system that firms using it can prudently invest in research over much wider areas of life, can invest more in applied research of the type that has a long time to pay-off, and can even in some cases invest in basic research. They can also encourage the development of applications which expand the market for their most profitable products, as the German glue manufacturers did with chipboard.[17] For all these reasons, modern innovation is increasingly something done by existing large firms, and it is their pattern of innovation which turns already large firms into giants.[18]

State Support of R & D

This trend is reinforced by the other dominating factor in innovation financing in the 20th century, Government R & D expenditures. Theoretically, these could lead to the foundation of new firms, but in practice they have helped the existing ones to

[17] C Freeman, Young & Fuller in *National Institute Economic Review* (1963) 22.
[18] cf. E. Dahmen *Entrepreneurial Activity in Swedish Industry* 1919-39 (1950) 412.

grow even faster and to keep out new competitors. This is particularly evident in the U.S., since it has been British policy to channel money for research to Government-owned research laboratories. These have consequently been very important in terms of expenditure (though not comparably important in terms of results). One U.S. survey uncovered that 60% of U.S. Government R & D awards were on a `sole source' basis, i.e only one firm was involved in tendering. In one year, more than half of all the money spent on military R & D contracts was on this basis. 11 out of 15 awards studied in the survey were made in cases where no more than three firms were competing against one another. The existing - and generally large - firms have thus also become the typical vehicle for innovation paid for out of public funds.[19]

This way of looking at the industrial history of the last two and a half centuries, can be expressed schematically as follows:-

Approximate dates	1750-1870	1870-1930	1930 -
Characteristic Industries	Textiles Steam powered transport Metal working	Steel-making Inorganic chemicals Electricity	Aerospace Pharmaceuticals Electronics Organic chemicals
Keynote	Trial-and-error and ingenuity; Science secondary	Science and trial-and error in rough balance.	Science-based
Characteristic Means of Protecting new Information	`Capability' market power	Patents	Persuasive Market Power plus Secrecy,
Organized R & D	Non-existent	Growing	Predominant
Government Support of R & D	Non-existent	Meagre	Largest single factor
Market and Marketing research	Extremely rare	Beginning	Widespread
Typical vehicle for innovation	Individual, partnership or family tradition	Firm newly formed often to exploit a Patent or Trade Mark	Already existing and usually large firm

[19] D. Allison ed. *The R & D Game* (1969) 294

The `Paris' Convention

It is suggested in this that economic growth at present tends to reflect growth on the part of existing firms through their own innovations. However, it is a matter of common observation that firms that grow in this way tend not only to be big, but international also. This is largely because of an agreement between many countries which is as important as it is little known - The International Convention on Industrial Property.[20] It was signed at Paris in 1883, and now has almost as many members as the United Nations. It is very simple, being to the effect that any signatory country will treat citizens of any other signatory country in exactly the same way as its own, in the matter of industrial property. This means that a firm can extend the Patent or marketing (Trade Mark) monopoly which it may have under the law of one country, almost automatically to any other country in the Convention. It is no longer only the national market, therefore, from which returns can be expected because of entry barriers, to justify investment in innovation. It is the world market. The Convention has internationalized innovation, and in doing so it has made the typical innovating firm, which is already characteristically large, characteristically multi-national as well.

Because industrial property is made world-wide through the International Convention, modern science-based industries are `footloose'. Sometimes, basic research is done in one country, but production commences in another. The traditional theories of international trading, based upon principles such as that countries export products which contain a lot of what they possess more plentifully than others, or products for which they have a large home market or have been making for a long time, are no longer adequate. A whole new set of explanations must be developed for the location and performance of innovatory industry with world markets open to it.[21]

No discussion of innovation and money, therefore, can ever move far from the links that bind innovation to monopoly, and this becomes very clear when the financing of innovation is considered.

---

[20] For text, see www.wipo.org
[21] cf. R. Hufbauer *Synthetic Materials - A Study in International Trade* (1966).

Innovation just does not happen in practice unless there is common ground between the inventor, who is the source of ideas, and the investor, who is the source of money. In this general area, wherever the risks can be quantified, they are found to be very high indeed. No procedure that conforms to strict lending rules can cope with risks that are really high. Such risks *can* be coped with, but only by the combination of a continuing firm and equity participation.

Firms Indispensable

The continuing firm is needed for two reasons: It possesses and deploys an array of information of a detailed and specialized nature concerning one particular field, and this information, and skill in handling it, can reduce the risk of acting in that field considerably. Secondly, the firm remains in being, so that the continuing returns from its innovative activity to-day will accrue to it over time. It will live to enjoy the comparatively easy pickings of B-phase innovation after the hard A-phase struggles. Because of the ownership of the firm by those who subscribe its capital, returns that (in the long run) may be commensurate with the risk they take, can be anticipated by those who put up the money for it.

Any firm can be considered as a continuing entity which acts so that the law of large numbers applies to its transactions. When this happens, its losses are insured by its gains, and every viable firm is successful in controlling its transactions in this way. A bank has to do the same with its own transactions. This is easy enough to do when these are short-term loans to traders, but it becomes vastly more difficult if there is question of advancing money for entrepreneurial activity. The time-scale is longer, and (except for the largest or most specialized banks) the number of projects is too few at any one time to enable a proper 'insurance' operation to be run between them. What is true of banking for entrepreneurship is even more so for innovation. Here the risks are so high that no fixed rate of interest could possibly recompense an investor for them. If money is to be made available for innovation, then, it can only be on the basis of participation in the eventual returns.

Venture Capital Providers

Since the end of the second World War, there has been some development of banks which do just this. One reason for their establishment may be to fill the vacuum left by the effect of high taxation on private patronage. Another has undoubtedly been to take advantage of the innovation possibilities arising from University research, and from research in other laboratories financed from public funds, generally for Defence purposes. Almost always, these opportunities arise through individual research workers turned technological entrepreneurs; frequently, they involve Patents granted to such individuals after they have left their specific employment, but which involve discoveries which were either made earlier or which would not have been possible if they had not been active in a specific research programme. In one study of staff members who had left four laboratories of the Massachusetts Institute of Technology, more than 100 founders of new firms were identified, and when the M.I.T. academic departments were added in, this figure passed 160 companies. 24 firms were found to have been started up by men from two U.S. Air Force research organisations, and 39 by men from a single large electronics firm. Two particularly interesting aspects of these essentially innovating firms is that their failure rate has only been 20% over the first five years of their existence, in contrast to roughly 50% for all new companies established in the U.S., and that the men who start them have a strong tendency to be sons of fathers who are self-employed.[22] It cannot be said that these new financial institutions (for providing Venture Capital) have generally prospered. Among them, there has been only one unquestionable success, American Research and Development Corporation of Boston. In Britain, a much trumpeted attempt to emulate ARD, backed by a large number of banks and insurance companies, Technical Development Capital Ltd., had a disastrous start, and the firm became the very mildly speculative wing of the giant Industrial and Commercial Finance Corporation. It was said that the main cause of TDC's initial failure was the slowness with

---

[22] E.B. Roberts and H.A. Wainer in *Science Journal* (Dec. 1968) 79.

which they reached their decisions, and the timidity of these decisions when they were eventually made. This inevitably meant that the best projects were lost to them, as their promoters turned elsewhere for finance, and the projects in which they eventually invested were not the really profitable ones which alone would compensate for the failures. An area of uncertainty cannot be dealt with by people and procedures adapted only to coping with high risk, and an area of high risk cannot be treated in the same way as one of low risk. The moral from TDC's early experience seems to be that in financing innovation, too much caution can be every bit as costly as imprudence.

On the Continent, European Enterprises Development Co. S.A., also failed. It was founded under the leadership of, and with equity participation by ARD, the principal shareholders being a number of commercial banks in different countries. Participation in a firm of this kind has advantages for banks. It means that they do not have to bother further with innovation, since all approaches to them for finance for this purpose can be directed to the specialist institution in which they have an investment. There, any proposal may be expected to receive more expert evaluation than any individual bank could give it itself. In Canada and Australasia, there were similar firms with ARD participation. Even within ARD itself, it is very striking how few investments made up its success, and how many did little more than pay their way. Its original investment in Digital Equipment Corp., of $70,000 for 60% of the equity, had multiplied a thousandfold by 1970, and formed such a large part of ARD's assets that stock exchange analysts used to regard ARD stock more as a way of taking a hedged share in Digital Equipment, than anything else. Another outstanding investment success of ARD was High Voltage Engineering Corporation, where an original stake of $56,000 became worth several millions. However, these triumphs have to be seen in a context of many other ventures in innovation where the results were less startling, to say the least. When it is borne in mind that the ARD management showed itself to be the best in the world in this particular field, the pattern of its results. shows just how high the risks are in financing innovation. No ordinary bank management can be blamed if it is reluctant to undertake them.

Financing Inventions

What applies to innovation is true with even greater force to invention, since here uncertainty has not yet been quantified, that is, reduced to risk, at all. It has even been argued that with invention there is no practical possibility that even the largest firm can `insure' its failures against its successes by having a wide enough `spread' of projects. This is because very few inventions are successful, but these few can be of enormous economic importance. With this kind of distribution of results, the law of large numbers does not apply, and, in fact, risk increases rather than decreases with the number of projects in hand.[23] No bank can have the specialized knowledge that reduces risks from what may be astronomical levels to manageable ones, which is the most valuable asset of an individual firm. Sometimes a bank has not even the resources to monitor an equity interest (although, of course, merchant banks frequently do so, and in some countries, notably Germany and Japan, such a practice is the rule). Rejection by the Bell company of Fessenden's important telephony patent in 1907 has been blamed on bankers having replaced technical men in control of the firm by that time.[24] Yet the subsequent history of Bell is full of innovation, and since the bankers are hardly likely to have relinquished control, it must be assumed that they have since learned something about how to finance innovation successfully. On this, one important reservation must be made. At the time of being offered Fessenden's patent, and before, the Bell firm was operating under the conditions of the second industrial revolution, when the monopoly characteristically available was the Patent system, with the limitations that have been mentioned already. The period when bankers and innovation have seemingly gone together in Bell has been that of the third industrial revolution, when marketing activity combined with capability market power and secrecy has been the characteristic protection means. It can be argued that this new kind of protection is so comprehensive that it enabled even bankers to run an innovative company; or alternatively that it had made Bell and Western Electric

[23] W. D. Nordhaus *Invention, Growth & Welfare* (1969) 56.
[24] W.R. MacLaurin in *American Economic Review* (1950) 103.

so big that the law of large numbers applied to their R & D projects, so that they could effectively operate an insurance arrangement between the costs of their failures and the revenues from their successes, with the result that invention and even more importantly, innovation, were made more or less routine. This is the most advanced form of market power of capability imaginable. Such factors can be taken into account, without necessarily depriving bankers of the benefit of the doubt that they have indeed learned something about how to finance innovation and its diffusion.

From all this, it should be clear that it is a waste of time for an inventor to seek backing from a bank, and why even innovators, who may at least be said to be offering an investor risk rather than uncertainty, often have great difficulties in raising money. No bankers beat a path to Chester Carlson's door when he needed money for Xerox, and it is perhaps symbolic that the London merchant bank that helped Sir Frank Whittle with his jet engine in the early days, has since disappeared. Much of such support as there has been for the private inventor has come from individuals. Probably this was often because the individuals concerned were unable to see how the odds were stacked against them, or did not bother to look, or were unconcerned because in any event they were putting up the money on non-rational grounds. During the period when Patents provided the characteristic means of protecting investment in information production, much money was put up to back inventions in this way, and by no means all of this was lost. Elmer Sperry, for example, was able to set up successive companies to exploit his inventions in fields such as arc-lamps and streetcar equipment, by finding individuals to subscribe the capital. The fortunes made by those lucky enough to finance Edison made it rather easy to get support for exploiting inventions at one time, at least in the U.S.

Obviously, large private fortunes and low taxation are necessary if this way of financing innovation is to be important, most probably because of a particular way of thinking about money which is associated with these. Everything points towards a connection between finance at high risk and decisions being made personally by people who are deploying their own money. There is a factor at work here which Business Schools invariably, perhaps inevitably, ignore. People can be taught the techniques of financial management and control, but no external teaching can enable them to approach the investment of money as if it were their own, if it is not. The gap between the mental attitudes of the individuals who are investing their own money and the person who is investing someone else's, is fundamental, and no feat of imagination can overcome it.

Element of Gambling

This is one reason why decisions regarding innovation have to be made so near the top of the firm, and why `originative' inventions tend to be innovated in firms where stockholding and management coincide. Nevil (Shute) Norway considered, on the basis of his experience as both entrepreneur and innovator, that British industry at one time gained a great deal from the leisure pursuits of the upper classes, because this produced a number of men who were not alone wealthy enough to own racehorses, but were used to betting on them, and were therefore open to consider risky propositions in business matters and to weigh up odds, even if these were long. His view may not be altogether far-fetched. Even in the largest research laboratories to-day, it seems that there is `always a gambler in the act'.[25] This is understandable, if invention is to do with uncertainty, not risk, and if the opportunities of obtaining `insurance' by increasing the scale and number of projects are limited, if indeed they exist at all. From the financing aspect, the advantage of capability and marketing barriers over Patenting is not to be found in the replacement of uncertainty by risk at the invention stage, but in providing better protection for information when this is required. Even the large continuing firm with its research laboratories is not able to remove the uncertainty from invention – certainly not from `originative' invention, in Ravenshear's sense. But because of the availability within it of theoretical knowledge, which in the case of the largest firms, may be backed up by actual fundamental research, the area where `originative' invention is necessary for economic progress is reduced. Correspondingly, the area of `intensive' invention, which is a matter of risk rather than uncertainty,

[25] D. Allison (ed.) *The R & D Game* (1969) 17.

is broadened, and the actual risks of this type of invention are lowered. B-phase innovation - the making of the actual production pattern approximate to the potential one - is therefore accelerated. Profits are high upon the products which emerge, because market power from capability or from marketing, or both, gives good protection to the information which has been produced either by luck or by good applied research.

The way in which basic research can open areas of life to innovation which would otherwise need invention, is analogous to exploration of virgin territory for minerals. In the absence of a means for geologically mapping this territory, the minerals, if there are any, will only be discovered by the random searchings of individual prospectors. There is no way of quantifying the chances of any particular prospector's chances of striking it lucky, and so no way of putting up prudent financial backing for such an individual, who must therefore `wild-cat' speculatively. If, however, a geophysical survey of the territory was made before the prospectors entered it, not only could they direct their efforts toward the most promising areas, but some estimates based upon previous experience, could then be made of their likely success. They would still need luck, but much less than before. The odds would be improving towards a point where it becomes a reasonable proposition for a firm to support their explorations, either as employers or otherwise.

In the same way, when `fundamental' knowledge is available, those who work in applied research can advance without needing so much luck, their chances of success are more quantifiable, and consequently finance can prudently be made available to provide them with resources.

Uncertainty

When Whitehead spoke of `invention of the method of invention' as the supreme achievement of the nineteenth century, he was talking about the combination of the scientific approach with better means of protecting whatever useful information was generated (he might not have seen it in precisely these terms, but they can now be seen to be the important elements in the reality to which he was referring). It must be remembered, though, that even if these developments make it possible to calculate the risks of finding many new things which before would have been in the realms of extreme uncertainty, and also materially improve the returns from finding many other new things of a more prosaic nature, they do not completely eliminate the area where invention remains as much a matter of uncertainty as it always was, nor can they do so. From at least the middle of the 19th century, there has been a long series of firms in different countries, established to take up and exploit inventions rather than innovations. Sometimes, these were founded by successful inventors, who felt that they could use the experience they had gained in obtaining backing for, and exploiting their own ideas - Sperry is again an example - in doing the same for the ideas of others.

There is no record of a single one of these firms surviving, much less growing into any kind of importance, and the most likely reason is that there was a fatal flaw in the thinking which lay behind them: They were expecting a return from money invested not merely at high risk, but in the face of actual uncertainty. The provision of finance for invention cannot be a fully rational activity, and if the only finance available is `rational' finance, the range of ideas that will be turned into concrete reality will be limited. The removal from the scene of wealthy individual backers through taxation policy can only mean that some kinds of invention are just no longer being innovated. Given a sufficiently large population of rich individuals, any idea, however crazy, will eventually find a backer. Most of these will lose their money, but occasionally one will find that their gamble has led to the enrichment of the world in some unique way. The loss of this kind of patronage is most evident in the arts, but it should not be forgotten that it applies to invention, the activity which lies between art and innovation, as well.

Public Backing of Inventions

Those who suspect that Government patronage has been a poor substitute for individual taste in the arts, can point to the actual record in the case of invention. Since the War, there have been set up in many countries, State-sponsored bodies to provide finance for innovation and invention, the British National

Research Development Corporation being typical. But a study of
N.R.D.C'.s results showed that only 3% of the ideas offered to
them - 9% of those which they took up - (between 1953-60) ever
earned any revenue at all.[26] A later study of 20,000 proposals
from private inventors which they had received, reported that no
more than 30 had been considered worth investing in, and only
one of these had made any money.[27] N.R.D.C. really had only one
outstanding financial success, which was a range of drugs, and in
this case it can be argued that the invention stage at Oxford
University had been financed from another source, and that
N.R.D.C. made money precisely because they came in at the
innovating stage, when risks were calculable, rather than at the
invention stage, when they were not. Further support for this view
comes from the poor return on their biggest investment, in the
Hovercraft, where they did come in very early on. In fact, it could
be claimed that they were involved here at the pre-inventive
stage, since it was the incorporating of `skirts' that gave the
hovercraft whatever commercial potential it possessed, and these
had not been invented when they made their first commitment to
the project.

Wherever public money is involved in invention or innovation,
there is need for special caution in interpreting whatever figures are
available. To begin with, a body such as the N.R.D.C. is an investor
of last resort. Many inventions, and among them some of the best,
will never reach them at all for consideration. Researchers may
have been employed to invent by a firm which has all the resources
it needs to innovate the commercial product. Or they may have
enough resources themselves, or be in contact with a firm which
will put up the necessary backing. Their instinct may warn them
that they will not find the support they need from people who have
to account for the investment of money that ultimately belongs to
the public, even more carefully than bankers have to account for
money that ultimately belongs to their depositors and shareholders.
Consequently, the overall picture for success and failure in invention
is not as bad as might appear from study of those inventions for
which Government aid is sought. A second reason why statistics in

[26] K. Grossfield in *Economic Journal* (1962) 15.
[27] R.A.E. Walker in *Financial Times* 7th July (1970).

this area are suspect is that there is a tendency for the profitability of such successes as there are to be overstated, and this is especially pronounced in the smaller countries. For these, the run of the figures is even more adverse than in the case of a body like N.R.D.C., yet the activity still has to be justified in the face of a public opinion that is simultaneously wholly ignorant of the economics of backing invention, and convinced of the existence of vast and untapped inventive capacity in its population. It can therefore happen that the very few partial successes receive indirect support in terms of executive time or laboratory or workshop services, which is never fully charged out to the particular project. This hidden subsidy may help the innovation in its early stages, but it means that there will never be growth in it once it has to stand on its own feet.

Multiplicity of Decision Points

The odds against success of Government-sponsored bodies for encouraging invention are therefore high, and their actual record has been extremely disappointing. Wherever progress can be made only by trial and error, especially in a situation of uncertainty, it seems to be dangerous to centralize decision-making, especially in regard to financing. Even those who are unwilling to accept one economic historian's judgment that `those economies grew fastest that were freest', must give due weight to the evidence that in any situation of high risk, or in one which cannot be reduced to risk at all, `there is most progress where the number of independent thought centres is greatest'.[28] When Government attempts to bring about innovation by direct intervention, the disadvantage of centralized financing is compounded by the way in which conditions are highly unsuitable for the emergence of product champions:

> In England, after World War II, the Government established a number of industrial institutes, nearly fifty of them, whose prime purpose was to help create new products and to introduce modern technology and modern processes in British industry. This was done because the British recognized that their industry was not on a par with

[28] C. K. Mees *The Path of Science* (1947) 200.

with most modern American industry. With a great deal of imagination and energy they set out to do something about the situation. But the results of these activities in 1961 and 1962 showed that most of them had been failures. They had done a number of very interesting but largely unimportant things.

This whole assembly of institutes, which had spent a great deal of money, had not developed any really important new products or new ideas that had been introduced in industry. To say that these institutes had made no contribution at all would be unfair, but it is a fact that they did not revitalize British industry, as had been the initial hope.[29]

There is now very strong evidence that the American approach to subsidising R & D through development contracts awarded to private industry, is very much more productive of results than the British system. Apart from this, in financing innovation, the U.S. has a great advantage from the number of different sources of capital for backing new things which exist there. The number of banks and other firms which are active in the venture capital area, now supports no less than three directories, and there is even a monthly publication in this field. It has long been thought that the number of European inventions which have been innovated in the U.S. reflects more perceptive financial support for innovation in America, the electric lamp industry being a case in point.[30] In any situation of uncertainty, the very multiplication of points of attack increases the chances of success, even if no improvement in perceptiveness is assumed - and competition can be counted upon to sharpen this too. There is little mystery about American supremacy in this field.

The U.S. `SBIR' Programs

The United States Small Business Innovation Research (SBIR) Act of 1982 is a good illustration of how legal structures influence the amount and kind of innovation there will be. This Act changed the law so that seed capital could be provided by public funds in a market context. It arose from awareness that the

---

[29] J.B. Weisner in D. Morse & A.N. Warner (eds.) *Technological Innovation and Society* (1966) 15.
[30] A.A. Bright *The Electric Lamp Industry* (1948) 488.

very first money that is put behind an idea has to face uncertainty, not risk. To this extent, it can never be rational investment, and since venture capitalists are in the business of investing rationally on the basis of portfolio theory, they cannot be expected to be significant providers of seed capital. Only the State can do this, and all State action encounters the twin problems of `cover' for employed investors and the need for a multiplicity of decision-points, referred to earlier. The programs that have been developed under the SBIR Act use public funds in ways that recognize and deal with these in a most effective way.

Program Structure

The program format was devised by Roland Tibbetts of the National Science Foundation. It was then developed and tested there over several years, until legislation imposed it on every Federal Agency with an extramural R & D budget of more than $100 million annually. Each of these must establish a Small Business Innovation Research (SBIR) program to divert a proportion of this budget (originally 1.25%, now double this) to the financing of R & D projects in firms with no more than 500 employees. This support is not for basic research, but must have the objective of eventual production of marketable products and processes. SBIR programs have a clearly defined three-phase structure. In phase I, grants of up to $75,000 are made for feasibility studies. Winners of these are eligible for Phase II, with awards of up to $750,000 to bring projects to the prototype stage.

In Phase III, it is intended that private financing of projects will take over from SBIR financing, because the uncertainty has now been removed from the original idea, and venture capitalists have consequently been put into position to calculate the risk of taking it on to commercialization.

Since it is virtually certain that smaller firms will not themselves have all the resources they need to develop worth-while projects, they are actively encouraged to obtain specialized help through use of external experts. Up to one-third of a Phase I award and up to half of a Phase II award may be spent in this way. About 15% of applications win Stage I awards, and of these, about one-third go on to receive Stage II money. No proposal for a Phase I award may be longer than 25 typewritten pages. This is not only to enable large numbers of proposals to be assessed relatively quickly; it also ensures that firms with good projects do not suffer in comparison with those which are merely skilled in proposal-writing.

Another realistic feature of the programs is that they recognize that R & D has an opportunity cost, which is especially burdensome to smaller firms. For this reason, award budgets can include, not only provision for the firm's normal overhead element, but also a fee of 7% as a contribution towards the distraction from the firm's ordinary activity which doing the research will inevitably cause.

All applications are peer-reviewed, decisions are published within 6 months, and those who fail are de-briefed and encouraged to apply again, often to more than one Agency. The website for these programs is http://www.sba.gov. Because the Small Business Administration wants the results of SBIR awards to be widely commercialized, it makes full information about them available on another website, http://tech-net.sba.gov.

Caution and Creativeness

By bankers' standards, innovation is risky, and invention is simply a certain way of losing money (there is a saying in the City of London that whatever it may do for the inventor or innovator, it gives far less pleasure, pound for pound, than money thrown away on women or horses). Even for the continuing firm, innovation remains risky, in spite of the fact that a firm is organized precisely to reduce risks as far as possible in its own specialized area, and the corpus of positive law (especially Corporation and Industrial Property law) gives it powerful support in reaping the rewards of its investments in information production. It is quite wrong to think of managements of innovating firms as typically swashbuckling, daring individuals who risk millions on their hunches. Those who do, naturally attract attention, but business history suggests that caution has been as much a characteristic of innovating business people as creativeness. The most radical innovators preached extreme caution, in fact, and the summing up of one detailed study of nineteenth century innovations in the U.S. was that the pattern was one of `no heroic gambling, but cautious exploitation'.[31] Inventors are invariably astonished at how low a level of risk business people will sheer off. 91% of a U.S. survey expected to get a pay-off from money invested in R & D within five years, the `payback period' for Drugs, in fact, is typically three years.[32] It should be remembered, of course, that any R & D Department deals with much pedestrian work which has a rapid pay-off, such as minor development and `trouble-shooting'. Sometimes, the problem is to find even the right economic measure for an innovation. It was cost per capacity-ton-seat mile, not absolute engine efficiency, that was the determining factor in acceptance of the jet engine by airlines.[33] The procedures and experience of Imperial Chemical Industries, as representative of a modern multinational firm, show the need there is for caution in this area.

Using Discounted Cash Flow methods, I.C.I calculate the present worth of an innovation, using the rate of interest they have to pay on marginal cash, or alternatively, they find the rate of interest which makes the innovation's present worth zero. (The first approach, they find, is more useful if cash is plentiful). The record shows that even with all their resources and experience, they have frequently set the present values and returns from innovation too high, neglecting to make enough allowance for failure, because sales and other forecasts are necessarily very crude, and because with long term projects one is dealing with high pay-offs at low probabilities. In their risk analysis, I.C.I. use, not a point estimate of the present value of an innovation, but a probability distribution of the present value.[34] Estimates can err, of course, on either side. Those made in 1939 for Nylon and Polythene for the 1950s and 1960s were *short* by two orders of magnitude.[35]

[31] W.P. Strassmann *Risk and Technological Innovation* (1966) 77.

[32] D. Hamberg *Essays in the Economics of R & D* (1966) 77.

[33] G. Wills, Ashton & Taylor (eds.) *Technological Forecasting and Corporate Strategy* (1969) 11.

[34] J.R.Lawrence in *Management Decision* (Winter 1968) 244-50. H.A. Edge, Roeslen & Sherlock in *R & D Management 2* (1972) 91.

[35] D. Davies & C. McCarthy *Introduction to Technological Economics* (1967) 108.

Forecasting and Innovation

Although the enthusiasts for technological forecasting make strong claims for their techniques, there is no evidence that they can yet provide a sound basis for investment decisions regarding innovation. Too many forecasts were produced on the assumption of cheap oil for a whole generation of forecasters and their techniques to retain credibility.[36] Gilfillan, as always in this area, has made original and useful contributions. He quotes W. F. Ogburn's experiment on innovation in the aviation field, where the actual results of the latest 10-year period were suppressed, and mathematicians were set to work to extrapolate from the earlier data. Of 30 estimates, 16 were too great, with an average error of 74%, and 14 were too small, the average error being 43%.[37] It must be remembered that the requirements for prediction on the part of a banker or investor are much more stringent than they are for an economist, since their money is involved in a particular instance, and what happens in the general case is of no help to them. It is easier to foresee the effects of innovations than it is to foresee the shape of the innovations themselves; and the principle of equivalent invention, whereby the same results are achieved in different ways, may provide justification for the predictor but is poor consolation to an investor. It also happens frequently that a global estimate can be correct through compensating errors in its parts. The Ridley Committee on Energy in Britain arrived at a correct forecast in 1952 for total energy demand from 1959-63, but *every single one* of the component estimates was wrong.[38] Since no investment decision is made in respect of `energy' as such, but only in respect of a particular way of producing it, such as `oil', `natural gas' and so on, it is the error in the micro-forecasts, rather than anything in the macro-ones, that is important from the aspect of financing innovation. All investment is attempted prediction, and since the `product champion' or his equivalent can be a better predictor than any other, as explained in Chapter II, an investment in innovation which is made without the involvement of this key

---

[36] e.g., in Britain, the White Paper Cmnd. 3438 para. 26.
[37] In J.R. Bright (ed.) *Technological Forecasting for Industry.*
[38] T.M. Fry in Wills, Ashton and Taylor, op. cit. 149.

individual, is correspondingly more risky. This, of course, is not to say that the presence of the `champion' is all that is needed; cranks, as well as innovators, become obsessed with their subject, and lost causes, as is well known, have a special kind of attraction, sometimes even for born leaders. All that can be said is that if it is desired to minimize the risks inherent in investment for innovation, the judgement of a sane and experienced individual who is committed wholeheartedly to it may be a better guide to the uncertain future than any `scientific' forecast so far developed. The specialist venture capital firms are well aware of this, and are noted for making a point of backing a person as much as a project.

In financing innovation, the deficiencies in the present market power laws make it vital to sell developed hardware, rather than just information, as far as possible. This is yet another way in which the odds are against private/small firm inventors, whose chance of getting even adequate recompense for their time, from royalties, is very small indeed. The financial return to invention when only royalties are payable is `trivial' according to one student of the field, `miniscule' according to another, who estimates that the true value of an invention is on average about 30 times the royalty revenue paid for it.[39] These figures suggest that an individual or firm should always have the clear objective of selling any information generated in the form of an embodiment as far as it is possible to do so. The corollary to this, which is just as relevant to getting a return from money invested in innovation, is that no firm should ever think of developing anything itself if it can copy, buy, license, modify or otherwise obtain it from some external source. As the law of intellectual and industrial property stands at present, any useful information which can be bought in disembodied form, especially on a royalty basis, is cheap. The growth of licensing of `know-how' has been remarkable in recent years, and has been accelerated by the establishment of many active and experienced consultants in this field, as well as publications to spread knowledge of information for sale. In almost half of all cases where a Patent is licensed, the information in the Patent Specification has to be supplemented by

---

[39] K.J. Arrow in R. R. Nelson (ed.) *The Rate and Direction of Inventive Activity* (1962) 355. Nordhaus op. cit. 40.

`know-how'. When secrecy combined with either the market power of capability or marketing monopoly are used as the means of protecting new information, of course, there is not even a partial disclosure initially, and the `searching' role of the licensing consultant is even more important.

The most advanced innovating firms are well aware of these facts of financial life, and look to their investments in information production to be productive in three ways: There are the embodiments of the information, designed to be sold by the firm itself. Then there are other results, which for one reason or another, are not suitable for being embodied in products in the firm's own range. The policy with these will be to use them as counters with which to obtain from some other firm, corresponding new information which can be turned into a suitable embodiment for sale. This results in cross-licensing, and its practice marks out a major difference between the large, innovative, generally multi-national firms, and the rest, which is greatly to the advantage of the former. In so far as there exists a market for new information, there are two currencies, only one of which is coin of the realm. No matter how much money a European firm may have to offer some American firms for the rights to a new product or process, the latter will be even more interested if the European firm can offer as well some information which the American firm can put into a saleable product. The situation is rather like that in the property business, where the big operators have an important advantage over the small ones in that they can exchange amongst themselves parcels of land which otherwise can block major developments.

Valuing Inventions

It is the same in innovation with cross-licensing. `Know-how' is extremely difficult to pin down in a legal agreement. The Banks Committee on reform of the Patent Law in Britain was asked to consider the question of `know-how', and did so at length. However, it reported that it could see no way of dealing with the complexities. A firm, then, which enters into a license agreement which gives it certain rights to new information developed by another firm, is in a weak position if the licensor,

for whatever reason, turns unco-operative or drags *their* feet.
Arguments as to whether a hold-up is due to A's bad design or B's
poor operation can be long drawn-out, and can be very costly to
the licensee. However, when there is a cross-licence, both
participants are on a more equal footing. Good service from one
side is likely to meet a response in good service from the other,
and vice versa. The use of cross-licensing is at its most extensive
when there is what is called a `Patent pool' into which every
member of a particular trade association agrees to put all its
Patents at the disposal of the members. Perhaps the best known of
these is the pool operated by the Manufacturers Aircraft
Association in the U.S., which included every significant firm in
the industry except Hughes Aircraft and Lear Jet. Ironically,
although this Association was established under Government
prompting in 1928, the Department of Justice filed an anti-Trust
suit against it in 1972, calling for its dissolution on the ground of
being a combination to eliminate competition in research and
development. In this pool, each member submitted all new
Patents to the Association, which classified and reported on them
to all other members, and then enforced compulsory arbitration to
settle licence terms between them. MAA members claimed that
the world dominance of the U.S. aircraft industry owed much to
the resulting elimination of wasteful duplication in R & D,
coupled with rapid diffusion of innovation into the products of
member firms.

In financing information production, therefore, it is prudent to
assume that information that is not immediately usable will be
generated, to give some thought to who else might be able to turn
it to profit, and to look not just for money, but also for new
information in payment for it. The third way in which innovative
firms expect their investment in the production of new
information to produce a return is through what is known as
`serendipitous benefits' - or simple good luck. It frequently
happens that research directed towards one particular objective
throws up useful discoveries in quite unexpected ways -
occasionally more valuable than the original objective itself.
Within the Corning glass firm, for example, it is held that <u>all</u> their
most significant advances have come about through research
accidents. This was certainly the case with Pyrosil (Corningware

as it is known in the U.S.). If Glass-Reinforced Concrete fulfils the predictions of a great future that have been made up for it, this would support their view. It was a type of glass that Corning had developed for quite another purpose which had the alkali-resistant properties that Majumdar required for his invention, subsequently the subject of a joint development programme between the Building Research Station and Pilkington's, with N.R.D.C. backing. The implication for policy is that no firm should ever be so deeply committed to one line of enquiry as to deprive itself of resources to take up and profit from any lucky chance which might befall during the course of the investigation.

Licensing and `Know-How'

Some further light on the financing of innovation comes from the following diagram:

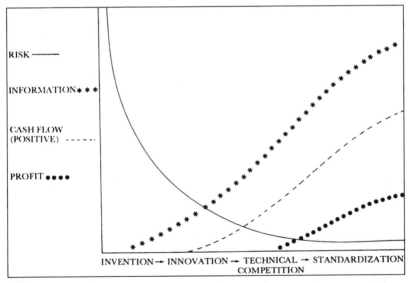

In this, the various stages of turning an idea into concrete reality and diffusing this reality widely are plotted horizontally, and the corresponding risk, information generated, revenue, and profits, are on the vertical scale. Risk, of course, is at its highest for invention, and in fact,. as has been seen, for the very first money that is invested in a new idea it goes beyond the bounds of rational calculation altogether. Once the idea is embodied in a working prototype, the risk drops sharply, and thereafter declines more gradually as the process of 'intensive' innovation takes place, until, when the product has become perfected and standardized, the risk is little more than that of ordinary trading. The curve for information is the mirror image of that of risk, starting almost at zero, and rising to a maximum when standardisation is achieved. At some point after the invention stage and during the innovating stage, the cash flow will change from negative to positive, and this will probably be accompanied by the emergence of competition based upon imitation. Because of earlier losses, real profits will not usually start to be made until well into the stage of technical competition. As this intensifies, these profits will reach a maximum and then decline, during the era of standardisation. Taking all these factors into account, it is easy to see why, to a financial mind, the most attractive time to invest is about half-way along the bottom line, around the end of innovation and the beginning of imitation.

This is why individuals and firms that find it almost impossible to raise money for new ideas in the earlier stages, often find investment money being pressed on them once it becomes clear that an innovation is nearing the standardisation stage. The phrase about the world beating a path to your door, it should be remembered, is related to your being able to make a better mousetrap, not to having an idea - or even a Patent - for one. It is only in the later stages of innovation that financiers begin to penetrate to the middle of the wood. What every investor is looking for is an innovation just after what in flying jargon is the 'unstick' point. Apart from this, there is no good or bad time for investment in innovation. A time of rising prices may be conducive to the adoption of factor-saving innovations; on the other hand such a time offers more outlets for speculative profits in other fields.[40]

Information, Cash Flow and Profit

It has been argued earlier that there is a sense in which money for invention and the early stages of innovation cannot be justified by ordinary investment criteria at all. Either there is a stage of uncertainty, as with invention, or of very high risk, as with

---

[40] W. B. Bennett *The American Patent System* (1943 repr. 1972) 36.

the first part of any innovation. As long as there are any alternative outlets for investment, these will almost always be preferable. Consequently, there are only two ways in which money becomes available at all for inventive and innovative activities. The first is when the investment decision is not strictly dominated by rational considerations. This is the case when inventors mortgage their homes to get a very first working prototype made, for example, or when, as so often in the past, wealthy patrons provided backing simply because they believed in particular individuals without scrutinising their ideas too closely.

The second way is by sequestrating funds so that they can only be invested in these uncertain or high risk areas. Some merchant banks have what they call `racing money', a small proportion of their funds to which their normal criteria for investment do not apply. In a modern large company the R & D budget as a whole can be looked at in much the same way. The Board decides that sane investment criteria are observed by appropriating a certain proportion of turnover to R & D (typically 2½%-5%). Although the main guarantee of sanity is often no more than that competitors are spending much the same proportion, the bulk of this percentage can be rationalized as follows: The first commercial plants for new products often cost ten times as much as the development work, and since liquid capital available is frequently 10%-20% of total current sales, this indicates 1%-2% for development costs on major new products designed to provide outlets for the firm's retained earnings. Work in the laboratory is only about one-tenth as costly as such scaling-up, but 80% leads nowhere, so the percentage justified here is ½ - 1 ((0.1 or 0.2) x 5). `Intensive' innovation of the existing product line, including factory optimisation, can reduce standard costs by 1% a year, so a further ¼% - ½% of sales can be justified for this.[41] Within such a budget, a project is competing for funds only against other projects of similar uncertainty or high risk; consequently, money can be spent on projects which would stand no chance except in the context of `this money is going to be spent anyway in breaking new ground, so it may as well be spent upon this project as on any other'. Being able to set aside funds in

---

[41] Davies & McCarthy op. cit. 108.

this way is another advantage of the large firm in the innovation field; for the small firm, expenditure on innovation is more likely to be in competition for finance with other activities which can meet rational investment criteria far better than it can. The result is that the decision to innovate in the small firm almost always has to be based upon the non-rational factors referred to above to one degree or another. This in turn calls for a relatively higher calibre of management - and more luck - if it is to be successful.

Irrational Investment

Just as B-phase innovation is economically at least as important as A-phase, so innovation diffusion is as important as making the innovations in the first instance. From 1925, I.G. Farben (whose international ramifications alone probably more than made up to Germany for the loss of her colonies at Versailles) spent more on research than it distributed in dividends. Even to-day, its successors, such as Bayer, BASF and Hoechst, spend more than 4% of their total turnover in this way. But some firms, and indeed countries, specialize in innovating and diffusing innovations, based upon new information that they have not themselves developed. Japanese productivity has increased three and a half times as fast as Britain's even though it spends hardly more than half as much on R & D. In Japanese manufacturing industry, payments for licences and knowhow average more than half R & D expenditure; in the important petrochemical field, they are more than the total spent on R & D. Japanese innovators (or innovation diffusers) have been taking far more out of the Patent system internationally as a source of information, than they have been putting into it in terms of inventions. As an activity, diffusing of innovations may be closer to entrepreneurship than it is to innovation itself. A firm which tries to make money by using information which it has not paid to generate is acting as an entrepreneur or even as a trader, hardly as an innovative firm, still less as an inventive one. The commonest form of this is what is known as 'inventing around' a Patent, in order to escape paying for a license, and which is only too possible because of the inadequacies of the Patent system. Not surprisingly, there is no record of any worthwhile invention ever having come about through this type of activity - which is not to say that a great deal of money has not been made at it. One source from which there is little to be learned for innovation purposes, is the general public. The U.S. consulting firm, Arthur D. Little, investigated this, and found that only one in 2000 unsolicited ideas reaching firms was of any value. The U.S. General Electric Co. receives 2500 ideas a year from the public, employs a full-time staff of three to screen them, and finds only 2 or 3 interesting ones every year. In the light of these figures, it is not surprising that most large U.S. firms will only accept an idea from an outsider on condition that he signs a `Confidential Disclosure Waiver' whereby he leaves all question of reward for the idea to the firm's benevolence. What a firm stands to gain by accepting ideas on any other basis is far less than what it might lose through litigation. The use of CDW's may be expected to become world-wide with time, and those who produce ideas can expect to get very little for them, because an idea is economically worthless without market power.

Once it is understood that innovation of the type which has money as its appropriate measure is a matter of market power, there is little difficulty about understanding why some inventions are innovated and some – apparently equally or more worth-while - are not. The political power which grants monopolies thereby sets the pattern of innovation that is linked in any way to money - the pattern of ideas that are `money-making as well as ingenious' which Matthew Boulton found so attractive. If the pattern is unbalanced, or results in too much innovation in one area and too little in another, or is inhumane, the remedy can only be a political one. For their part, investors have to take the market power world as they find it.

Better links between Creativity and Money

However, existing market power arrangements badly need to be reformed. Protecting ideas and information by scale of investment in productive assets or in marketing, i.e., sheer size and ability to be first to the market, opens up a gap between creativity and economic innovation. As organisations grow, they cannot escape becoming progressively more bureaucratic, and therefore less capable of providing congenial environments for creative individuals.

This has been recognized by some progressive firms, which have set up arrangements to allow employees with new ideas to try to develop these outside the established hierarchical arrangements. For example, 3M's program for this resulted in `post-its' amongst other innovations. When IBM grasped how late it was in joining the micro-computer revolution, it set up a completely independent management group to develop its PC, because it recognized that this simply could not be done quickly within its existing bureaucratic organisation.

The other side of this innovatory coin is that because neither individual originators of new ideas nor smaller firms have scale in productive or marketing resources, they simply cannot do without intellectual property to protect their ideas and information. Unfortunately, the arrangements for this have developed in ways which are progressively less capable of responding to this need. In fact, much of the functioning of intellectual property now is to reinforce the capability and persuasive market power of larger firms which - except in the pharmaceutical industry - can innovate without it.[42]

It was explained in the last Chapter how current patent arrangements originated in the 1952 Act in the United States, which was quickly copied in the rest of the world. As discussed there, the new `non-obviousness' criterion for patentability suits industries such as pharmaceuticals which can operate a portfolio approach to their R&D. It does not suit engineering, which can only do so partially, and of course such an approach is altogether out of the question for individual inventors or small firms. The result is an enormous waste of creative potential, either because effort is put into economic innovation which can result in heartbreak and bankruptcy because the results are pirated; or creative people are deterred from becoming involved in economic innovation through becoming aware of its dangers.

Improvements Easily Made

However, it would need little legislation to change this situation radically for the better. Firstly, applicants could be given the option

[42] D. Kash and W. Kingston `Patents in a World of Complex Technologies' (2001) 28/1 *Science and Public Policy* 11-22.

to use a different measure of patentability. For much of the type
of innovation which can be expected from smaller firms, a test of
`non-availability in the ordinary course of trade', has been argued
to be much more appropriate than the present criterion.[43]

Secondly, the grant of a patent could be made unchallengeable
for at least part of the grant term. There is a useful precedent for
this in the U.S. 1983 Orphan Drug Act, which was designed to
encourage investment in R&D related to diseases which affect less
than 200,000 patients. This permits the Health Department to agree
with the originator of a drug for such diseases that it will not
license a competitor for 7 years - in other words, absolute
protection is being offered for this period. It has been outstandingly
successful, resulting in a twelve-fold annual increase in new
relevant drugs, and both absolute and relative declines in death
rates. All that would be needed to transfer this approach to other
technologies would be to introduce a short period for public
opposition to an application prior to examination of a patent, to
ensure that the latter takes account of all relevant information. This
is already the practice in Japan.

Thirdly, arrangements could be put in place to deal with the
costs of defending patents. Grants are worthless to those without
resources to litigate, and there is strong empirical evidence that
those who do have such resources practice deliberate intimidation
of financially weaker patentees.[44] It is impossible to obtain any
worthwhile insurance against this at an acceptable cost. The
cognate reality, of course, is that for a firm which can afford to
litigate, and so frighten off opposition, a patent that would be
found to be invalid if it was ever tested in litigation is just as good
as a genuinely valid one.

Compulsory Arbitration

This could be dealt with by compulsory technical arbitration,
with legal aid for the respondent party in the event of an appeal to
the Courts. Weak firms would never appeal, because to do so would
move the battle to where their opponent has the advantage; strong

---

[43] For a full multi-expert discussion of this, see Kingston, W. (ed.) (1987) *Direct Protection of Innovation.*
[44] Kingston, W. *Enforcing Small Firms' Patent Rights* (2001).

ones would be very cautious about appealing, having lost the arbitration. Consequently, legal aid would be called upon very infrequently.

Once again, there is useful precedent from the United States, this time from certain compulsory technical arbitration procedures in the Patent Office. Over 12 years' of decisions studied, only 5% of those which were appealed to the Courts were even *partially* changed.[45] This shows how well compulsory technical arbitration could work if it was applied to the patent system as a whole - indeed, to all intellectual property.

Every innovator who has been through the grinding and dispiriting search for support for any project, tends to despise financiers for their short-sightedness and craven caution. It should now be clear that this is due to lack of understanding on his own part of the problems of innovating as looked at from the financier's viewpoint. Innovators who try to share in the thought processes at work not alone have the best chance of obtaining the backing they need, but will also save themselves much heartbreak. And this, considering how much `heart' is needed for success in innovating, is not the least important way in which they can learn things to their advantage.

---

[45] Kingston, W. `The Case for Compulsory Arbitration: Empirical Evidence' *European Intellectual Property Review* (2000) (4) 154-158.

CHAPTER V

Creativity in Business

Once academic research into technological innovation had identified the importance of the contribution made by individuals, it was inevitable that attention would be turned to creativity in this area. However, the positive achievements in this direction so far have hardly gone beyond techniques which are more relevant to `intensive' rather than to `originative' innovation. This could be because research into creativity in business has been too self-denying in its terms of reference.

Arnold Toynbee's famous Study of History was written out of his conviction that states or nations in themselves simply were not intelligible units of study; a wider perspective was needed. It is precisely the same in every way with technological innovation, entrepreneurship and business. Attempts to study creativity in these fields on their own are bound to fail, because in any such attempt the order of reality has been inverted. There is not a reality called `business' within which it is possible to find and study a component called `creativeness'; it is the creativeness that is the primary reality; business is only one of countless ways in which it can be expressed. The reward of getting these priorities right is escape from the intellectual prison where those who let practical affairs assume disproportionate importance, have to serve their sentences.

Schumpeter on Bourgeois Values

This prison does not only include the simple-minded who preach on `the social role of business' or who have never found Fortune magazine even faintly ridiculous. It also holds some sophisticated and thoughtful writers whose cultural time-scale is too short to enable them to realize that the explosion of technical and economic growth in recent centuries has parallels in other cultures in their later periods. Rostovtzeff, in his great study of the Hellenistic world, was among the first to advert to this aspect of cultural history. In recent centuries, our own culture has seen the emergence of a special class of people, noted for creativeness of a particular kind, expressing themselves through business and technology with confidence and style, but otherwise haltingly, to the point of being inarticulate. It has been called the bourgeoisie, and its philistine approach to the things which relate to the upper half of the rectangle of Chapter I has been the subject of countless attacks and satires. Yet bourgeois society cannot be understood, and this means that a great deal of what we mean to-day when we talk about innovation cannot be understood - unless the extent of bourgeois creativeness is also appreciated, even if this creativeness can be seen to have been constricted within limits which stunted human growth in other ways. 'The capitalist arrangement, as embodied in private enterprise, effectively chains the bourgeois stratum to its tasks', said Schumpeter. And again, confirming the tendency in recent times for energy to be expressed in technological innovation and entrepreneurship:

> Wherever the bourgeois way of life ... dims the beacons of other social worlds, these promises (of wealth) attract the large majority of supernormal brains and identify success with business success.[1]

Schumpeter's thought, of course, was formed in the era when new ideas typically resulted in the foundation of new firms for their exploitation. He was not unaware of the later pattern, when innovations are more likely to take place *within* large continuing firms, but he never incorporated it fully into his system. For example, sometimes he sees what he calls `trustified' capitalism as requiring a new type of `post-bourgeois' or `organisation' man; sometimes he justifies the large firm because it provides the most economic use of the scarce resource of `the better brains'.[2] But it should be clear from earlier chapters that what Schumpeter thought of as the bourgeois spirit is always found where there is economic innovation, even within today's typically large organisation.

---

[1] J.A. Schumpeter *Capitalism, Socialism & Democracy* (1943) 73.
[2] ibid. 20.

Marx's `Panegyric'

The bourgeoisie can hardly ever have had a more formidable critic than Karl Marx, yet Marx was quite unusually well aware of how much creativeness there was in it. Schumpeter commented that it was the Communist Manifesto which contained `a panegyric upon bourgeois achievement that has no equal in economic literature'. Concerning this famous document, he urges us to `observe, in particular, the emphasis upon the creative role of the business class. Never, I repeat, and in particular by no modern defender of the Bourgeois civilisation, never has a brief been composed on behalf of the business class from so profound and so wide a comprehension of what its achievement is and what it means to humanity'.[3] This points towards why the word `innovation' as commonly used, has come so largely to mean `technological innovation'; because, as Marx wrote, the bourgeoisie

> has been the first to show what man's activity can bring about. It has accomplished wonders far surpassing Egyptian pyramids, Roman aqueducts, and Gothic cathedrals; it has conducted expeditions that put in the shade all former exoduses of all nations and crusades.
>
> The bourgeoisie cannot exist without constantly revolutionising the instruments of production, and thereby the relations of production ... during its rule of scarce one hundred years (it) has created more massive and more colossal productive forces than have all preceding generations put together. Subjection of Nature's forces to Man, machinery, application of chemistry to industry and agriculture, steam-navigation, railways, electric telegraphs, cleaning of whole continents for cultivation, canalisation of rivers, whole populations conjured out of the ground - what earlier century had even a presentiment that such productive forces slumbered in the lap of social labour?[4]

Why did the achievements of the Western bourgeoisie so far outstrip those of similar groups in other cultures? Another way of putting this question is the one to which a number of serious economic historians have recently been addressing themselves,

---

[3] J.A. Schumpeter in *Journal of Political Economy* (1949) 209.
[4] *The Communist Manifesto* (Penguin Edn. 1967) 83.

which is: Why was it only in the West that self-sustained economic growth took place, and that even there it was a comparatively late development? The assumption made by all these writers is that such growth will be permanent, which suggests that what has been called the Whig interpretation is more difficult to exorcize from economic even than from political history.[5] This view reduces the past to a justification of the present, and in relation to science, business and technology, its assumption of continuing progress fails to face up to the reality that earlier cultures too have made their advances in these areas, and then lost them. A simple, though telling example is the way in which the early canal-builders in the United States had to re-discover for themselves techniques of puddling clay which the Romans had perfected.[6] The assumption of technological and economic advance into an indefinite future now looks a lot more shaky than it used to do, so it is possible to suggest that the reason why our `technological' stage has been so much in advance of the comparable stage of any other culture is no more than that, even in decline, Western culture is by far the greatest that mankind has known. However radical this may seem, it is worth study at least as much as some of the approaches to `take-off' which have actually been made. The movement of human creative energy into the lower half of the Chapter I rectangle, that is, into those activities which are `business' or close to it, is undoubtedly associated with social cultures that have begun to live on their intellectual and emotional past. In historical culture after historical culture, the clear evidence is that whatever technological and commercial flowering is to be found in it, will be found in its *later* stages. There is never a case where a society's engineers and merchants emerge as characteristic types earlier than its priests and artists. This is why the economic interpretation of history, particularly associated with Marx, is so good at rendering the later stages of a sociological culture intelligible, but useless in regard to the mysterious, early stages in cultural growth. For the same reason, whatever we can learn from Marx and his followers about B-phase innovation, or quantitative change, is of no help at all in understanding A-phase, or qualitative change.

---

[5] Herbert Butterfield *The Whig Interpretation of History* (1931) Especially Ch. IV.
[6] Elting Morison *From Know-how to Nowhere* (1975) Ch. II.

How Important is Deprivation?

One tantalising aspect of this shift in the direction in which creative energy is expended, is the apparent association of innovation in the lower half of the rectangle *with deprivation*. Deprivation is not simply lack, it is lack associated with feeling that whatever is missing was possessed in the past, or ought to be possessed now, for some reason: Creativeness and consciousness of having a raw deal appear to be linked, as far as those activities which can be measured by money are concerned. There is almost unanimity amongst economic historians, for example, that the first industrial revolution depended quite disproportionately upon the energy of the Nonconformists, which was blocked in expressing itself along the traditional roads to status. Not blocked totally, note, as had been the case in France with the comparable group, the Huguenots, whose expulsion Rostow has called `the critical margin for economic `take-off' which France denied herself in 1685'.[7]

Thus, Birmingham, though disadvantaged geographically, became the centre of metal-working primarily because `it became known as a place where people could settle without interference and take advantage of the absence of craft restrictions. Perhaps because non-conformists who had altered the pattern of their lives tended to be strong-minded men (it) became a lively and inventive business community'.[8] Deprivation's effect upon creativity in business also appears in Marris's study of African business men in Kenya. He found that those who were entrepreneurs `were in a sense reacting to loss' which brings him to ask `is innovation itself, paradoxically, an attempt to restore the continuity of expectations?' He suggests that

> even at the point in history where people attempt something new, their underlying motive is still, in a sense, conservative. They displace into original enterprises the purposes they learned from the society in which they grew up, but cannot satisfy within its orthodox framework.

[7] W.W. Rostow *How It All Began* (1975) 188.
[8] Nicholas Goodison *Ormolu: The Work of Matthew Boulton* (1974) 2.

Parallels which he quotes include the way in which the Japanese samurai `turned to business to recover the purpose and prestige they had lost in the disintegration of feudal society', and the development of large-scale business by the aristocracy of Bali, when Dutch rule deprived them of political power.[9]

In Barron's wide-ranging studies of creativity, a factor which is apparently always present is `the need for achievement', and it certainly seems plausible that deprivation will stimulate this and consequently increase the amount of creative energy which flows into business.[10] But there is a further, and highly intriguing aspect. What happens when deprivation is positively linked to above-average capacity? From Coleridge to Barnes Wallis, for example, few schools in the world can have a record of achievement amongst their alumni to equal that of Christ's Hospital in London, which is bound by its Charter only to educate the poor. However, a study of its rolls over the centuries has shown that virtually all its pupils have been of what would be called `middle-class' background to-day.[11] A typical case would be the son of a father of some achievement who dies before he has been able to make provision for education. The school has therefore tended to be made up of pupils who are poor only in material terms; genetically, they have been rich. This combination, on the face of it, would tend to intensify `deprivation' in the sense this has been used above, and thus result in an unusually strong need and ability to achieve. There might be much to be learnt about creativity from studies of institutions such as Christ's Hospital School. In any event, there are a convincing number of hints that creativity in business (perhaps all creativity?) is exercised in the shadow of a set of values that are quite apart from the ostensible object of the activity.

Sharing Creative Excitement

When discussing the Chapter I rectangle, it was stressed that the distinctions between the listed activities were not sharp, but blurred, and this is because each activity as it is found in practice,

---

[9] Peter Marris *Loss and Change* (1974) 105, 116, 114.
[10] F.W. Barron *Creative Person and Creative Process* (1969).
[11] cf. *The Christ's Hospital Book* (1953).

includes some degree of other activities in the spectrum, more particularly those on either side of it. Innovation as it is encountered in the real world generally involves some degree of entrepreneurship, as well as some degree of invention. An innovator is, above all else, a person who can become excited about the concrete possibilities of ideas. Most frequently in his case, the ideas are other people's, but no one can be sufficiently excited by an idea which is not his own to have the energy to turn it into practical reality, unless in some way he is able to share, on a basis which is not too far off equality, in the creative excitement of the person who originated it. When innovation was being considered as a learning process, support was found for this view of the common ground that exists between the capacity to originate and the capacity to imitate - `good innovators make good imitators'. This parallels experience in literature, science and the creative arts:

> The poem or the discovery exists in two moments of vision; the moment of appreciation as much as that of creation; for the appreciator must see the movement, wake to the echo which was started in the creation of the work. In the moment of appreciation, we live again the moment when the creator saw and held the hidden likeness ... We re-enact the creative act, and we ourselves make the discovery again. At bottom, there is no unifying likeness there until we too have seized it, and we too have made it for ourselves. [12]

This can be said also of the creativity that is present in all the activities of the Chapter I spectrum, albeit in different degrees, and which is the common element in them. Such a perspective greatly expands the list of activities which are labelled `creative' in any society - even in modern industrial society. That whole society, from this standpoint, represents an aggregate of creative energy, expressed in so many different ways, in technological innovation as well as the fine arts, in literature and entrepreneurship and public administration, even in its own measure, in mere trading.

The part creativeness plays in all these activities has tended to be overlooked, just as in education until quite recently the difference

---

[12] J. Bronowski *Science and Human Values* (Penguin ed. 1964) 29.

between creative ability and intelligence tended to be overlooked. It was really only in the 1950s that educational psychologists woke up to the fact that their widespread use of I.Q. tests in selecting children for further education, was in fact eliminating from the educational process precisely those individuals upon which society most depends for both social and economic progress. `Will', which Schumpeter saw to be so important in innovation, and which by extension can be taken to be vital in any creative act, is even less capable of being measured objectively than `intellect'. No test has yet been devised which engages the depth of an individual's being in the way creative activity always does. It is hardly surprising, therefore, that the correlation of creativity with intelligence by current testing methods is no more than 0.20.[13] It was G. H. Hardy, one of the great mathematicians, whom consequently no one could accuse of jealousy of brainpower as a gift of the gods, who said that there was no really valuable human achievement in which intelligence played more than a minor role.[14] Thinking back over the examples quoted in earlier chapters should be enough to show how frequently high intelligence may be less important in carrying an innovation through to success than the commitment of the innovator.

Technology and Beauty

Giving due importance to the creative element in innovation, in entrepreneurship, in ordinary business activity, helps not only to make sense of these activities, but goes to the core of what we call culture. An interesting practical recognition of this is to be found in the objectives which the venture capital firm, American Research and Development Corp., set for itself:

> Creation of processes and products, of ideas and industries, depends on men more than money, on imagination as well as initiative. Seek out creative men with the vision of things to be done. Help breathe life into new ideas and processes and products with capital - and with more than capital - with sensitive appreciation for creative drive; with support in management and manpower: with loyalty to the idea and to its initiator, the creative man.[15]

[13] Barron op. cit. 37, 49.
[14] C. P. Snow *Variety of Men* (1969).
[15] A.R.D. was very much the creation of one man, Georges F. Doriot.

The view of innovation which insists that it is simply human creative power expressed in a particular context, finds confirmation even in technical and technological advances themselves, for its rejection of any irreconcilable opposition between art and usefulness, between beauty and good engineering, or even, as was seen in Chapter II, between knowledge as power and knowledge as delight. Gilfillan goes so far as to erect into a principle that `the perfecting of a type of object mechanically is evidenced by its attainment of beauty', and holds that we can actually tell when an artifact has reached its technical climax when it not alone works well, but looks well also: `Grace and mechanical perfection hanging together, either one is useful to verify and measure the other'.[16] Hints that he is right come from many sources. For many years, Barnes Wallis was one of Britain's most outstanding inventors and aircraft designers. It was fundamental to his engineering credo that aesthetic and technical perfection were inseparably linked.[17] A psychological test originally developed to measure feeling for good design and form in Art school applicants, has been found to be the best single predictor of creative performance in the physical sciences and engineering.[18]

No theory of aesthetics fails to stress the importance of simplicity, and Edison said that he always knew if any inventive or innovating development was going in the wrong direction, if it was not heading towards simplification. In basic science, the test of a theory is not primarily its elegance, but the power it confers to predict events. Even the layman can appreciate that better predictions can be made on the basis of Einstein's physics than of Newton's (it was, after all, a remarkable piece of astronomical prediction in 1919 that enabled Einstein's views to conquer the contemporary scientific wisdom). Yet those who can grasp both, say that, all other factors apart, Einstein's theory is also the more `beautiful' in the sense that scientists and mathematicians use that word. In such a case, there is no conflict between knowledge for its own sake (which, of course, is knowledge as beauty) and knowledge as power: Conceptual elegance and predictive capacity are simply two aspects of the same reality.

[16] S.C. Gilfillan *The Sociology of Invention* (1935) 8.

[17] J.E. Morpurgo *Barnes Wallis* (1972) 177.

[18] H. G. Gough in *Journal of Value Engineering* (Aug. 1964) 7-12.

The `Business Culture'

Contemporary culture is characterized by specialisation, and thus by people set in intellectual compartments, with little or no contact with others outside them. In a famous lecture, C.P. Snow called attention to the way in which one group of people, educated in science, and another, educated in the humanities, have no intellectual common ground. As a result, they necessarily live in isolation from each other, the scientists - `who have the future in their bones' - pressing on with the building up of a world in which all will be technology, largely in ignorance and disregard of humane traditions, while the humanists retreat into contemplation of the past, unable and unwilling to come to grips with the changes brought about by scientific progress. Humanists characteristically react to what the scientists are doing, Snow holds, `by wishing that the future did not exist'. He contrasts Rutherford and T.S. Eliot as archetypal figures of his two cultures, calling attention to the social optimism of scientists and the pessimism of literary men. Some kinds of twentieth century art, he claims, are actually linked to anti-social feeling, and literary intellectuals are `natural Luddites'. In spite of the fact that `there is a moral component right in the grain of science itself', many people who are concerned with values, are quite `tone-deaf' to science. [19]

Snow called his book `The Two Cultures'. Although he did not advert to it, there is in existence yet a third culture, which is every bit as insulated from the other two as they are from each other. This is the modern business culture, and it meets every one of the anthropologist's criteria for a self-contained world in which people live their lives with little if any need to look outside. It would be interesting to follow through an analysis of the business culture in anthropological terms, but it is quite unnecessary to do so. Anyone with the slightest experience of it knows how it has its own value system, structures, initiatory and celebratory rituals (what else is the business lunch?) and even language. Millions of men and women do in fact live out their lives completely within the cocoon of this business culture, conditioned by the mores of

---

[19] C.P. Snow *The Two Cultures and a Second Look* (1964) 11, 10, 13.

their firms as thoroughly as any primitives have ever been conditioned by the laws and taboos of their tribe, finding a marriage partner within the firm, living in a company house, playing for the works team, oblivious of the scientific culture except in so far as it may impinge upon them through the firm's activities, and of humanist culture only peripherally if at all. There are three cultures, then, not two, as Snow claimed, and each of them is set apart from the others by seemingly impassable barriers. The perennial lack of mutual comprehension between engineers and accountants can stand for the barrier between the scientific and business cultures, just as the disaster which seems always to ensue when an attempt is made to beautify a modern office block symbolizes the divorce between the business culture and the humane tradition of loveliness in man-made things.

Has this fragmentation of culture to be accepted as a sad fact of life, or can these separate sociological cultures be reconciled? Is there any way in which people could move easily between them so that increased material wealth is not matched by mental and emotional impoverishment? Deprivation is inevitable as long as the three cultures are so well insulated from each other, as they are at present. Reconciliation *is* possible, at the level of creativeness. It is creative energy which is the common ground between all three cultures, and if each of them is looked at as being an expression of creativity, not alone can the individual cultures be better understood, but the elements which are shared between them can be seen.

Snow and Bronowski

Snow was able to discern the reality of his two cultures and write with such understanding about them and their mutual isolation, because of being by training a scientist, by calling a civil servant, and by choice a writer. Consequently, he knew what it is to be active in several worlds. Another distinguished scientist, already quoted in this chapter, was Dr. J. Bronowski, and he also crossed the barrier between the worlds of science and of literature, by making the study of the poet Blake a life's work. Nobody has ever written better upon the way in which these apparently quite separate worlds are linked at their foundations, as islands may be the visible peaks of a submarine mountain chain:

> The discoveries of science, the works of art, are explorations - more, are explosions, of a hidden likeness. The discoverer or the artist presents in them two aspects of nature and fuses them into one. This is the act of creation, in which an original thought is born and it is the same act in original science and original art ... Science, like art, is not a copy of nature but a re-creation of her. We re-make nature by the act of discovery, in the poem or in the theorem. And the great poem and the deep theorem are new to every reader, and yet are his own experiences, because he himself re-creates them. They are the marks of unity in variety; and in the instant when the mind seizes this for itself, in art or in science, the heart misses a beat.[20]

The small book in which these extracts are to be found should be a first priority for anyone who is at all concerned with these questions. Snow points out that creativity of exactly the same sort is found in technology as in pure science. Molecular biology needs little mathematics, as the physical sciences do. Indeed, it seems to demand the same kind of visual and three-dimensional imagination that painters and sculptors use.[21] As with science and art, so with business, because imagination is also involved there. It is nothing else than fertility and resource in imagination that is at the root of material progress.[22] This is why so many of the truly revolutionary inventions or innovations are made by outsiders. The power loom was invented by the Rev. Edward Cartwright, Fellow of Magdalen, Oxford, classicist and poetry lover. Einstein was an Examiner in the Swiss Patent Office. Kodachrome was invented by two musicians. Rolt has called attention to the surprisingly high proportion of the leaders of the industrial revolution who came from remote rural areas:

> But is this, after all, any stranger than the inexplicable flowering of poetic or artistic genius? For the truth is, surely, that these pioneer engineers were the artists of their profession whose careers were determined by the artist's compulsive need to fulfill his creative endowment.[23]

[20] Bronowski op. cit. 29, 30.
[21] C.P. Snow *The Two Cultures* 67.
[22] G.C. Allen in *Economic Journal* (1950) 469.
[23] L.T.C. Rolt *Tools for the, Job* (1965) 105.

Even in the day-to-day run of business, all decisions are made, not between realities, but between realities as presented to us by our imagination. Consequently, the creative rythm which students of scientific activity have identified - preparation, incubation, illumination, verification - has parallels even in prosaic business activity. The definition of science as `an aspect of Nature seeking realisation in our minds' can be applied equally well to artistic activity or to economic innovation. The world - even in its business aspects - is made by creative imagination and creative activity. Business can be made intelligible to the scientist and the artist in so far as it can be described in terms of the same creativeness which provides the only possible common ground for their own mutual understanding. And once creativeness becomes the element of interest (which means when innovation becomes important) those in business are no longer locked away in their own world, insulated from those other worlds which they know are there, but whose beauties and secrets have to be closed books to them. In the three cultures, it is awareness of creativity as common to them all, that unlocks the prison doors and breaks down the barriers of incomprehension.

Orders of Creativity

All this, however, is subject to one condition. Creativity is indeed indivisible, it is the same in business as in literature, in science as in art, but it is not the dominant force in all these activities to the same extent. Referring again to the rectangle of Chapter I, the ranking of the activities reflects the importance of the creative element in them. There are, in fact, orders of creativity and nothing but confusion follows from ignoring this; it is naive to think that because there is creativeness in artistic work and also creativeness in trading, there is no difference between one and the other. There is a tremendous difference, because the order of creativeness in trading is altogether lower than the order of creativeness involved in producing a work of literature or of art. What then, are the factors which distinguish `high-order' creativity from `low-order'?

It is possible to list as least some. The first can only be the level at which the particular activity affects us. In a world where sponges are now almost always synthetic, some minimal creativeness must be granted to the work of the trader who finds a still-remaining source of natural sponges, imports them, and puts them on sale in a shop. But this affects people only in an extremely superficial way. The majority may not advert to it at all, and even the few devotees of natural sponges could return to the synthetic variety, if they had to, with little diminution in their sum of pleasure. Contrast this with the way in which great art moves people in the very depths of their being so that they remain marked by the experience of the contact with it for a lifetime. Clearly, when this happens, there is need to accept the presence of creativity of a quite different and higher order. Even if we grant cooking much of the status of an art, to make people laugh and cry is still a far greater thing than to make even the lightest soufflé for them. How deeply we are moved by the results of an activity, is one measure of the order of creativeness that it involves. In fact, a good working measure of the order of creativeness in any activity is to be found in the level of its effect. There is creativeness of a higher order in engaging people's emotions than in causing them to think, and more again in either of these activities than in housing them or providing them with food, under ordinary economic circumstances. (Of course, in an unexpected disaster situation, such as a typhoon, creativeness of a higher order will almost certainly be called out in response to people's exceptional need for things such as food and housing, which they can normally take for granted. And a well-designed building provides food for the imagination, and not just shelter).

Another measure of creativeness is the intensity of experience which is being communicated. What is to be expressed in terms which will make others think or feel, has first of all to be felt and thought. Creators must put their own excitement into a work of art if we are to be able to take theirs and our own excitement out of it. The pleasure of reading, or viewing or listening, is in some sense a recreation of the pleasure in expressing. So many great works of art seem to have been made when artists were totally absorbed in enjoyment of what they were doing, or when their satisfaction from creative activity was so great as even to outweigh some especially intense suffering on their part, with their enjoyment or their power to overcome suffering passing over to others through the work of art. When this happens it does not have to be spelled out to us that there is creativeness of a high order at work.

A third measure of creativeness is universality, with which is linked timelessness. High-order creativeness results in things which are valued by people almost irrespective of their geographical situation, which also escape being time-bound and which at least partly transcend cultural boundaries. Shakespeare might almost be a German or a Russian writer, so much attention does he receive in those countries, and his attraction appears to be affected neither by language problems nor generation gaps. When people want to express how powerful an effect a particular work of art has on them, they frequently say 'It will last' - thus testifying to the power to escape from domination by time as a measure of high-order creativity. In contrast, human action in which the creative element is of a lower order, is more constrained both in terms of place and of time. For example, any creativeness there might be in trading, is exercised in a particular environment and context. It is a solution of a specific problem for a specific time - this is why it can be measured adequately by money - but it makes no pretence to a solution for everywhere and always. Its creativeness, through being space-and-time-bound, is not at all of the same order as a work of art, which escapes these limitations. All scientific theorists know that their work will be superseded, but the 'timelessness' of the higher order of creativity in science is shown by the way in which progress is made, not so much by theories being shown to be wrong, or to explain only a limited range of phenomena, considered separately, but rather by their being taken up and absorbed into theory of more general applicability.

Fourthly, the order of creativity of a particular expression of human energy is indicated by something which is analogous to 'value added' in economics. This is easily explained in the light of earlier chapters. In discussing the diagonal of the Chapter I rectangle, attention was first called to the way in which this distinguished each ranked activity from others according to the extent to which it is exclusively an 'interior' one. It was pointed out in relation to trading, that all the components already exist physically; all the trader does is contribute one last element, which increases the value of the whole ensemble somewhat. In trading, the value added by the trader's action is generally small. It is greater in the case of the entrepreneur, still greater in that of the innovator. At the level of artistic activity, the pre-existent elements are so small in relation to what the artist adds to them, that they may virtually be disregarded. The physical ingredients in what brings people flocking to any great art galley consist only of very small quantities of clays, oils and dyes; all the rest is the mental, emotional and technical contribution of the artists. Creation from nothing has not traditionally been regarded as a human activity; but creation from little very definitely is - in fact, it is a prerequisite of all high order creativeness. Related to the high `value added', is the individual and unpredictable nature of the artist's work. No one can say beforehand how artists will use their materials. All writers start with no more than paper and means for making marks on it, and the results reflect their personalities and individual experiences; no two good writers express even what is apparently the same experience in the same way. But what a trader does, any other trader could do, and the elements of the problem are so comprehensively `given' that no trader can solve it in any very different way to any other. There is little more there after the trader has acted than there was before and what more there is, is easily definable. What there is in the new situation would have come about whether or not this particular trader had acted, and all this action does is ensure that this trader and not another, has some place in the outcome. In contrast, at the artistic level, there is a great deal more there when the work is complete than when the artist began, and what it is, is often impossible to define, save that it is in some way related to the artist's individuality. All creativeness results in a whole that is in some way greater than the sum of its parts - a little greater with low order creativeness, a lot greater with high order.

Business as `Low-Order Art'

Now, it must be perfectly clear that by all these measures, business cannot involve anything other than fairly low-order creativeness. Acceptance that creativity is indivisible and that there is creativity in business too, only makes sense if it is also accepted that there are different orders of creativity, and that business is not too high on the list. The escape from the isolation of the business culture is through awareness of the creativeness which it has in common with the humane and scientific cultures. Once they become aware of this quality as an element in their own work - at however humble a level - as well as in that of artists, inventors, scientists and writers, those in business see access for the first time to those other worlds of human activity to which otherwise they must remain an outsider. They have at least the beginnings of a common language with the people who work in those other worlds. They have a key which opens up the riches of the worlds of literature and art and science, and they are no longer disinherited from the achievements of human creative energy in the past, no matter in what area. But there remains the inescapable condition. This condition is that they accept that creativity, which is the common factor in all these worlds, is to be found in their business world, only in a lower order version. For them, getting business into perspective is, more than anything else, an exercise in humility. The lowest proportion of creativity to be found in business (which every business person instinctively knows) is when business is no more than trading. The highest proportion (which they also know) is when it involves innovation. Entrepreneurship, which is innovation adequately measurable by money, comes in between: `The truly creative individual is not an outlaw, but a lawmaker'.[24] To impose order upon the chaos of experience through artistic activity is a greater thing than to reduce uncertainty to risk in innovation or entrepreneurship. Yet if the difference in `orders' and levels is accepted, it is the same thing.

Creativity in Commerce

The greatest advantage of looking at business from the point of view of the content of creativeness in it, is that it integrates business activity into the mainstream of higher cultural life, and in doing so, provides a context in which innovation can be understood, indeed one in which technological innovation can be made to follow a humane pattern. Hitherto, business has been outside this stream, being either neutral or even positively antipathetic to it. The viewpoint

[24] J.W. Gardner *Self-renewal* (1963) 39.

has also a number of practical advantages for business itself, the most important of these relating to its capacity to deal successfully with innovation. Many failures in innovation come from trying to apply standards to it that are only appropriate to other areas. The `invention' element in innovation involves uncertainty, and so proper financial control of it cannot be maintained through the techniques which have evolved for dealing with risk, even high risk. For the same reason, the tight control of research which may work at the level of `intensive' innovation, will not produce results at the level of `originative' innovation. Even more so is it the case that the mere deployment of physical resources, however great, will not achieve success in innovation except in so far as these resources are directed by individual creative energies.

People in business who have learned these lessons will not embark on any innovative venture unless they are sure of having the necessary resources in creativeness. If they see creativeness in business simply as part of creativeness in the whole of life, they will be the more able to recognize and foster it in their staff. The power to do this comes far more from contact with creativity in the arts and in science than it does from techniques of personnel selection. The firms which see themselves as providing an environment for the expression of creative energy must inevitably be those in which innovation, as an expression of intermediate order creativeness, will be taken seriously. If for no other reason, such firms are able to use applied science better than others. Creative people are drawn to such a working environment, which by its very subordination of creativeness in business to higher orders of creativeness, is attractive to them, and gives them a means of fitting their work intelligibly into the rest of their cultural life.

In firms where the philosophy of management gives primacy to creativeness and hence to innovation, practical steps are taken to ensure that staff understand this. In recent years, indeed, there has been quite a growth of interest, especially amongst large firms, in encouraging `creative analysis' on the part of their managements. All the techniques which have been developed, such as `lateral thinking', `brainstorming' or `synectics' are attempts to bring about, at the mental level, the `leap' or discontinuity which Schumpeter identified as being intrinsic to innovation.[25] The usefulness of these techniques to large businesses which have been experimenting with them, is often limited by the firms' own structures.

Their selection procedures for management trainees simply cannot be successful unless they filter out a high proportion of creative people, since, after all, organisations do need organisation people. No set of techniques can put back what the firm's structure has eliminated, any more than training alone can make a winner on the Flat out of a horse which was bought for his steeplechasing pedigree. Secondly, as mentioned in an earlier chapter, the rewards for success in such firms do not at all match the penalties for failure, when weighted by their respective chances. This militates against the degree of commitment to a project, which is the most prolific source of original ideas. And thirdly, the fatal tendency for people who talk most about creativity to be uncreative themselves, is at its worst when it is a matter of taking low order creativity seriously.

Importance of Leisure

There is one type of incentive scheme in this area, however, which is well suited to a firm which is seeking to be innovatory: The award of *leisure*. This should be made only by the highest level of management, in recognition of an innovation regarded as significant to the firm, to the individual who 'championed' it (who is always identifiable, it will be recalled, in the smallest as in the large projects). The award recognizes that revolutionary ideas are born in leisure and freedom from external pressures, away from work, by not being too absorbed in the completion of day-to-day tasks. Leisure, freedom of spirit, being 'distanced' in some way from the source of major pre-occupations, is a key element in all creative work. It was 'while walking near the golf course on the Sabbath' that Watt had the inspiration that ended his long wrestling with the problem of how to improve the Newcomen engine.[26] Hankey, the remarkable Secretary to so many British Cabinets,

---

[25] They are succinctly described in Tudor Rickards *Problem-solving Through Creative Analysis* (1974).

[26] E.K. von Fange *Professional Creativity* (1959) 94, 98.

records how his best ideas always came when relaxing in the country, but always, too, after a period of intense concentration. *The source of new ideas is the unconscious mind, tilled by conscious labour.* It is to allow time for this 'tilling' to take effect that some people advocate attacking problems on a two-stage basis, with time between for the ideas of the first stage to germinate, as it were, as a result of deliberate inaction. As Renoir put it, 'you must know how to loaf a bit' - and his output as a painter shows that this has nothing to do with laziness.[27]

There are many advantages to a firm in awarding leisure. Recipients have already shown ability to be innovators, and the odds are that the firm will benefit through further innovations which they will be more free to make. The award can be made at any level, from Director down to shop-floor worker or salesman, and so it creates an elite within the firm whose membership and lines of communication run *across* those of the organisational structures. This is important, as shown by the way one firm of Consultants in the U.S. insists that for a firm to cope successfully with innovation it is essential for it to build up informal communication channels alongside the regular ones. The leisure award system does this better than any other method, by linking the innovators within a firm through a special form of recognition. The creativeness expressed in innovative work, at whatever level, the common experiences of failure and of the need for persistence, the problems of coping with uncertainty, all provide a common bond and language between award winners, thus providing a still better environment in which more new ideas can be turned into concrete realities. Award of leisure has the further advantage of being obvious to others on a continuing basis and is thus far superior to a money award which is made once and then easily forgotten. The innovation for which the award was made will also be known, so that others in the firm will have regular reminders of the importance the firm attaches to innovation, and of the way in which individual commitment to it is necessary.

[27] J. Renoir *Renoir My Father* (1958) 180.

Management Development

Looking at business in terms of the creativeness it contains, even if this is creativeness of a lower order, also explains why it is that education for the highest levels of management, from which the energy to get new things done must come, cannot be purely practical, but must contain strong 'liberal' and cultural elements. It also shows up much contemporary advocacy of management development schemes and management 'education' for the nonsense it is. Charles Kettering, when he became General Motors' great innovator, expressed an analogous problem in the following terms:

> Some years ago a survey was made in which it was shown that if a person had an engineering or scientific education, the probability of his making an invention was only about half as great as if he did not have that specialized training. Now that is very interesting, and I have spent a great deal of time wondering why it is so. As a result, I have arrived at a definition of what an inventor is. An inventor is simply a fellow who doesn't take his education too seriously. You see, from the time a boy is six years old until he graduates from college he has to take three or four examinations a year. If he flunks once, he is out. But an inventor is almost always failing. He tries and fails maybe a thousand times. If he succeeds once, he is in. These two things are diametrically opposite. We often say that the biggest job we have is to teach a newly hired boy how to fail intelligently. We have to train him to experiment over and over and to keep on trying and failing until he finally learns what will work. We also have to teach him that everything is not in the books. In his education he invariably gets the idea that this is so because his textbook is always the last word and final authority on whatever he is studying. If we fail to do this, sooner or later he will say, 'There is no sense trying this experiment because page 284 of this book says it won't work'. Then we have to explain that these things we are doing have never been done before. If they had, we wouldn't go to all the trouble of repeating them.[28]

There can be few top managements in any advanced country who by now have not had cause to weep over some of the products of

---

[28] C. Kettering *Address to the 1943 Annual Meeting of the American Society of Mechanical Engineers.*

business schools, who know all the jargon but who are simply unable to get things done - much less new things. People are best prepared for coping with problems which need a creative approach to solve, by bringing them into contact with creativity. Not with diluted, low-order creativity, as in `business case studies' but with the highest achievements of human creative energy, in literature, in art and in science - with creativity `neat' so to speak. The student who has achieved a trained mind and the power to feel some of the excitement of great art is far better equipped to play a positive role in innovating business than his counterpart who has done no more than absorb `management subjects'. The knowledge of these, and the associated techniques, can easily be obtained, whereas creative capacity as such cannot be taught, only absorbed by actual contact with creative people and with the work in which it has been embodied. If the power to do anything that really matters can be passed on at all, it is only through apprenticeship in one form or another. All any teacher can do is bring his students to sit at the feet of the real Masters.

This general viewpoint, that creativity is indivisible, but that there are higher and lower orders of it, can also offer a unifying theme for general education, which has been adversely affected, like business and other aspects of life, by disintegratory forces. To contemporary teachers, the world of business, which will eventually absorb most of those they teach in one way or another, is puzzling and in some way inimical. Even if they do not regard it as actually opposed to what they are trying to achieve in and for their pupils, they see no common ground on which the two activities can meet, no line of communication by which those involved in one activity can grasp properly what those in the other are doing. And if such teachers have the misfortune to be concerned with a programme to show schoolchildren what industry is about, with its deadly boring visits to mineral water bottling plants and button factories, they will be confirmed in their view that the world of business and that of anything remotely resembling intellectual culture have nothing whatever in common, and that it is better for them not even to attempt to break down their mutual isolation. If it is explained to such a teacher that there is creativity in business, he or she will quite justifiably say that they are unable to see it. The problem is that at the end of economic activity which they and their students generally see, the order of creativity involved is the lowest possible. Products have long since moved into the stage of standardisation, where they no longer even have the interest of the preceding stage of technical competition. At the `top' end of the business, where there may be active innovation, where creativeness is still the most important factor, it is both impossible for outsiders to be admitted, and even if they were, they would lack the very specialized knowledge to enable them to appreciate what was going on.

This is where industrial archaeology has much to commend it as a school subject in the senior years. For all but a few, the imaginative leap required for ordinary archaeology to be an enthralling subject is too great. There is too wide a gap between the way of life of which the student has first-hand experience and that demonstrated by the artifacts. However, if the archaeology is industrial, almost all students have enough imagination to make the necessary mental connections. What is more, they are brought into contact with developments at the moment when creativity is most evident in them, and in a form which their teachers are able to explain and which they are able to grasp. For example, science to-day is so specialized that only those who are working in intimate contact with one area where advances are being made, can appreciate and share in the creative excitement which discoveries in that area generate. Yet any schoolboy or schoolgirl whose knowledge of science has reached the stage of grasping what latent heat is, or the most elementary hydraulics, can come to imaginative awareness of Watt's achievement in inventing the separate condenser, or Bramah's in his press. What is more, any science teacher has the necessary knowledge to play his or her part.

Restoring Cultural Integrity

Much more is involved here than simply the advantages of the historical approach to the teaching of science. If the students can see, study and sometimes even handle or work the actual old things, something of what went into them passes into their own capacities and sense of values - and what went into them, of course, was creative energy. Science tends to be taught as a subject without a past, when in fact it can be every bit as much a way of bringing students into contact with creativity 'neat' as their studies in the humanities. It is perfectly possible to make education relevant to practical life, without the slightest watering down of its intellectual and cultural standards or content. Once it is realized that what business reflects to-day more than anything else is a certain power to innovate, and that innovation presupposes creativity, the long-standing divorce between 'liberal' and 'practical' education is over; from the standpoint of innovation the most liberal education can have the most practical implications. In Europe (apart from Germany; and above all, in England) this divorce has undoubtedly been a primary cause of the 'technological gap' as compared with the United States. It is why there is such a lack of innovatory power and why many European inventions become reality only when they are taken across the Atlantic. Healing this divorce could transform the technological balance of payments.

Much more important than this, however, is that such a breaking down of the barriers between the business and intellectual culture must inevitably modify both - and this modification is now vital if business is to continue to be able to supply our material needs. Literature and art have progressively suffered (after a brief honeymoon at the start of the first industrial revolution) from failure to take into account the creativeness which is at the heart, not only of technological advances, but of the entrepreneurial activity which made these advances relevant to masses of people in terms of new things to be bought and used. Applied science and business also suffered through being isolated from the humane tradition which includes most of the finest expressions of human creativeness. The result is that innovation has gone ahead in an unbalanced fashion, so that in some areas of life there is more innovation than people want or can cope with, whereas in other areas there is far less innovation than is needed. The consequent lack of *social* innovations has now come to be regarded as crucial.

Regected Innovation Patterns

The actual pattern of economic innovation, based upon a system of positive law of industrial and intellectual property which has become fossilized, is increasingly being rejected. In more and more countries, this rejection --- for want of an alternative - involves the acceptance of increasing amounts of State control at the expense of economic freedom, and, consequently, of innovation itself. Because of this, there is no more important creative task at the present time for those who want to see new things done than that - intellectual at first and then political - of making the law of industrial and intellectual property more sophisticated. It is this law which provides a degree of power over the market. It is market power which makes economic innovation possible. If the resulting pattern of innovation no longer fulfils true human needs and purposes, then the proper remedy is to change the underlying legal foundation.

It may be said that such matters need not concern business people, nor need they figure in education for business. However, if they do not, the result is a complete disproportion between the quality of creative energy and the objectives towards which this force is expended. Many individuals who should be grappling with the difficulties inherent in creative activity of a relatively high order, suffering the failure and exhaustion that are inevitable in such an effort, will instead be restricted to trading or entrepreneurship simply because they are unaware of the full range of challenges to innovation that are on offer. Their energy, which is capable of overcoming genuine obstacles, is used up at a level where success - of a kind - comes easily, and which provides them with poor satisfaction, even though they fill days and nights with toil.

Everyone has met business people to whom all this applies, and it is only possible to guess at the loss to humanity, as well as to themselves, from the lack of correspondence between what such individuals are doing and what they could achieve if `new things' in a wider sense could be made their objective. An educational system, from which most of those who go into business receive no awareness of the reformable nature of the economic framework in which they will work, is clearly flawed. Unless this is repaired, they will have little chance of escaping the influence of a legal system which draws them towards trading or entrepreneurship with their short time-scale where results come easily to them, or technical innovation in the unbalanced forms in which we know it, instead of towards innovation over the whole range of political and social life which could provide difficulties and obstacles that match their gifts.

Such a lack of proportion between the talent dedicated to the achievement of an objective, and the frequent meretriciousness of that objective, even when measured in economic and social terms, is itself no new thing. Commenting on the world of business in the 19th century, the perceptive Walter Bagehot wrote of `the excessive energy natural to half-educated men who have but a single pursuit'. This, he could hold at that time, was `kept in check by the close vicinity of an educated world'.[29] It is precisely this `close vicinity' of the worlds of educated people and of business - the one now largely unaware of the existence of creativity in practical affairs, the other oblivious to orders of creativity other than its own - which no longer exists. Consequently, the actual patterns of innovation are increasingly suspect, and often with good reason. Nothing can bridge this gap again except exploration at every level, of all the meanings and nuances of creativeness, the indivisible common ground of all that gives meaning to activity, and the indispensable element in all innovation. For - and here the pointers from the past are altogether unambiguous - unless enough creative energy is directed to more important things, it must eventually become impossible to exercise creativity even in business.

---

[29] W. Bagehot *Biographical Sketches* (1881) 89.

BIBLIOGRAPHY

A.S.L.I.B. *Accelerating Innovation.* Nottingham Symposium, 1969.

ALLEN, T.J., MEADOWS & MARQUIS *M.I.T. Working Paper* 313-68. Cambridge, Mass.: Sloan School of Management, 1968.

ALLISON, D. *The R & D Game.* Cambridge, Mass.: M.I.T. Press, 1969.

BAGEHOT, W. *Bibliographical Sketches.* London: Longman's, 1881.

BARRON, F.W. *Creative Person and Creative Process.* London: Holt, Rinehart & Winston, 1969.

BASALLA, G. *The Evolution of Technology.* Cambridge Univ. Press. 1988.

BENNETT, W.B. *The American Patent System.* Port Washington, New York: Kennikat Press (1941) reprinted 1972.

BEVERIDGE, W.I. *The Art of Scientific Discovery.* London: Heinemann, 1950.

BIGGER, J.W., BOLAND, C.R., O'MEARA, R.A.Q. *Variant colonies of Staphlococcus aureus.* J. Pathol. Bacteriol. 30, 261-268.1927.

BLACKETT, P.M.S. *Technology, Industry and Economic Growth.* Southampton: University Press, 1966.

BORLAUG, W.E. *Nobel Lecture.* Stockholm: Nobel Institute, 1970.

BRIGHT, A.A. Jr. *The Electric Lamp Industry.* New York: Macmillan, 1949.

BRIGHT, J.R. (ed.) *Technological Forecasting for Industry.* Englewood Cliffs, NewJersey: Prentice-Hall, 1968.

BRONOWSKI, J. *Science and Human Values.* London: Penguin Books, 1964.

BUD, R., *Penicillin and the new Elizabethans.* British Journal for the History of Science 31 (Part 3),1998.

BURNS, T., & STALKER, G. M. *The Management of Innovation.* London: Tavistock Publications, 1966.

BUTTERFIELD, Herbert *The Whig Interpretation of History.* London: George Bell & Sons, 1931.

CARDWELL, D.S.L. *From Watt to Clausius.* London: Heinemann, 1971.

CARTER, K.C., Carter, B.R. *Childbed Fever: a scientific biography of Ignaz Semmelweis.* Conn. Greenwood Press, Westport.1994.

CAVES, R.C. (ed.) *Britain's Economic Prospects.* London: Allen and Unwin, 1968.

CHAIN, E.B. *Thirty years of penicillin therapy.* Proc. R. Soc. London 179,293-319.1971.

CHAIN E.B., In: Parascandola, J. (Ed.), *The History of Antibiotics: A Symposium.* American Institute of the History of Pharmacy, Madison, WI, pp. 15-30. 1980.

CHAIN, E.B., Florey, H., et al., *Penicillin as a Chemotherapeutic Agent.* Lancet, August 24, pp. 226-228. 1940.

Christ's Hospital Book, The. London: Hamish Hamilton, 1953.

COMROE, J.H., *Am. Rev. Resp. Dis.* pp. 117, 773-781, 957-968.1978.

CRELLIN, J., *In: Parascandola, J. (Ed.), The History of Antibiotics: A Symposium.* American Institute of the History of Pharmacy, Madison, WI, pp. 5-14. 1980.

DAHMEN, E. *Entrepreneurial Activity in Swedish Industry 1919-1939.* Stockholm: Industriens Utredningsinstitut, 1950.

DAVID, P.A., *Technical Choice, Innovation and Economic Growth.* Cambridge Univ. Press.1975.

DAVIES, D., & McCARTHY, C., *Introduction to Technological Economics.* Chichester, Sussex: John Wiley, 1967.

DAWSON, Christopher *Medieval Essays.* London: Sheed and Ward, 1953.

DENISON, E.F. *The Sources of Economic Growth in the U.S.* Washington D.C.: Committee for Economic Development, 1962.

DUBOS, R., *Studies on a bactericidal agent extracted from a soil bacillus.*J. Exp. Med. 70, 1-17. 1939.

FESSENDEN, R. *The Deluged Civilization of the Caucasus Isthmus.* Boston: T.J. Russell, 1923.

FLEMING, A., *On the antibacterial action of cultures of Penicillium, With special reference to their use in the Isolation of B. Influenzae.* British Journal of Experimental Pathology 10, 226-236. 1929.

FLOREY, H.W., *Application to the Rockefeller Foundation for a Research Grant,* 20th November 1939. Copy on file with author.

FLOREY, H.W., *Letter to Dr. W. Weaver of the Rockefeller Foundation,* enclosing Notes on the growth of the mould which produces penicillin. 1941. April 18: Copy on file with author.

FLOREY, H.W., *Report to Dr. W. Weaver of the Rockefeller Foundation* on visits to U.S. and Canadian pharmaceutical firms. 1941, September 9: Copy on file with author.

FOSDICK, R.B., *The Story of the Rockefeller Foundation.* Harper and Brothers, New York. 1953.

FRIDAY, J. *Huxley and antibiosis in 1875.* Br. J. Hist. Sci. 7, 61-71. 1974.

GALDSTON, I., *Impact of antibiotics.* I.U.P., New York. 1958.

GARDNER, A.D., *Morphological effects of penicillin on bacteria.* Nature 146, 837-838 1940.

GARDNER, J.W. *Self-renewal.* New York: Harper, 1963.

GAUSE, G.F., *Gramicidin S. and early antibiotic research in the Soviet Union.* In: Parascandola, J. (Ed.), The History of Antibiotics: A Symposium. American Institute of the History of Pharmacy, Madison, WI, pp. 91-96.1980.

GILFILLAN, S.C. *Inventing the Ship*. Chicago: Follett Publishing Co., 1935.

GILFILLAN, S.C., *The Sociology of Invention*. M.I.T. Press, Cambridge [1935]. 1970. - *The Sociology of Invention*. Chicago: Follett Publishing Co., 1935.

GOLDSMITH, M. *Technological Innovation and the Economy*. Chichester, Sussex: Wiley-Interscience, 1970.

GOODISON, Nicholas, *Ormolu: The Work of Matthew Boulton*. London: Phaidon, 1974.

GOVERNMENT PUBLICATIONS
- *Hindsight Project* No. AD 6424017. Washington, D.C.: Clearinghouse for Scientific and Technical Information.
- *Invention and the Patent System*. Washington D.C.: United States Government Printing Office, 1964.
- *Research Program Effectiveness*. Washington, D.C.: Conference of Naval Research, 1966.
- *Hearings Pursuant to Senate Resolution. No. 70, 89th Congress, 1st Session*. Washington, D.C.: U.S. Government Printing Office.

GRUBER, R.E., *Penicillin and streptomycin*. M.I.T. Technology Review 49. 1947.

HAMBERG, D. *Essays in the Economics of R & D*. Westminster, Maryland: Random House, 1966.

HARE, R. *Birth of Penicillin*. London: Allen and Unwin, 1970.

HARE, R., *New light on the history of penicillin*. Medical History 26, 1. 1982.

HARRIS, S.E. (ed.) *Schumpeter, Social Scientist*. Cambridge, Mass.: Harvard University Press, 1951.

HELFLAND, W.H., et al., In: Parascandola, J. (Ed.), *The History of Antibiotics:* A Symposium. American Institute of the History of Pharmacy, Madison, WI, pp. 31-56. 1980.

HOBBY, G.L., *Penicillin: Meeting the Challenge*. Yale Univ. Press, New Haven. 1985.

HUFBAUER, R. *Synthetic Materials - A Study in International Trade*. London: Duckworth, 1966.

HUGHES, T.P. *Elmer Sperry*. Baltimore, Maryland: Johns Hopkins University Press, 1971.

IRVING, R.M. (ed.) *Crisis*. New York: Macmillan, 1971.

JEWKES, J., *Public and Private Enterprise*. Routledge and Kegan Paul, London. 1965.

KASH, Don E. and W. Kingston, `Patents in a world of complex technologies', *Science and Public Policy* , 28, 1 (2001), 11-23.

KEYNES, J.M. *General Theory of Employment, Interest & Money*. London: Macmillan, 1936.

KINGSTON, W., *Innovation or bureaucracy?* Creativity and Innovation Management 4 (3), 184-194. 1995.

KINGSTON, W. (ed.) (1987) *Direct Protection of Innovation.* Dordrecht/Boston, Kluwer Academic Publishers.

- `The Case for Compulsory Arbitration: Empirical Evidence' *European Intellectual Property Review* (2000) (4) 154-158.

- (2001) *Enforcing Small Firms' Patent Rights,* Luxembourg, Office for Official Publications of the European Communities.

KIPLE, K.F. (Ed.), *Cambridge World History of Human Disease.* Cambridge Univ. Press.1993.

KUECKEN, J.A. *Creativity, Invention & Progress.* Indianapolis: Howard W. Sams, 1969.

LANDES, D.S. *The Unbound Prometheus.* Cambridge: University Press, 1969.

LANGLOIS, R., *Schumpeter and Personal Capitalism.* In: Eliasson, G., Green, C. (Eds.), Microfoundations of Economic Growth. University of Michigan Press, Ann Arbor.1998.

LANGRISH, J. et. al. *Wealth from Knowledge.* London: Macmillan, 1971.

LECHEVALIER, H.A., *CRC Crit. Rev.* Microbiol. 3, 359-397. 1975.

LECHEVALIER, H.A., In: Parascandola, J. (Ed.), *The History of Antibiotics:* A Symposium. American Institute of the History of Pharmacy, Madison, WI, pp. 113-124. 1980.

LEHMANN, J. *Para-aminosalicylic acid in the treatment of tuberculosis.* Lancet 251 (1), 15-16., 1946.

LESLIE, C.R. *Memoirs of the Life of John Constable, R.A.* London: Medici Society, 1937.

LOASBY, B.J., *The imagined, deemed possible.* In: Helmstadter, E., Perlman, M. (Eds.), Behavioral Norms, Technological Progress and Economic Dynamics. University of Michigan Press, Ann Arbor, 1996.

MACFARLANE, G., *Howard Florey: the Making of a Great Scientist.* Oxford Univ. Press. 1979.

MACFARLANE, G., *Alexander Fleming: The Man and the Myth.* Ghetto and Wintus, London. 1984.

MANSFIELD, E. (ed.) *Monopoly Power & Economic Performance.* New York: W.V. Norton, 1969.

MARDER, A.J. *From the Dreadnought to Scapa Flow.* Oxford: University Press, 1970.

MARRIS, Peter *Loss and Change.* London: Routledge and Kegan Paul, 1974.

MARSCHAK, T. et. al. *Strategy for R & D.* New York: Springer Verlag, 1967.

MEES, C. K. *The Path of Science.* London: Chapman and Hall, 1947.

MOKYR, J., *The Lever of Riches.* Oxford Univ. Press, New York. 1990.

MORISON, ELTING *From Know-how to Nowhere.* Oxford: Blackwell, 1975.

MORPURGO, J. E. *Barnes Wallis.* London: Longman, 1972.

MORSE, D., & WARNER, A.N. (eds.) *Technological Innovation and Society.* New York: Columbia University Press, 1966.

NELSON, R.R. (ed.) *The Rate and Direction of Inventive Acitivity.* New Jersey: Princeton University Press, 1962.

NELSON, R.R., PECK & KALACHEK *Technology, Economic Growth & Public Policy.* Washington D.C.: Brookings Institution, 1967.

NEWMAN, ERNEST *Wagner.* London; Cassell, 1933-47.

NEWMAN, J.H. *Grammar of Assent.* Toronto: Longman's, 1947.

NORDHAUS, W.D. *Invention, Growth & Welfare.* Cambridge, Mass.: M.I.T. Press, 1969.

OGBURN, W.F. *Culture and Social Change.* Chicago: University of Chicago Press, 1964.

OLSON, M., *The Rise and Decline of Nations.* Yale Univ. Press, New Haven. 1982.

ORKIN, L.A., *Urology 4,* 80-84 1974.

PARASCANDOLA, J., *The History of Antibiotics:* A Symposium. American Institute of the History of Pharmacy, Madison, WI. 1980.

PASSER, H.C. *The Electrical Manufacturers 1875-1900.* Cambridge, Mass.: Harvard University Press, 1953.

PORTER, R.W., *Streptomycin Engineered into Commercial Production.* Chemical Engineering, October 1946.

RAVENSHEAR, A.F. *The Industrial and Commercial Influence of the English Patent System.* London: T. Fisher Unwin, 1908.

RENOIR, J. *Renoir My Father.* London: Collins, 1958.

RICHARDS, A.N., *Production of Penicillin in the United States, 1941-1946.* Nature, February 1.1964.

RICKARDS, Tudor *Problem-solving Through Creative Analysis.* Epping: Gower Press, 1974.

ROCKEFELLER FOUNDATION, 1941. April 14. Report by Dr. W. Weaver on visit to Prof. Florey's Laboratory in Oxford. Copy on file with author.

ROCKEFELLER FOUNDATION, 1941. Extract from President's Report. Copy on file with author.

ROCKEFELLER FOUNDATION, 1943. October. Extract from Trustees' Bulletin. Copy on file with author.

ROGERS, E.M. & SHOEMAKER *Communication of Innovations.* London: Collier-Macmillan, 1971.

Innovation

212 Innovation

ROLT, L.T.C. Tools for the Job. London: B.T. Batsford, 1965.
- *From Sea To Sea*. London: Allen Lane, 1973.
ROSEN, G., *A History of Public Health*. Johns Hopkins Univ. Press, Baltimore [1958]. 1993.
ROSSMAN, J. *The Psychology of the Inventor.* Washington, D.C.: Inventors Publishing Co., 1931.
ROSTOW, W. W. *How It All Began*. London: Methuen, 1975.
SCHATZ, A., BUGIE, E., WAKSMAN, S.E., *Streptomycin, a substance exhibiting antibiotic activity against Gram-positive and Gram-negative bacteria*. Proc. Soc. Exp. Biol. Med. 55, 65-9.1944.
SCHUMPETER, J.A., *Economic Journal,* pp. 38-64.1928.
SCHUMPETER, J.A. *Capitalism, Socialism & Democracy.* London: Allen & Unwin, 1943.
SCHUMPETER, J.A. *Business Cycles.* London: McGraw-Hill, 1939.
SCHUMPETER, J.A., *Journal of Economic History*, p. 150. 1947.
SCHWARTZMAN, D., *Innovation in the Pharmaceutical Industry.* Johns Hopkins Univ. Press, Baltimore.1976.
SHEEHAN, J.C., *The Enchanted Ring.* M.I.T. Press, Boston. 1982.
SINCLAIR, W.J. *Semmelweis - His Life and Doctrines*. Manchester: Victoria University, 1909.
SNOW, C.P. *Variety of Men.* New York: Charles Scribner's Sons, 1969.
- *The Two Cultures and a Second Look.* Cambridge: University Press, 1964.
STEWART, O. *Aviation, The Creative Ideas.* London: Faber and Faber, 1966.
STRASSMANN, W.P. *Risk & Technological Innovation.* Ithaca, New York: Cornell University Press, 1959.
SYLOS-LABINI, P. *Oligopoly and Technical Progress.* (English translation). Cambridge, Mass.: Harvard University Press, 1962.
TAUSSIG, F.W. *Inventors and Moneymakers.* New York: Macmillan, 1915.
TAYMANS A. *L'homme agent du développement économique.* Louvain: E. Nauwelaerts, 1951.
TEMIN, P., *Taking Your Medicine: Drug Regulation in the United States.* Harvard Univ. Press, Cambridge, MA. 1980.
VEBLEN, T. *The Instinct of Workmanship.* New York: Macmillan, 1914.
VON FANGE, E.K. *Professional Creativity.* London: Prentice-Hall, 1959.
WALKER, P.B. *Early Aviation at Farnborough.* London: Macdonald, 1971.
WAKSMAN, S.A., *Scientific Monthly,* November. 1940.
WAKSMAN, S.A., *My Life with the Microbes,* Robert Hale, London. 1958.

WAKSMAN, S.A., *A Most Fruitful Connection.* Merck Journal.1963.
WAKSMAN, S.A., *The Conquest of Tuberculosis.* Univ. of California Press, Berkeley.1964.
WAKSMAN, S.A., *The Antibiotic Era.* The Waksman Foundation of Japan, Tokyo. 1975.
WAKSMAN, S.A., WOODRUFF, H.B., *Bacteriostatic and bacteri cidal substances produced by soil actinomycetes.* Proc. Soc. Exp. Biol. Med. 45, 609-614, 710, 1940.
WAKSMAN, S.A., FOSTER, J.W., HUTCHINS, J.J., *Associative and antagonistic effect of microorganisms.* Soil Sci. 43, 51-92. 1937.
WHITEHEAD, A.N. *Science and the Modern World.* Cambridge: University Press, 1947.
WILLIAMS, T.I., *1984. Howard Florey: Penicillin and After.* Oxford Univ. Press.
WILLS, G., ASHTON & TAYLOR (eds.) *Technological Forecasting And Corporate Strategy.* London: Crosby Lockwood, 1969.
WILSON, D., *Penicillin In Perspective.* Faber and Faber, London.1976.
WOLF, J., *Structures of a Scientific/Technological Revolution: Coincidence, Order and Creation of Latitude for Action in the Evolution of an Innovation: Penicillin and Antibiotics.* Wissenschaftszentrum Berlin für Sozialforschung, Berlin, Publications series of the Research Unit Public Health Policy, ISSN-0935-8137.1996.
WOODRUFF, H.B., *A soil microbiologist's odyssey.* Annu. Rev. Microbiol. 35, 1-28. 1981.
WOODRUFF, P. *The Guardians.* London: Jonathan Cape, 1954.
YOUNG, ROSAMUND McP. *Boss Ket: A Life of Charles Kettering,* New York: Longman's, 1961.

PUBLICATIONS WHICH DEVELOP
TOPICS DISCUSSED IN 'INNOVATION'

Readers, who wish to pursue some of the ideas in this book further, may like to consult some later writings which develop them. Several of these relate to intellectual property, in particular to the need to reform this. The first was an edited book, `Direct Protection of Innovation',[1] which argued that the existing criteria for granting patents are inappropriate. Then, concern with how the cost of litigation reduces the value of patents to those who need them most, led to `Compulsory Arbitration: Empirical Evidence',[2] and to another book, `Enforcing Small Firms' Patent Rights'.[3] Growing awareness of the potential value of bringing a financial dimension into measuring grants, instead of using only time, culminated in `Intellectual Property Needs Help from Accounting',[4] which also proposed a way of doing this. Some unintended consequences of institutional arrangements in this field are discussed in `Intellectual Property's Problems: How Far is the U.S. Constitution to Blame?'[5]

Institutions in a wider context are the subject matter of two books, `The Political Economy of Innovation'[6] and `Innovation, Creativity and Law'.[7] One aspect of these arrangements which was touched on in `Innovation' and which has been growing rapidly in importance, is bureaucracy. `A Running Repair for the Civil Service'[8] and `An Alternative Agenda for Public Service Reform'[9] argue for needed and practical changes. More on Schumpeter can be found in a book Chapter, `Schumpeter and the Future of Capitalism'.[10] This future is discussed in `A Spectre is Haunting the World: the Spectre of Global Capitalism',[11] which is the background of work in progress on property rights and responsibility.

[1] 1987, Dordrecht, Kluwer Academic Publishers for the European Commission.
[2] 2000, *European Intellectual Property Review* 22 (4) 154-158.
[3] 2001, Luxembourg, Office for Official Publications of the European Communities.
[4] 2002, *European Intellectual Property Review* 24 (11) 508-515.
[5] 2002, *Intellectual Property Quarterly* (Issue 4) 315-341.
[6] 1984, Dordrecht/Boston, Kluwer Academic Publishers.
[7] 1990, Dordrecht/Boston, Kluwer Academic Publishers.
[8] 2002, *Political Quarterly* 73, 2198-207.
[9] 2004, *Administration.*
[10] 2001, In *Economic Theory in the Light of Schumpeter's Scientific Heritage,* eds. Vittorangelo Orati and Shri Bhagwan Dahiya, Rohtak, India, Spellbound Publications Pvt. Ltd., 227-243.
[11] 2001, In *Capitalism and Democracy in the 21st century,* eds. Dennis C. Mueller and Uwe Cantner. Heidelberg, Physica-Verlag, 89-114.

INDEX